Midwatch in Verse

Midwatch in Verse

New Year's Deck Log Poetry of the United States Navy, 1941–1946

DAVID E. JOHNSON *and*
GARY GUINN

McFarland & Company, Inc., Publishers
Jefferson, North Carolina

Library of Congress Cataloguing-in-Publication Data

Names: Johnson, David E., 1953– author. | Guinn, Gary, 1948– author.
Title: Midwatch in verse : New Year's deck log poetry of the United States Navy, 1941–1946 / David E. Johnson, and Gary Guinn.
Other titles: New Year's deck log poetry of the United States Navy, 1941–1946
Description: Jefferson, North Carolina : McFarland & Company, Inc., Publishers, 2023. | Includes bibliographical references and index.
Identifiers: LCCN 2023001101 | ISBN 9781476689265 (paperback : acid free paper) ♾
ISBN 9781476648118 (ebook)
Subjects: LCSH: World War, 1939–1945—Naval operations, American. | Logbooks—United States—History—20th century. | World War, 1939–1945—Poetry. | War poetry, English—United States—History—20th century. | Sailors' writings, English—United States—History—20th century. | BISAC: POETRY / American / General | HISTORY / Wars & Conflicts / World War II / General
Classification: LCC D773 .J625 2023 | DDC 940.54/5973—dc23/eng/20230110
LC record available at https://lccn.loc.gov/2023001101

British Library cataloguing data are available

ISBN (print) 978-1-4766-8926-5
ISBN (ebook) 978-1-4766-4811-8

Front cover images from the U.S. Navy and Shutterstock

Printed in the United States of America

McFarland & Company, Inc., Publishers
Box 611, Jefferson, North Carolina 28640
www.mcfarlandpub.com

This book is dedicated to the men who stood the midwatch on U.S. Navy ships in World War II. On every ship at every midnight hour, they responded to the call. In cold, rain, ice, snow or tropical heat, they stood the watch. And every New Year's Day they accepted the challenge to wax poetic in the middle of war. Their humanity, humor and inexhaustible faith in their cause inspire us even today.

* * *

And of course, to Simone and Mary Ann, who finally admitted it was good to get us out of their hair for a while.

Acknowledgments

We are indebted to many people for providing information contained in this book. We relied heavily on the National Archives for deck logs and photographs. Dr. John A. Arnold's company, NICOM, managed to obtain the documents we needed in the middle of the Covid-19 pandemic when the Archives opened and closed at unpredictable times. Chris Tucker, archivist–collections manager of the Battleship *South Dakota* (BB 57) Memorial, provided useful logs from that ship's collection.

Fred Sheller, a survivor of the USS *Murphy*–SS *Bulkoil* collision in the Atlantic, graciously allowed us to use his words about his experiences during that nighttime event. David Brennen served with one of the mid-watch poets (Lilly) while aboard the USS *Gridley* and gave us insights into his captain's leadership style.

During the course of our research, we had the good fortune to make contact with family members of the men who braved the hazards of war and managed to wax eloquent in verse. These individuals gave us first-hand insights into them: Kris Adams, Kandy Agee, Philip Axten, Alice Beal, George Beal, Thaddeus Beal, Harvie Combs, Victor Crowe, James C. Eschen, David Harvie, Robert (Bob) Hayes, James Howard, Jr., Rick Inghram, Paula Kortkamp, Mary Ann Kreitzer, Steve Lamborn, David McCabe, Rick Otto, Gail Thawley, J.C. (Curtis) Tyler III, Jack R. Wall, Steve Wessells and Linda Wyman.

Unique to the poems we selected for inclusion in this book was one written by L.C. Brogger while aboard USS *Gilmer*. Brogger mentioned six of his enlisted crew by name, mostly in humorous ways. We managed to locate family members of four crew members who were mentioned, and they gave us information about what happened to them after the war. Thanks to Candace Burley, Paula Cox, Jim Judkins and Larry Sheller for their contributions.

Table of Contents

Preface

The idea for *Midwatch in Verse* grew out of a personal research project by Dr. Dave Johnson in the fall of 2016 when he did extensive research on the provenance of a USS *Patterson* (DD 392) officer's napkin ring used by his father-in-law during World War II. Dave's father-in-law, the last person off the ship as its first lieutenant, took his napkin ring along with him. He used it every day at home until his death in 2000. After his research, Dave and his wife donated the ring to the Museum of the U.S. Navy in Washington, D.C. It was during the research on *Patterson* that Dave encountered poems written by American sailors in the unusual circumstance of a deck log. His discovery marked the beginning of the project that has become this book.

Midwatch in Verse will look at the manifestation during World War II of the little-known Navy tradition that began before that war, continues today, and has had very little attention: the tradition of writing the New Year's deck log on U.S. Naval ships in verse. U.S. Navy ship deck logs embody the term "administrivia." Designed to inform commanding officers and others of minute details of the ship's operations and serving as official legal documents, they are at best tedious and at worst unintelligible to the casual reader. Navy regulations determine the information that should be included in a deck log. That list is long, but most commonly, logs during World War II included geographical coordinates for ship's position, which boilers were lit and providing power, the ship's official readiness condition, average steam pressure, and any information that might involve a change in condition (e.g., General Quarters).

This attention to minute and mundane detail in deck logs, important in maintaining constant readiness in the fleet, held for all watches and all days of the year except one. The Midwatch (midnight to 4:00 a.m. or 0000–0400) on New Year's Day provided the Officer of the Deck (OOD) a chance to exercise creativity by entering the log in verse.

After a brief introduction to the long tradition of poetry in and about warfare, and a look at how New Year's deck log poetry on U.S. Naval ships fits (or more appropriately doesn't fit) into that tradition, the book will focus on the Midwatch poetry written during the years 1941 to 1946. That timeframe was chosen not only in response to clear reader interest in World War II, but for the inherent incongruity and interest of the tradition being practiced during the massive conflict that consumed the world at the time. The years 1941 and 1946 were included in order to bookend, or frame, the deck log poems written during the war with examples produced in the "innocence" of pre-war and the relief of post-war.

Each chapter will focus on a ship that engaged in combat during the war. The chapters begin with an overview of the history of the ship, focusing only on the most important and most engaging actions and experiences. Then the chapter will offer a midwatch poem (or poems) written during the specified years and consider the poem as it represents that moment in history. And finally, the chapter will offer a biographical sketch of the writer(s), attempting to bring a note of the humanity of the person caught up in the inhumanity of war. It is important to understand that this book is not a traditional history of World War II. The authors have brought a significant level of research to bear on the ships and the young officers who stood the first Midwatch of the year aboard those ships. But the book uses the inexplicable tradition of writing the first deck log of each year in verse to lay bare the humanity—in particular the American humanity—that persisted in the most inhumane of endeavors, warfare. For, as a writer for the Naval History and Heritage Command said in a 2018 article in the *January Landmark*, the tradition "appears wholly American in nature, with all the informality and irreverence that often brings" (Prose, p. 18). This book is therefore intended for a general audience as well as a scholarly one.

Though scattered articles have been written on the topic of New Year's deck logs over the years, there seems to have been no extended treatment of the tradition. One early endeavor, a 1959 article in the USNI *Proceedings* by Captain Robert W. McNitt, USN, offers a good overview of the style and tone of poems, from the earliest he could identify, in 1926, through World War II. The genesis of the tradition seems to be shrouded in the mists of history. McNitt suggested that junior officers condemned to endure the midwatch on January 1 while their mates celebrated were forced to find some means of compensation (McNitt, 1959).

After searching hundreds of deck logs from the middle of the 19th century up to 1926, the authors have as yet found no earlier deck log poems nor any further specific mention of the tradition. The earliest reference to the New Year holiday in a deck log obtained so far is from the USS *Jeannette* in 1880. The midwatch log states, "The New Year was ushered in by the rapid ringing of the ship's bell at midnight and with three cheers given by the crew for the 'Jeannette.'" The crew celebrated the New Year even though the ship had been and would continue to be trapped in pack ice during her Arctic expedition. She remained trapped for two years until her hull was crushed and she sank. While the deck log for New Year's Day in 1880 did not contain a poem, Captain George W. De Long's journal described a party and minstrel show that night: "One of the features of the evening was the reading of a prologue proposed by Mr. Collins [Jerome J. Collins, the ship's meteorologist], in which each one of the crew was made the subject of a rhyme in turn" (De Long, 1884). The celebration occurred despite the fact that the temperature outside was -40 degrees.

Jeannette's 1881 log for New Year's Day was almost identical to the 1880 log. The following excerpts are taken from logs found in Logbooks of U.S. Navy Ships, ca. 1801–1940 (Logbooks).

Reference to New Year's Day appears in the log of USS *Kearsarge* in 1890: "The Birth of the New Year was being celebrated on shore by the display of fireworks during the greater part of the watch." It appears again on the USS *Yorktown* in 1892: "From midnight until 12:20 the New Year was celebrated by the ringing of bells, the firing of guns and rockets and the burning of lights from the towns, the forts and Chilean war vessels in the harbor." Then again on the USS *Adams* in 1894: "Great pandemonium on shore and in harbor for a few minutes after 12:00 to usher in New Year." The New Year's deck log on USS *Albatross* for 1908 (mislabeled as 1907) reveals that "U.S. Flagship Rainbow made general signal to the fleet by the Ardois System: 'A happy new year to all.'"

After further mentions in 1913 and 1914, an intriguing reference appears on USS *Villalobos* for 1915: "As before, holiday routine as per Article R. 1289, U.S. Naval Regulations, 1913." According to Article R. 1289, relatively new at the time, January 1 (and several other days) "shall be regarded as holidays on board ships of the Navy and at naval stations. Of these, only the 22nd of February and the 4th of July shall be observed ceremoniously" (Regulations, 1913). It appears that at some point prior to 1926, perhaps inspired by meteorologist Jerome Collins' 1880 New Year's poems on USS *Jeannette*, Officers of the Deck began celebrating New Year's "unceremoniously" by writing the deck log in verse.

The tradition itself has waxed and waned over the decades. In 1968, the *Navy Times* promoted a deck log poem contest, and by 1970 *All Hands* claimed that the midwatch poems were "a growing Naval Tradition." But by 2016, fewer than 30 ships participated and by 2017 less than 20 (Prose, p. 18). In 2021, the Naval History & Heritage Command, fearing that the tradition was fading away, initiated a New Year's Deck Log Entry Contest which generated a flurry of articles on the topic. The authors hope that *Midwatch in Verse* will contribute to the tradition and will keep alive the memories of the ships and the men who participated in the tradition while serving in World War II.

The authors have attempted to include a range of ships—from the most decorated of the war, which may be familiar to most readers, to those ships that are little known but performed heroically in obscurity; from the giants of history, like the USS *Enterprise*, down to the small and nameless craft, such as *PC 1264*. Not every poem from every ship is included. Criteria for choosing poems included the level of interest of the material, readability, quality and at times the biography of the writer.

The deck logs themselves, as well as information about the ships and the men, were pulled from the National Archives in Washington D.C., a crucial source. Biographical information came from a variety of publicly available sources, including government records, high school and college yearbooks (especially the Annapolis *Lucky Bag*), newspapers, blogs and veterans' organizations. Unless otherwise cited, ship histories were taken from the *Dictionary of American Naval Fighting Ships*. Most photographs are from the National Archives and the Naval History & Heritage Command. The poems as presented in the book follow the punctuation and spelling of the original deck logs, right or wrong.

To assist those who are unfamiliar with Navy jargon and routine, we have included several appendices: "Material Conditions in Navy Ships," "How Ships Get Their Names," "U.S. Navy Hull Designations," "Candid Comments by Poets in the Poems" and "Non–World War II Poems." The final appendix includes a selection of poems from other eras, giving readers access to a bit broader context.

Introduction

Poetry and war have been strange but intimate bedfellows for thousands of years. Poets in every age have been drawn to the inexpressible power and tragedy of war. Poems of war have become touchstones of Western literature as poets have tried to express the horror of war or to inspire patriotic fervor.

Rage—Goddess, sing the rage of Peleus' son Achilles,
Murderous, doomed, that cost the Achaeans countless losses,
Hurling down to the House of Death so many sturdy souls,
Great fighters' souls, but made their bodies carrion,
Feasts for the dogs and birds,
And the will of Zeus was moving toward its end.

So begins the first great poem of war in the Western world: *The Iliad*. Homer, long believed to be the blind bard, records the story of the Greeks' ten-year assault on the edifice of Troy. Their quest to recover Helen, the face that launched a thousand ships. The destruction of the great citadel of Troy. The deaths of countless warriors.

The long tradition of poetry about war is perhaps most poignant when the poets themselves are warriors. From ancient China to the early Arab world, from the Norse to the knights of Medieval Europe, the warrior poet tradition has thrived. In modern times, a powerful expression of the tradition developed in the World Wars of the 20th century, which produced many soldier poets, too many to do justice to here. In World War I, Wilfred Owen published the haunting poems "Anthem to Doomed Youth" and "Dulce et Decorum Est." Other poets from that war included John McCrae ("In Flanders Fields"), the American Alan Seeger ("I Have a Rendezvous with Death"), Rupert Brooke ("The Soldier") and Siegried Sassoon (anti-war poems). World War II saw Randall Jarrell ("The Death of the Ball Turret Gunner"), Henry Reed ("The Naming of Parts"), Keith Douglas ("Desert Flowers"), Alun Lewis ("All Day It Has Rained") and many more. But each of these wartime poets was a soldier *and* a professional bard, and their war poetry, like Homer's, expresses in beautiful and poignant language the horror of war.

But what happens when an *amateur* poet is called on to produce a poem that describes not the towering emotions of the warrior in battle, but the mundane hours of a midnight watch aboard an American Navy ship during wartime? Amateur poets have never been in short supply. In fact, the modern amateur poet has become almost a cliché—the lovesick youth, the angst-filled teenager, the maudlin lover of nature. And with the onset of the Internet and the ease of self-publishing, almost anyone can become a published poet.

Midwatch in Verse unites the long tradition of warrior poets with the modern expression of the amateur through a little-known Navy tradition, a tradition so non-standard and unmilitary that it seems out of place: the tradition of writing the first ship's deck log of each New Year in verse. On the first watch of the year, the Midwatch from midnight to four a.m., the Officer of the Deck on Navy ships was given the leeway to write the deck log in poetry. Deck logs have always been mind-numbing recitations of technical details, describing weather conditions, ship conditions and readiness. A listing of the ship's speed, direction, propellers, boilers, position and so forth. While a ship is moored, deck logs often appear like alphabet soup when indicating the abbreviations of those in command such as SOPA (Senior Officer Present Afloat), COMDESRON (Commander, Destroyer Squadron) and COMPACFLT (Commander, Pacific Fleet).

The following is a *part of* a typical deck log, written on the USS *Patterson* near the close of World War II by Lt. j.g. E.A. Schroder, the father-in-law of one of the authors of this book:

> U.S.S. Patterson (DD 392) Sunday 1 April 1945
>
> 0–4
>
> ComDesRon 6, ComScreen, in BAGLEY. Ship is darkened and in Condition of Readiness IIM. Boilers #3 and #4 in use. Sonar gear out of commission. 0210 Ceased zigzagging and resumed base course. 0215 C/c to 001°T, 000° pgc, 005° psc. 0230
>
> Resumed zigzagging. 0310 Proceeded on various courses and various speeds to plane guard station astern of SANGAMON. 0315 Formation ceased zigzagging, C/c to 030°T, 029° pgc, 028° psc. 0325 C/c to 075°T, 074° pgc, 075° psc. 0353 C/c to 355°T, 354° pgc, 358° psc. Flight operations completed, proceeded to former screening station. 0359 C/c to 345°T, 344° pgc, 349° psc.

No creativity was allowed in this quasi-legal document, just the facts, which are indecipherable to the uninitiated reader. The content of the deck log is strictly controlled by Naval regulations. Except, that is, for that one four-hour stretch launching the new year. In those four hours, young sailors, amateur poets all of them, tried to turn the base metal of mundane details into literature.

A reader may well ask, "Why would the Navy allow such an unmilitary thing as a deck log in verse? How and when did the tradition get started?" The origins of the Midwatch in verse tradition and its *raison d'être* are shrouded in mystery. Captain Robert W. McNitt, USN, speculated in a 1959 article in the U.S. Naval Institute's *Proceedings*,

> Bad enough, when the ship is in port to forego a big time ashore; worse still to stand chilled to the bone on a deserted quarterdeck and glumly greet the still celebrating shipmates who manage to make it back before dawn.
>
> And so grew up the custom of logging the first watch of the New Year in verse, providing some diversion for the wretched watch officer, and amusement for his shipmates the next day [McNitt, 1959].

McNitt shared part of the 1926 midwatch in verse by Ensign E.V. Dockweiler on USS *Idaho*:

> We are anchored in Pedro Harbor
> Tho there isn't much of a lee,
> And why they call it a harbor
> Is something I never could see!
>
> That's all the dope this morning,
> Except just between us two
> If the Captain ever sees this log,
> My Gawd, what will he do.

McNitt then added that Captain Arthur St. Claire Smith (USNA class of 1897) wrote the following above Ensign Dockweiler's signature (italics added): "The Captain is glad to see that *the old Navy custom* of writing up the first watch of the year in rhyme is known to the younger members of the Service. The watch stands as written." The captain's reference to the "old Navy custom" suggests that it was well known at the time.

But writers of deck log poems have not always been so fortunate as Ensign Dockweiler. In a 1972 issue of *Shipmate*, Lt. j.g. Arthur Ageton told of his unsuccessful attempt: "Skipper was a humorless fellow who had never heard of this tradition and sent the deck log back to me for rewriting in less rhythmical style." The skipper recommended he submit the poem to the ship's paper (Prose, 2018).

The writers of New Year's deck log poems sometimes recruited fellow sailors to help create the poem. The immediate copy of the deck log is kept by the Quartermaster of the Watch and then prepared by the Officer of the Deck. The poets displayed their amateur poetics in everything from tortured attempts at rhyme to sophisticated imitations of classic works. In an era when regular, rhymed poetry was more the standard than it is today, amateur poets tended to fall back on what they probably knew best, the old ballad stanzas of the hymns they sang in church. English and American hymnody had widely used the medieval ballad form.

Occasionally, a writer attempted something more challenging, imitating the style or meter of a famous poem. A great many of the young officers who wrote the poems were well-educated Annapolis grads. Lt. P.E. McArther, on USS *Washington*, began his midwatch poem in a tribute to Edgar Allan Poe's "The Raven":

> Once upon a midnight dreary, while I slumbered, weak and weary,
> Dreaming of such far-off places as New York and good old Philly,
> Suddenly there came a tapping, and someone opened up my chamber door,
> "Tis a visitor," I muttered as he uttered—"Twelve to four."
> Only that, and nothing more.

Lt. j.g. R.E. Hayes' poem, entered in the January 1, 1945, deck log of USS *Pennsylvania*, adopted the style of Rudyard Kipling's 1890 poem "Gunga Din":

> Oh a look beneath our keel will at a glance reveal,
> The water there is 18 fathoms deep.

And the Navigator's fix says we're in Berth 26,
A position that he really wants to keep.......

But regardless of style, certain constants run through the midwatch poems: their sense of humor, their optimism and their desire to turn the soul-withering requirements of military details in wartime into an expression of the poet's humanity. Ensign J.T. O'Neill, writing in 1941 on USS *Dewey* after the ship had two collisions while in port, demonstrated humor and ingenuity in the following deck log lines:

So here we sit in the whale-struck *Dewey,*
With our engines and steam lines all Ker-flooey.

At a time when these warriors could lose their humanity with little or no warning in the middle of war, the poems ring out with it.

The poems expressed something as old as *The Iliad*—in this case, the humor and humanity of the American men caught up in conflict. Rather than attempt to reveal the horror of war, which was very real to them—their ships were often damaged or destroyed and their shipmates wounded or killed—the *Midwatch in Verse* poets expressed the inexhaustible resilience, optimism and irreverence of the American spirit. They used the opportunity of turning a deck log into a poem to share a moment during war in which they were released from the regulations that dictated their actions in all the other midwatches of the year. The result was archetypically American.

The poems often bemoan the fact that it is New Year's and the writer is on watch rather than reveling like most other crew members. The lack of alcohol for such a festive time and the lack of female companionship appear on a regular basis. Writers often yearn to be back home celebrating. New York, Times Square and San Francisco commonly appear as wishful destinations. Not surprisingly, New Year's logs often mention the ongoing war, and they typically convey confidence and hope for ultimate victory for the U.S. Many entries express the hope that peace will soon be achieved.

The urge to express emotion and experience in poetry is almost as human as breathing and speech itself. Carl Schoettler, a national correspondent for *The Orlando Sentinel,* offered a deck log poem from an unexpected source in a 2001 article. "With his Russian crewmates at his side," Schoetller says, "Cmdr. Bill Shepherd, a Navy captain, did something much like that aboard the International Space Station in the ship's log for 0000 01 Jan 2001:

On this ship's deck sits no helm now
Rudder, sheet and rig long since gone
But here still—a pull to go places
Beyond lines where sky meets the dawn
Though star trackers mark Altair and Vega
Same as mariners eyed long ago
We are still as wayfinders of knowledge
Seeking new things that mankind shall know.

The men featured in this book, who took the time to compose midwatch poems with humor and feeling in wartime, were not the famous names we know from the histories and cultural productions that look back at the war. They were simply the men who answered the call, who left behind their peacetime lives and found themselves in the middle of the greatest conflict in American history. They are all dead now, yet their lives, especially relating to their service, are worthy of note. The ships they fought on are all gone now, some sunk in the heat of battle, most sold for scrap after the war, a few transformed into museums. Most of them are known only through the National Archives and the *Dictionary of American Naval Fighting Ships*. Yet each of those ships performed memorable duty in service of the country and in the process became living entities to the sailors who manned them.

The men and the ships deserve to be remembered.

None of these poets' families knew about the tradition or about the poem written by their father or grandfather or uncle. During the writing of this book, poems were shared with many families, and they were surprised and delighted to learn about them. The ships have fascinating stories after living for a short time in the crucible of history. The poems make no attempt to be *The Iliad*, were never written with an eye on publication in *The New Yorker*, but they reveal the American humanity of the citizen sailors who wrote them. Some of the poets did not survive the conflict.

It's a story that needs to be told.

USS *Detroit*

The Dashing "D"

USS *Detroit* (CL-8) off Port Angeles, Washington, on April 14, 1944. Her camouflage pattern is Design 3D in the Measure 31-32-33 series. National Archives photo 19-N-63828.

The Ship

USS *Detroit* (CL 8) was an Omaha-class light cruiser, sponsored by the daughter of the mayor of Detroit and commissioned July 31, 1923. During her early years, *Detroit* spent time on diplomatic missions in Europe, North Africa and the Middle East as the flagship for U.S. naval forces in Europe. She visited ports throughout Europe, North

Africa and the Middle East, hosting numerous dignitaries, including the kings of Norway, Denmark and Spain, and the president of the Irish Free State. In the early 1930s, *Detroit* moved to the Pacific fleet where she remained until the end of World War II.

On December 7, 1941, *Detroit* was moored in Pearl Harbor along with USS *Raleigh* (CL 7), USS *Utah* (BB 31/AG 16) and USS *Tangier* (AV 8). While the attacking Japanese focused on Battleship Row on the other side of Ford Island, they also came after *Detroit* and the ships with her. *Raleigh* suffered one torpedo hit, while *Utah* took two torpedo hits and capsized. According to *The Detroit News*' Jim Lynch, many of *Detroit*'s sailors were on shore leave, and "getting up to steam was huge to begin with with the reduced crew.... But she got up to steam and got underway with guns blazing. It was pretty dramatic." She managed to begin firing at the attacking aircraft with 3" guns and 50-caliber machine guns. In the action report, the C.O. claimed the ship had a part in downing two aircraft and that two men were superficially wounded. A torpedo from a Japanese plane passed ten yards astern of *Detroit* and buried in the mud (Naval History and Heritage Command, 2018). Members of the crew used any available firepower, including rifles and pistols. The ship got underway at 10:10 a.m. and was ordered to proceed at once to the west coast of Oahu to defend against possible Japanese landing forces. On December 10 at 11:25 a.m., after taking part in the unsuccessful attempt to catch the retiring Japanese fleet, *Detroit* re-entered Pearl Harbor and moored to begin taking on ordnance and personnel.

In March 1942, *Detroit* transferred approximately 20 metric tons of gold and silver from USS *Trout* (SS 202). *Trout* had spirited the precious metals out of the Philippines to keep them out of Japanese hands. *Detroit* brought the fortune to the U.S. for safekeeping by the Department of the Treasury. She performed escort duty until later that year.

In November 1942, *Detroit* sailed from San Francisco to the Aleutian Islands, where she remained until 1944. While there, she assisted in preventing further Japanese incursions in the Aleutians. In January 1943, she covered landings on Amitchka, establishing a base to cut Japanese supply lines, and later she worked to intercept reinforcements headed to the Japanese garrisons on Kiska and Attu. From April to August, she provided bombardment and support for the assault and capture of both islands. In June 1944, she moved further south with Task Force 94 and participated in bombardment of shore installations in the Kurile Islands between Japan and the Kamchatka Peninsula of Russia. She then patrolled off the west coast of South America until December.

In February 1945, *Detroit* joined the 5th Fleet at Ulithi Atoll, a remote coral reef that the U.S. had just the year before turned into the largest naval base and staging area in the war. She participated in several campaigns, including the invasions of Iwo Jima and Okinawa. During this time, she served as flagship directing the Service Force Pacific Fleet, whose mission was to provide logistical support for fast carrier task forces. She was one of only two ships present at Pearl Harbor on December 7, 1941, that also moored in Tokyo Harbor at the signing of the Japanese surrender in

September 1945 (the other being USS *West Virginia* [BB 48]). She continued to direct the replenishment support of the occupation fleet until October, when she headed home with returning servicemen as part of Operation Magic Carpet.

Detroit was decommissioned at Philadelphia on January 11, 1946, and the proud lady was sold for scrap on February 27 at the age of 23.

She earned 11 battle stars for her service during World War II.

The Poems

The three midwatch poems written on *Detroit* offer a unique glimpse of the experience of American sailors in World War II. Three young officers each stood the January 1 midwatch on *Detroit* at three points in time—the first almost a year before Pearl Harbor, the second three weeks after the attack, and the third two years deep into a lengthening conflict, the resolution of which was anything but certain. The narrative moves from the carefree tone of Louis Adelard Perras on January 1, 1941, to the somber resolve of Raymond John Schneider on January 1, 1942, and finally to the hopeful weariness of Donald Goodrich on January 1, 1944. The three men were serving on *Detroit* at the time of the Pearl Harbor attack. Two of them were Annapolis classmates in the Class of 1940. The three could not know, when they wrote their deck log poems, that the war would drag on for almost four years after the United States was thrust into the conflict. But all three performed the mission they were called to do. All three saw the war out and lived their lives with courage thereafter. And for a brief moment in their careers, they did something only a small minority of sailors in their position were allowed to do: They wrote a poem and expressed their humanity in the deck log of a U.S. Navy ship. And though they didn't know it at the time, they left behind for later generations a small slice of the very human, very American experience of the war.

Poem One

The first log was entered on January 1, 1941, by Ensign Louis Adelard Perras. The poem consists of 27 lines, mostly rhymed couplets, divided into six stanzas. The poem is notable for its clear pre-war tone and content. Perras could not know what was coming. It would be 11 months and six days before the tragedy of Pearl Harbor. In an ironic twist, in the first line of Perras' poem, he refers to the ship as the "DETROIT Maru." The Japanese word "maru," meaning "circle" or "purity," was often applied to beloved things. Japanese sailors sometimes applied the appellation to the names of their ships.

The carefree tone of the poem is established immediately, with Perras' tongue surely firmly in his cheek. Though the midwatch crew is "lonely, cold and blue," they are actually "happy, joyous, gay" because they won't have hangovers in the morning from New Year's Eve celebrations; they won't feel "that way." The first stanza closes with a light-hearted jab at the quartermaster, who is in the galley "poaching the festive bird."

Perras offers some of the requisite information of a deck log: *Detroit* is moored at San Diego in seven fathoms of water, secured to buoys, the anchor at starboard side, with steam provided by boiler five: "Ah, It's great to be alive!" The war in Europe and Asia was certainly a threatening cloud, but it was far away, and there was no great conviction at that point that the U.S. would enter fully into the war. So, it's great to be alive. And as if to prove it is so, Seaman Second Class Poorker returns from leave "with a friendly wheeze." He shows "no hint of a list or weave," despite his undoubted celebrations. The poem closes with a happy New Year wish to the captain and crew from "ComAirScoFor" (Commander Airforces Scouting Force), who is the "SOPA" (Senior Officer Present Afloat), and a sigh of relief for the end of the watch, "a weary four hours and a half."

Perras' poem is a snapshot of a confident young officer's midwatch in peacetime. That secure and happy tone will change in the deck log written one year later, on the first day of 1942.

Here is Perras' poem.

On the midnight deck of the DETROIT Maru
Stands the midwatch, lonely, cold and blue.
Still they are happy, joyous, gay,
For on the morrow they'll not feel "that way."
While from the galley are stealthy noises heard,
Proclaiming the QM [Quartermaster] poaching the festive bird.

In the bay, San Diego
'Tis seven fathoms or so,
Moored bow to buoy number eighteen,
Stern to another, we stand in between

A stout eight inch manila preventer
With a one and an eighth inch wire,
Fast to our starboard anchor chain
Keep us from swinging on the blue Calif. Main.

There is steam in boiler number five,
Ah, It's great to be alive!

Aboard on time, with a friendly wheeze,
Poorker, seaman second, returned from leave,
With neither a list nor a weave,
And nary a rating on his sleeve.

The NECHES, CUYAMA, AVOCET,
SOMERS, NESHO and PLATTE
Join ComAirScoFor (the SOPA to you)
In wishing "Happy New Year" to Captain & crew.

Lo, at long, long last,
With various yard & district craft,
We end a weary four hours and a half.

L.A. Perras,
Ensign, U.S. Navy

Poet One

Midshipman Louis Adelard Perras, Jr., from the 1940 Naval Academy Yearbook *Annapolis Lucky Bag.*

Louis Adelard Perras, Jr., was born March 21, 1917, in New Bedford, Massachusetts. Both of his parents were born in Quebec, Canada, and emigrated to the U.S. Louis' father became a prominent New Bedford physician. His mother, Marie Eugenie Josephine Banville, died only a month after his birth.

He received an appointment to Annapolis and graduated in the Class of 1940. During his time at the Naval Academy, he was known as an excellent tennis player. He maintained this interest throughout his life and held both national and New England rankings for his tennis prowess. His entry in the 1940 Annapolis yearbook, *Lucky Bag*, mentions his penchant for cursing in French, most likely related to his parents' French-Canadian background.

During his time in the Navy, Perras served on USS *New Mexico* (BB 40) and USS *Gwin* (DM 33) in addition to *Detroit*. He rose to the rank of lieutenant commander before leaving the Navy. In 1950, Perras graduated from the Boston College School of Law and spent many years in practice. He was well-known for his work as a trial attorney and did considerable *pro bono* work.

He died on September 27, 2004, at the age of 87. He was buried at Massachusetts National Cemetery in Bourne with military honors.

Poem Two

The second deck log verse from *Detroit* was posted one year later, on January 1, 1942, by Ensign R.J. Schneider, USN. The clear shift in tone reflects a country now at war, still reeling three weeks after the Pearl Harbor attack. There is no celebration here as there was in the earlier poem. America is at war. Schneider describes the convoy of which *Detroit* is a part as "the life-blood of the nation" and says they are moving slowly: "We poke along at a meagre rate / That was barely eight-point-five." Two boilers supply the power, and two more stand at ready. For the members of Task Force Fifteen-Two, the New Year's toast does away with wine and replaces it with action as they "raised white spray instead of wine / in toast to our comrades true." The future is now uncertain, and he toasts the coming year, our great American nation, and the men in uniform serving her. A fierce battle is raging in the west. Our fighters are fearless and dauntless. The work ahead is "a job that's unfinished Until We Have Won!!"

Schneider's poem is technically one of the best poems among the deck logs. He shows perfect control of the old traditional ballad stanza, perhaps best known from Samuel Taylor Coleridge's famous 19th-century poem "The Rime of the Ancient Mariner," which would have been well-known to a Naval Academy grad. In English poetry, the traditional ballad carries the historical air of adventure and romance, of heroes and quests, of love and death and heartbreak. Schneider turns this undercurrent of emotional weight to his purpose—to inspire and sound the clarion call. Coming so soon after Pearl Harbor, the poem seems to embody the spirit of the statement attributed to Japanese Admiral Yamamoto, that all Japan had done in the attack was "awaken a sleeping giant and fill him with a terrible resolve."

Perhaps most impressive poetically in Schneider's poem is the way he closes. In the final four lines, he turns from the rocking narrative rhythm of the traditional ballad to what is known as the long ballad form. He presses forward to the conclusion by creating a driving rhythm and rhyme. The effect of the change is to give weight to the poem's final lines. And it is there that Schneider rings the clarion call most powerfully. The emotional pinnacle of the poem. The roar of the sleeping giant awakened.

Here is the poem:

The New Year came to Zone Plus Nine,
Without much celebration;
While a full moon shone o're our convoy line,
The life-blood of the nation.

The longitude was one-three-eight,
The latitude three-five.
We poked along at a meagre rate
That was barely eight-point-five.

The steaming firerooms on the line
Were numbers Two and Four,
With number Three on a five minutes call
And One on thirty more.

We steered a course of two-four-nine
In Task Force Fifteen-Two,
And raised white spray instead of wine
In toast to our comrades true.

So here's to the future, to Forty Two,
And our great American nation;
To the men of the service in Navy blue,
Whatever their rank or station;
Let us look to the West where fiercest is raging,
The battle our fearless are dauntlessly waging.
To the work that's ahead and the fight we've begun,
To a job that's unfinished Until We Have Won!!

R.J. SCHNEIDER,
Ensign, U.S. Navy

Poet Two

Midshipman Raymond John Schneider from the 1940 Naval Academy Yearbook *Annapolis Lucky Bag.*

Raymond John Schneider was born October 20, 1917, in Cleveland, Ohio, to parents Raymond Michael and Marie Catherine. He received an appointment to the Annapolis Naval Academy in 1936 and graduated in the Class of 1940, receiving his commission as an ensign. At the Academy, he was a classmate of Louis Perras, the writer of the deck log above. His entry from the *Lucky Bag* shows that he was on both the outdoor and indoor rifle teams, something that would serve him well on December 7, 1941.

Ensign Schneider's first post was to USS *Detroit*, where he served during the Japanese attack on Pearl Harbor. According to a blog post by Schneider's son Raymond Jr. (now deceased), he left *Detroit* in 1942 and pursued Navy flight training in Florida (Schneider, 2009). After successful flight training and carrier qualification, Schneider held a variety of posts and furthered his engineering education, including earning a master's degree in aeronautical engineering from MIT in 1946. He rose through the ranks, and in 1968 he received promotion to Rear Admiral. In 1972 he began his command of Naval Electronic Systems Command (NAVELEX), where he remained until his retirement in 1975. For excellence of service, Schneider received three Legion of Merit awards.

As an ensign on *Detroit* on December 7, 1941, Schneider participated in the attempt to repel the Pearl Harbor attack. In a 1981 article, he recounted some of his experiences (Naworzki, 1981): Awakened from a short sleep after his watch by the sound of an explosion, Schneider rushed topside, still in his underwear, and was engulfed in the chaos of battle. "[T]he boat behind us was burning. I could see the *Utah* going upside down. The two airfields were full of flame and smoke." His wry sense of humor surfaces in his retelling of the events when he writes, "You got the impression all was not well." But Schneider sprang into action, his first priority to clear the canvas awnings from the guns. "I sent a sailor down to the butcher shop and we cut the canvas down with cutlery, but that cleared out nine antiaircraft guns. Someone blew the lock off the ammunition storage locker with a .45.... Finally, we started the guns and we must have thrown a thousand shells into the air and didn't hit a thing."

Barefoot and firing a rifle at the Japanese planes swarming around them, Schneider stepped on a hot shell casing. He ran to his bunk to put on his shoes. Recounting the scene years later for Naworzki, he said, "The scene was such I was firing a rifle at the planes, still in my skivvies. Hardly a dramatic impression, but that's the way it was." After Pearl Harbor, Schneider slept in his shoes for several months, afraid of again going into combat with bare feet.

According to Schneider, he and *Detroit* were lucky to survive when the ships around them were taking serious damage. "There were two torpedoes fired at us," he said, "but they went in the mud. But they were headed for the forward area, where I was sleeping. If they would have hit, I would have been gone." His sense of humor still rang true as he told the story. "Before we cast off, the gunnery officer told me I wasn't wearing my tin hat. Now here I was, nothing but my underwear and shoes with a rifle, and he's asking about my following regulations" (Naworzki, 1981).

Schneider's children, after reading his deck log verse, confirmed the observation that he had a great sense of humor. It appeared in an address that Admiral Schneider gave at the *Precise Time and Time Interval Planning Meeting* in 1974, where he began by saying, "Good morning ladies and gentlemen. I have a few prepared remarks. I intend to slightly embellish them with a few unprepared ones." The talk contained many examples of a wry humor, but also a deep understanding of the topic at hand. He challenged his audience to pursue ongoing efforts to improve our ability to measure increasingly small intervals of time to advance technological development.

One of Admiral Schneider's daughters, Mary Ann, revealed that he frequently had those around him laughing heartily. She also said that her father was an excellent pianist, learning how to play at the hand of his father, who played the piano for silent movie theaters and was the organist and choir director at St. James Roman Catholic Church in Cleveland. Schneider also played the organ at the Naval Academy. His daughter fondly recalled times when she was a child sitting on a piano bench singing while her father played selections from operas (email, May 3, 2020).

Admiral Schneider was also, according to Mary Ann, a person who appreciated and lauded those individuals who toiled in obscurity: the common person. No job, no matter how menial it seemed to most individuals, was so small that it should go unappreciated.

Admiral Schneider died on July 5, 1985. He is buried at the Naval Academy Cemetery in Annapolis, Maryland.

Poem Three

The final deck log verse was posted on January 1, 1944, by Lt. Donald Charles Goodrich, USNR. Carrying the burden of two years of warfare, Goodrich looks hopefully toward the end of the conflict. His poem is short, two four-line stanzas separated by a three-line stanza. The first two stanzas simply offer the required deck log information. *Detroit,* which he calls the "Dashing 'D,'" is berthed at Iliuliuk Bay in the Aleutian Islands in 19 fathoms of water. The anchor is run out to port side, and the water is a bit dicey. The ship "yawed and we swung with plenty of sport." He names five other ships that are with them. They are in "Condition Y and readiness III," meaning the ship has a medium degree of watertight integrity (Y) and one third to one-half of the battle stations are manned (III). Power is supplied by boiler number two.

But the final stanza strikes a melancholy, wistful note. It begins with the traditional idea that the new year ushers out the old things and ushers in the new. But there is no joy in this fact, as the next line laments that they "stood and froze as we always do." Schneider prays for a fight that will end the war: "As we usher in Nineteen—Forty Four." The poem expresses a sense of weariness after two long years of conflict and yearns for the coming year to bring the war to an end. It would be 20 long months before the surrender of Japan.

Here is the poem:

At Iliuliuk Bay in Berth B3
In 19 fathoms rode the Dashing "D"
With 90 of chain run out to port
We yawed and we swung with plenty of sport

Commanding LUCE, ISHERWOOD, PICKING, PORTER and WICKES.
Condition "Y" and readiness III
Number Two's on the line to give light to see

So out went the old and in came the new
And we stood and froze as we always do
And we'll pray for a fight and the end of the War
As we usher in Nineteen—Forty Four.

D.C. Goodrich,
Lieut. USNR

The Poet

Donald C. Goodrich was born to Roy Selah Goodrich and Ann Estelle Murray on December 9, 1915, in Arizona. His family was very well-known in both Arizona and California. Roy was a Harvard-educated attorney who played a role in the process of the Arizona Territory becoming a state. His family, being rather wealthy, owned the Goodrich Building in downtown Phoenix for many years and enlisted renowned architect John Byers to design a home for them in Bel-Air, California.

Donald attended the Thacher School in Ojai, California, and the Milton Academy in Milton, Massachusetts. During his time at Harvard, he majored in history, was a member of the Hasty Pudding Club, and expressed an interest in a business career. At the time of the 1940 U.S. Census, he was living in Los Angeles and listed his occupation as Real Estate Agent. It is likely that some time during 1940 he attended Officer Training, since he received his commission as an ensign in the

Navy on December 12 of that year. His first posting was to USS *Detroit* shortly after his commission. He married Mary Frances Burkhard on January 13, 1942, in Honolulu, Hawaii, just five weeks after the Pearl Harbor attack. His best man was Edward Laurence Doheny III of the famous California Doheny family, who were prominent in the oil industry and owned the Greystone Mansion in Beverly Hills.

Goodrich was promoted to Lt. j.g. on June 15, 1942; to lieutenant on March 1, 1943; and to lieutenant commander on October 3, 1945. He retired at that rank in January 1954. City directories show that Goodrich was in the real estate business from at least 1954 through 1970. Most of this time, he was affiliated with the R.A. Rowan Company, one of the oldest real estate developers in the Los Angeles area. He died on June 13, 1985, in San Diego.

USS *Finch*

The Ultimate Indignity

USS *Finch* (AM 9) in the summer of 1934, off Tsingtao, China, while serving in the U.S. Asiatic Fleet. National Archives Photo 80-G-1025944.

The Ship

USS *Finch* (AM 9) was a Lapwing-class minesweeper commissioned on September 10, 1918. In her earliest deployments, she removed World War I–era mines from the North Sea near the Orkney Islands in 1919 and 1920. Later, she sailed back to the west coast of the U.S. for modernization. From 1921 through 1941, *Finch* spent winters in the Philippines and summers in China engaging in duties that included towing and salvage work, as well as participation in the Yangtze River Patrol. One of *Finch*'s distinctions during this period came in 1937 when Lt. Hyman G. Rickover took command on July 10 and captained the ship until October 5. Rickover, who eventually rose to the rank of admiral, became the United States' foremost proponent of nuclear propulsion. *Finch* was Rickover's only surface vessel command (Rickover, 2019). When tensions with Japan began in 1941, *Finch* joined other vessels in the Philippines in anti-submarine and mine exercises.

After being informed on December 8 of the Pearl Harbor attack, *Finch*'s crew performed heroically until April 10 to keep Manila Harbor navigable. This included sweeping for mines and shepherding untethered barges out of the navigation channel. By late February, Japanese planes began direct attacks on *Finch*, dropping bombs and strafing. She fought off these attacks with her anti-aircraft munitions, scoring hits but failing to shoot down the attackers. Minesweeping became a night-only activity to avoid the aerial attacks.

By early April 1942, fuel reserves became critical. Japanese shore batteries began shelling ships in Manila Harbor. *Finch* anchored near Corregidor to avoid the shelling. On April 10, at 1600 hours, *Finch*'s luck ran out. During an air attack, a large bomb landed close to her port side. According to her commander, T.W. Davison, "Near misses bashed in the port quarter of the ship and made several rips in her side. She settled to the bottom in 3 fathoms of water and took a heavy list to port" (Davison, 1942, April 10).

The day prior to *Finch*'s sinking, Allied troops on the Bataan Peninsula surrendered to the Japanese invaders due to shrinking provisions, high casualty rates, and the impossibility of re-supply. After *Finch*'s damage grounded her, the crew feverishly moved useful supplies off the ship to Corregidor. They also destroyed any equipment that might prove useful to the Japanese. The crew joined ground forces on Corregidor who attempted to prohibit Japanese capture of the island.

As April ended, Corregidor's ragtag garrison of Marines, Regular Army, Navy, Coast Guard and Filipino defenders faced the same conditions as the defenders of Bataan weeks earlier. Japanese ground forces attacked in the early days of May. On May 4, the submarine USS *Spearfish* evacuated 27 people from Corregidor. In an interesting sidenote, two unauthorized personnel stowed away on *Spearfish* and were taken into custody when the sub docked at Fremantle. Their names were redacted from the war patrol report. Those evacuated included Marine, Army and Navy officers as well as 13 nurses. Also evacuated was *Finch*'s commanding officer, Lt. Cmdr. Davison, who was awarded a Navy Cross and Silver Star for his actions.

On May 6, 1942, General Jonathan M. Wainwright ordered a surrender to avoid further needless bloodshed. The defenders of Corregidor thus began their time as POWs of the Japanese Empire. Colonel Samuel Howard, commander of the 4th Marine Regiment and ranking Marine on Corregidor, ordered the national and regimental colors burned rather than see them fall into enemy hands. Many of the men spent the rest of the war in Japanese prison camps in the Philippines, while others were taken elsewhere on the infamous Hell Ships, to spend the rest of their war as virtual slave laborers.

In a final gesture by the *Finch* crew, Captain Davison delivered *Finch*'s service

USS *Finch* partially sunk in Manila Bay in 1942. NH 73590 Courtesy of Naval History & Heritage Command.

funds of cash on hand to the Navy Relief Society for assistance to Navy and Marine Corps members and families. The amount of the donation was $878, the equivalent of over $14,000 in the year 2020 (Davison, 1942, April 28).

In the ultimate indignity, *Finch* was salvaged by the Japanese and put into service as IJN Patrol Boat 103 in April 1943. She was eventually sunk by U.S. carrier planes in January 1945 in the South China Sea.

The Poem

The following deck log for January 1, 1942, was entered by Warrant Boatswain Orion A. Hammett, USN, on USS *Finch* three weeks after Pearl Harbor, three months before *Finch* was sunk, and four months before Hammett became a prisoner of war.

Hammett's poem is highly competent in its simplicity and its lilting, regular rhythm. It consists of only 16 lines organized into two eight-line stanzas. The lines themselves are short, six syllables, three beats per line, using the rhythm of everyday speech. Hammett clearly attended to the rhythm of the poem—in line 13, he crosses out the verb "are," a revision that maintains the feel of the rhythm.

In addition to capably managing the rhythm, Hammett gives each of the two stanzas its own distinctive purpose and content. Stanza one describes with haunting simplicity the tragic circumstances of the U.S. forces in the Philippines early in the war, the ongoing battle in which they were embroiled and their increasingly desperate situation—under fire from Japanese artillery in the hills and low on fuel. The stanza ends with a turn to an upbeat, defiant assertion of optimism and courage as the new year begins: "Are we downhearted? No!"

Stanza two offers the required data for any log entry as it catalogues anchors, props, boilers, gun crews and weather. But once again, Hammett ends the stanza with a turn from the mundane ship data to a veiled reference to Pearl Harbor just three weeks earlier. The year 1942, he says, has been "pushed in with a shove." Just as the first stanza ends with defiance, the second ends in typical droll American humor, subtle but loaded with meaning.

Here is the poem:

Here we lie at war,
Within Manila Bay
With cannon in the hills,
As echoes of the fray.
The Japs are close at hand.
Our fuel is running low
The new years rolling in
Are we downhearted? No!

With ninety fathoms out,
To starboard anchor firm,
And Boiler number one,
The props all set to turn,
Gun crews ~~are~~ at their posts
A full moon high above
As nineteen forty two
Is pushed in with a shove.

O. A. Hammett
Boatswain, U.S.N.

The Poet

Orion Alexander Hammett was born to Gather Clyde Hammett (sometimes known as Gaither) and Mary Emily Allison on October 19, 1906, near Paragould, Arkansas. In the 1910 Census, Gather was listed as an engineer on a dredge boat. By 1920, Gather had apparently moved from northeast Arkansas to Memphis, Tennessee. The 1920 Census lists Orion's mother Mary as the head of household and unemployed. Thirteen-year-old Orion and his 14-year-old sister Pauline worked at a local cooperage making wooden barrels and casks. Their likely place of employment was the Booser Stave Factory in Corning, Arkansas.

Some time between 1920 and 1930, Mary Hammett moved to California with her children, while Gather stayed behind in Memphis. In 1930, Gather worked as a carpenter for the U.S. Dredge Fleet. Orion joined the Navy prior to 1930. That year he was listed as residing at the Coco Solo Submarine base in the Panama Canal Zone. On September 21, 1935, Orion married Olga P. Yeager in Los Angeles. They apparently had no children.

A muster roll for USS *Cachelot* (SS 170) indicated that Orion first served aboard that submarine in June 1937 as a Chief Quartermaster. In October 1940, he was transferred to USS *Barker* (DD 213). He arrived on *Barker* on November 18, 1940, where he remained as a Chief Quartermaster until March 1941, when he was transferred to USS *Pillsbury* (DD 227). In September 1941, Hammett received an appointment to the rank of Warrant Bosun and was transferred to *Finch*. This transfer was fortuitous for Hammett because *Pillsbury* was sunk on March 2, 1942, and all hands were lost with the ship.

After *Finch* was abandoned, Hammett likely joined the hodgepodge of forces defending Corregidor. He was among those captured by the Japanese when Corregidor fell and remained a prisoner of war until the Japanese surrender in 1945.

It is unclear in which POW camp Hammett was held in the Philippines from capture in May 1942 until March 1944. It was probably a camp near Cabanatuan. Records indicate that on March 6, 1944, 300 men, including Hammett, were taken from a camp near Cabanatuan to the railway station in town. The Japanese placed those men on railway box cars and took them to the infamous Bilibid Prison, where they spent a little over two weeks. According to an affidavit from Lt. Col. Arthur G. Christensen (U.S. Army), ranking officer of the group, they then boarded a small freighter, *Taikoku Maru*, for transport to the Japanese mainland.

Thousands of Allied POWs, as well as local civilians, were herded onto similar ships during the war. These ships came to be called Hell Ships. Conditions aboard proved to be horrendous. Often packed into ships' holds with little or no accommodation for sanitation, POWs experienced almost unspeakable conditions. Intense heat or cold, little food and water, dysentery, and random beatings accompanied many of these trips to places where prisoners would become forced laborers. In Gregory F. Michno's book *Death on Hell Ships: Prisoners at Sea in the Pacific War* (2016), many of these POWs described their experiences in detail, including the voyage of Orion A. Hammett. As one of the 300 men on *Taikoku Maru* during

March and April 1944, he experienced less severe conditions than many who found themselves on the Hell Ships. According to Christensen's affidavit, *Taikoku Maru*'s hold was crowded and cold. Many men experienced minor illnesses. But sanitation proved to be better than on other Hell Ships. Christensen wrote:

> Latrine facilities existed on the deck, consisting of a small shed built out over the side of the ship. Prisoners were allowed use of the latrines practically without restriction both day and night. Washing facilities were practically non-existent due to the shortage of water on the ship. Sufficient water was furnished, though, for the washing of mess equipment [Christensen, Arthur].

Some men complained that while using the latrines that hung over the side of the ship, they would at times receive a rear end washing when the swells were large. However, *Taikoku Maru* prisoners' unfettered access to the latrine helped them avoid the experiences of other Hell Ship passengers, who ended up sitting in their own excrement or the excrement of animals that seeped downward from decks above them (Michno, 2016).

Also, food was more readily available on *Taikoku Maru*. As Christensen described it,

> Food was comparatively good. Cooking was done on the after well deck by prisoner cooks under the supervision of a prisoner mess officer and without too great interference by the Japanese. Cooking facilities consisted of expedient stoves made by cutting 55-gallon drums in half transversely and using them as fire boxes. Upon these were placed large cauldrons in which the cooking was done. These proved adequate as long as the sea was calm and the weather good, but when bad weather was encountered, it was next to impossible to cook on them. Wood was used for fuel [Christensen, Arthur].

Hammett and his 299 compatriots completed their voyage in 17 days, arriving in Osaka on April 9. The next day, they boarded a train for Hitachi and arrived there after 18 hours, on the 11th. According to Christensen, "Rail travel was in coaches which were crowded. Food en route during the train trip was good and furnished in individual 'bento' boxes."

Hammet again fortuitously escaped death when *Taikoku Maru* was sunk the next month on May 17, 1944, by U.S. Submarine *Sand Lance* (SS 381). Hammett spent the rest of the war in the Tokyo 12B—Mitsushima Camp (also known as Tokyo Area POW Command, Detachment 2 Hiraoka). He was repatriated to the U.S. in late 1945. He remained in the Navy and rose to the rank of lieutenant commander in 1950. He retired in 1956.

Hammett and his wife Olga settled in the little town of Rogue River, Oregon. Just over a year after his retirement, he resurrected his position as a Naval officer by playing Captain Blakeley, president of the court, in a production of *The Caine Mutiny Court-Martial* produced by the Southern Oregon College Players. He ran an unsuccessful campaign for Rogue River City Council in 1962.

Orion A. Hammett died on September 3, 1991, at the age of 84. He was preceded in death by Olga in 1988. Both are buried in Hillcrest Memorial Park Cemetery in Grants Pass, Oregon.

USS *Dewey*

The Whale-Struck

A photo of USS *Dewey* (DD 349) taken on October 27, 1936. NH 63112 Courtesy of Naval History & Heritage Command.

The Ship

USS *Dewey* (DD 349) was a Farragut-class destroyer commissioned on October 4, 1934. During her pre–World War II duty, she shuttled back and forth between the Atlantic and Pacific engaging in fleet exercises and training. At the end of 1939, she sailed to Pearl Harbor where she remained until the Japanese attack in December 1941.

On December 7, *Dewey* fought to repel enemy planes, then cleared Pearl Harbor that afternoon. During the following weeks, she patrolled the Hawaiian Islands. In February, she joined a projected attack on Rabaul, the notorious Japanese naval base in New Guinea sometimes referred to as the "Japanese Gibraltar," but the attack was cancelled when the force was discovered and engaged by Japanese aircraft. She aided in the downing of several planes. In March, she was called to screen the carrier USS *Lexington* (CV 2) during the Air Action off Bougainville. That action led to cancellation of the U.S. plan to attack Rabaul and a delay of the Japanese plan to attack New Guinea (Lundstrom, 2005).

In May 1942, *Dewey* participated in the Battle of the Coral Sea in which the U.S. fought the Japanese in the first clash involving carrier-to-carrier action. When USS *Lexington* came under fire from Japanese aircraft, *Dewey* fired upon the enemy planes and claimed to have shot down three. She experienced considerable damage from Japanese plane strafing and shrapnel from bombs exploding close aboard. At least five men were wounded (USS *Dewey,* 1942). When the battle-damaged *Lexington* started sinking, *Dewey* began rescuing her crew. She picked up 13 officers, 93 men and 15 Marines. All rescued personnel were taken to New Caledonia for transfer.

Through the rest of the war, *Dewey* participated in many of the important campaigns in the Marshall Islands, the Marianas, Iwo Jima and Okinawa. She also survived the infamous December 18, 1944, Typhoon Cobra, which became known as Halsey's Typhoon because Halsey took the fleet directly into it, leading to over two dozen ships sustaining significant damage. Three ships from Task Force 38 sank in the storm—USS *Monaghan* (DD 354), USS *Spence* (DD 512), and USS *Hull* (DD 350)—and nearly 800 crewmen perished. The Navy's investigation cited Halsey's "error of judgment" but did not sanction him.

At 0820, *Dewey* lost bridge steering control and transferred control to the steering motor room. After regaining bridge control, the crew donned life jackets and began securing equipment to prevent damage and injury. By 0900, the ship was rolling heavily and began to list. First, she listed 20 to 40 degrees starboard, then 10 to 30 degrees to port. Bucket brigades helped maintain water levels that leaked into the steering motor room. By 1015, *Dewey* lost radar and radio contact with the rest of the ship formation and listing increased to 40 to 50 degrees. The ship's doctor reported many crew injuries due to falling. At 1130, the main engines went down, leaving the ship without electricity and lights. Dead in the water, *Dewey* took on an estimated 500 to 1000 gallons of seawater on every big roll. All living quarters contained at least eight inches of water. Just when the crew thought that things could not get any worse, *Dewey* listed 60 degrees and then eventually over 70 degrees, according to the ship's inclinometers. Engine room crew reported that at one point their inclinometer pegged at 75 degrees. Wind speed was estimated to be around 110 knots (127 mph). At 1230, the number one stack broke away.

Later in the afternoon, conditions began to improve, allowing *Dewey* to get underway again and assess injuries and damage. She was more fortunate than some other vessels by recording no fatalities and no serious injuries. Most injuries were broken bones and bruises.

Dewey was awarded 13 battles stars for her service in World War II, putting her in the top ten percent of active destroyers during the war.

The Poem

The deck log below was entered on January 1, 1941, 11 months and one week before the Pearl Harbor attack, by Ensign J.T. O'Neill, USN. Though Europe was suffering the calamity of war and the clouds of that war were blowing toward the Americas, O'Neill's mood was light. In fact, the entire poem, which is only 12 lines long, can be read as tongue-in-cheek. The ship is moored in Pearl Harbor, surrounded by the incredible beauty of the islands, but O'Neill laments that "Living here is awfully hard" and "The O.O.D. [Officer of the Deck, O'Neill himself] feels not so good." The problem troubling him is that he'd much rather be enjoying shore leave in paradise. Hawaii in 1940 was an exotic landscape and culture, offering young American sailors a taste of a life most of them had only dreamed about. But O'Neill says he won't complain *too* much about being stuck on board because all the rest of the crew are in the same situation.

Dewey had been moored at the Pearl Harbor Navy yard since November 12 for what was apparently planned maintenance on her starboard high-pressure turbine (Dr. John Arnold, email, November 18, 2021). O'Neill refers obliquely to the condition of *Dewey* when in lines seven and eight, he says, "So here we sit in the whale-struck *Dewey*, / With our engines and steam lines all Ker-flooey." There is no record that *Dewey* had in fact been struck by a whale, but it appears O'Neill may be using the term "whale-struck" metaphorically. A week earlier, on November 25, *Dewey* was indeed struck while she was moored at the yard, but not by a whale. She was hit by a covered lighter—a barge used for unloading (lightening) or loading ships offshore, usually in harbors. The damage was not significant. Then, as if being hit were not enough, that same day a tugboat struck her starboard power cable and a supporting block. Tugs had to move *Dewey* to a different berth (Arnold, email).

O'Neill mentions that *Dewey* is operating on shore power. The final section of the poem offers a wry observation about the gangway watch, who is pulling his hair out wondering which ship in the harbor is hosting the Commander in Chief of the U.S. Fleet (CinCUS Fleet). It is not clear why the gangway watch sailor, typically a Petty Officer, was so concerned about the location of the senior officer.

O'Neill closes the deck log with another tongue-in-cheek comment about the poem he has just written. The comment is an addendum to the poem itself, saying that he trusts the mooring lines holding the ship more than he trusts the poem.

Here's the poem:

Moored in Pearl Harbor, Navy Yard,
Living here is awfully hard.
The O.O.D. feels not so good,
He'd be ashore if he possibly could.
But he can't make quite all the noise,
'Cause that goes for all the rest of the boys.
So here we sit in the whale-struck *Dewey*,
With our engines and steam lines all Ker-flooey.
From the dock we get our water and air,
While the gangway watch is tearing his hair,
Wondering which ship of the old U.S. Fleet,
Was present aboard the CinCUS [Commander in Chief US Fleet] Fleet.
Note: Moored with the usual lines which we trust more completely than the foregoing.

J.T. O'Neill
Ensign, U.S.N.

The Poet

John Timothee Trezevant O'Neill was born on April 15, 1916, to Rue O'Neill and Eva Whitthorne Trezevant in Dallas, Texas. His grandfather, Col. John Timothee Trezevant, was a member of the Society of the Cincinnati, an organization founded by Revolutionary War Continental Army officers in 1783. The Society's goal was to commemorate the founding of the new United States and to continue to promote the remembrance of the reasons behind its founding. The Trezevant family had a long history of service to the country.

Midshipman John Timothee Trezevant O'Neill from the 1939 Naval Academy Yearbook *Annapolis Lucky Bag*.

O'Neill received an appointment to the Naval Academy at Annapolis in 1935, where he was christened, not surprisingly, as "Tex" or "J. T. T." Going by his *Lucky Bag* entry, he must have been an easygoing midshipman: "Tex has his own philosophy which does not permit him to overtax himself, and any study hour will find him curled up with a magazine." He was slated to graduate in 1938, but a football injury kept him at the Academy until 1939. He served on USS *Louisville* (CA 28) in 1939 and 1940 and then served on *Dewey*.

After flight training at Pensacola, Florida, O'Neill flew scout planes from cruisers like USS *Helena* (CL 50) and at one point he became the commanding officer of Cruiser Scouting Squadron VCS-9. Later, he became the Executive Officer of VBF-85, a bombing squadron that flew off USS *Shangri La* (CV/CVS/CVA 38). O'Neill continued to fly combat missions in World War II and then went on to do the same during the Korean War. Over that time, he amassed well over 5000 hours of flight time. In Korea, he was a particularly ardent supporter of close air support for the ground troops. He flew 92 missions in his F4U Corsair "Lady Luck." In an era when jets were becoming the norm in the skies over the battlefield, Tex and his men flew down "on the deck" bombing and strafing to protect the vulnerable infantrymen. O'Neill once had to have his plane repaired due to damage incurred when a North Korean infantryman tossed a hand grenade at him as he was flying at less than 50 feet above the ground. He was a fierce advocate for the Corsair, once writing in a letter to his mother when it appeared that the plane was headed toward its manufacturing end, "[P]lease get Chance Voight [*sic*] on the phone and tell them my plane has had three tails, 66 patches, and two engines, but I'll get it back to the plant if I have to swim and tow it" (*Fort Worth Star-Telegram*, 1953). The Corsair was legendary for its ability to absorb damage and still complete the mission.

In 1950, a reporter aboard USS *Philippine Sea* (CV 47) described O'Neill as "a person who looked like he had been cast for the role of squadron skipper by a Hollywood director...." A new, relatively untested pilot stated of O'Neill, "What a guy! He's a flier's flier." When a voice over the intercom system in the ready room informed the pilots that launching of planes would commence in two hours at 1200, O'Neill exclaimed, "Two more hours. How many times do they think I can get up my nerve?" (*Knoxville News-Sentinel*, 1950).

In late 1951, O'Neill became operations officer of Cabaniss Field near the Corpus Christi Naval Air Station. CCNAS was an advanced training facility for carrier pilots at one time. He retired from the Navy in 1959 as Commander of All Weather Fighter Squadron 3 (VFAW-3) in San Diego, California. In his career in the Navy, O'Neill earned four Distinguished Flying Crosses, 11 Air Medals, three Presidential Unit Citations, and many other awards. He died on November 29, 1980, in Santa Clara, California. In a series of tweets, his son Kevin referred to O'Neill as "the greatest fighter pilot you've never heard of" (O'Neill, 2018).

USS *Gilmer*

Chasing Subs in Puget Sound

USS *Gilmer* (DD 233/APD 11) in Hampton Roads, Virginia, in October 1922. Note her 5/51 guns. She was one of five flush-deck destroyers to carry these weapons. NH 53732 Courtesy of Naval History & Heritage Command.

The Ship

USS *Gilmer* (DD 233/APD 11) was a Clemson-class destroyer commissioned on April 30, 1920. During her early years, she engaged in many training exercises on both the east and west coasts. *Gilmer* was decommissioned in 1938 but, with the onset of World War II, recommissioned in 1939.

When Pearl Harbor was attacked in December 1941, *Gilmer* was patrolling off the northwest coast of the U.S. For most of December, the ship was in a constant hunt for enemy submarines in Puget Sound. According to the commander's war diary for December 7 through 18, frequent reports of sub sightings had *Gilmer* heading off at full speed to points all along the Strait of Juan de Fuca and Puget Sound at all hours of the day and night. The searches were hectic. In blackout conditions, there were regular near-collisions, and on December 13 *Gilmer* experienced a minor collision with another search ship. At one point, *Gilmer* herself was reported as a possible Japanese sub. Weather conditions were often terrible, and the ship's commanding officer complained about the deplorable state of affairs of the military communication system, creating difficulty identifying ships and planes. The supposed submarine sightings were so frequent in the area of Crescent Bay, a few miles west of Port Angeles on the Strait of Juan de Fuca, that the Commanding Officer joked, "The Japs must have established a submarine base there" (USS *Gilmer*, 1941).

Gilmer participated in the Aleutians Campaigns beginning in June, when the Japanese invaded the islands of Attu and Kiska. The Aleutian Islands were important to the U.S., since they stretched southwest from Alaska far into the Pacific toward Japan, reaching to within 750 miles of the closest Japanese military base. The campaign to control the islands was not concluded until August 1943, when the U.S. retook Kiska.

Gilmer next headed west to Pearl Harbor. She began amphibious landing training with the Marines, and in January 1943, like many other older destroyers, she was reclassified as a high-speed transport. Her training for landing forces on beaches led to the role in which she served for much of the remaining war. Underwater Demolition Teams (UDTs—what are now called SEALs) in their nascent stages needed a platform for deployment. *Gilmer*, having practiced landing combatants on islands, became one of those ships that deployed UDTs and eventually became the UDT flagship during the Okinawa Campaign. On March 26, 1945, she suffered a hit on her galley deckhouse by a kamikaze, killing one and wounding three crewmen.

After the Japanese surrender, *Gilmer* carried former POWs from Japan to Okinawa and escorted ships moving Chinese troops to new deployments. She returned to the U.S. in January 1946. The Navy decommissioned her on February 5, 1946. She was struck from Navy lists later that month and sold for scrap in December.

Gilmer earned seven battle stars for her action in the Pacific Theater as well as the Navy Unit Commendation.

The Poem

The following deck log was entered by Lt. j.g. L.C. Brogger, USNR, on January 1, 1942. The poem consists of 39 continuous lines with no stanza breaks, but Brogger creates four-line units of the old ballad stanza, generally alternating four- and three-beat lines and rhyming the second and fourth lines of each unit.

Three weeks after Pearl Harbor, *Gilmer* is still patrolling off the northwest coast of the U.S., responding to America's intense concern about potential attacks on the Pacific Coast by Japanese submarines. As Brogger writes his poem, *Gilmer* is anchored in Puget Sound at Port Townsend in a state of high preparedness. He establishes the ship's position, moored with 30 fathoms of anchor chain in seven fathoms of water.

The ship's commander is getting his first good night's sleep in a long time because of constant false sightings of enemy submarines. In an apparent response to the commander's joke about the Japanese at Crescent Bay, Brogger says, "We've hunted Nippon submarines / From their base at Crescent Bay." Actually, *Gilmer* engaged no Japanese submarines, though she was kept busy by false sightings: "We haven't found a single one, / Despite what fliers say; / Their logs and roots and trees and stumps / Have kept us underway."

Following his complaint about the frustrated search for Japanese subs, Brogger does something unusual in deck log poems, referring by name to six of his shipmates and their activities on board. First, he mentions Seaman Albert C. Blatz, who is on the sound gear. Albert was the great-grandson of Valentin Blatz who founded Blatz Brewery in Milwaukee. Albert eventually became a sonarman on *Gilmer*. In December 1943, he was sent to the Navy V-12 program for officer training and was commissioned in 1944. The next shipmate mentioned in the poem is Yeoman Armour P. Bowles, who is on the phones. He also received a commission in 1944 and later served in the Korean War. He retired in 1958 at the rank of Lieutenant Commander (Paula Cox email, June 27, 2121). Next up is Gunner's Mate Lawrence E. Sheller, who is manning a machine gun and, according to Brogger, thinking of home. Sheller was eventually commissioned, served for 26 years and, according to his son Larry, retired at the rank of Commander in 1956 (email, June 16, 2021).

In the mention of his next shipmate, Brogger uses a play on the opening lines of the classic poem "The Night Before Christmas" to poke fun at Signalman James W. Judkins: "'Tis the night before New Years / And all through the ship / Not a creature is stirring—/ Except Judkins—the drip." Judkins is breaking into the galley to "rustle up some Joe" to combat the cold temperature and wind. According to his son Jim, Judkins enlisted on his 17th birthday, served 20 years and retired as a Chief Signalman (email, June 17, 2021). He is buried with his wife in Arlington Cemetery. Next up is Metalsmith Albert E. Morton, who is in the engine room "[k]eeping his turbines hot." Morton served on the USS *Yosemite* in the late '40s and attained the rank of Chief Metalsmith. The last shipmate Brogger mentions, Coxswain Norbert A. Rink, is the Boatswain's Mate and is "Sleeping—like as not." Rink also served in the Korean War and retired as a Chief Boatswain's Mate (Candice Renee-Rink Burley, email, July 9, 2021).

Brogger closes the deck log by saying that he has tried to write his entry as a poem, but that the Navigator will probably make him rewrite it in the standard form. But the Navigator did not do so. As with some other deck log poems, the reading is made poignant by the fact that Brogger did not survive the war.

Here's the poem:

We're anchored in Port Townsend,
With the anchor at short stay.
Ready for any emergency,
In a minute to get underway.
Point Wilson bears three sixteen true
From where the anchor lies;
The bearing of the light-on-dock
Is two seven nought, likewise.
The chain is thirty fathoms long
The water, seven deep;
The Skipper's in his nice soft bunk
Deep in a New Year's sleep.
He hasn't had one like it
For this is the thirtieth day,
We've hunted Nippon submarines
From their base at Crescent Bay.
We haven't found a single one,
Despite what fliers say;
Their logs and roots and trees and stumps
Have kept us underway.
Young Blatz is on the sound gear,
And Bowles is on the phones,
Sheller's on a machine gun
But his thoughts are on his home.
'Tis the night before New Years
And all through the ship
Not a creature is stirring—
Except Judkins—the drip.
He's breaking in the galley
To rustle up some Joe,
'Cause the wind is blowing briskly
and the temperature is low.
Morton's in the engine room
Keeping his turbines hot.
The Boatswain's Mate is Coxswain Rink—
Sleeping—like as not.
I've tried to rhyme my log today
But the Navigator's sure to say,
"Write it up in the regular way."

L.C. Brogger,
Lieut. (j.g.) DE-V(G), USNR

The Poet

Lloyd Christian Brogger was born on July 2, 1913, in Butterfield, Minnesota, to Norwegian-born Eivind Brogger and Cora Belle Fromm of Iowa. Brogger graduated from Butterfield's high school in 1930 and received an appointment to attend the Naval Academy at Annapolis. Listed as an Annapolis graduate in the 1935 *Lucky Bag,* he was also listed in the "resigned" section as a midshipman in a Navy Directory. The resignation was dated June 1935.

On February 4, 1939, Brogger married Delores Jane Meagher in Ottumwa, Iowa. At the time, Brogger was the manager of a commercial credit company in Des Moines. By 1940, Mr. and Mrs. Brogger moved to Milwaukee, Wisconsin, where he worked with Commercial Credit Plan, Inc. By 1941, he was in the U.S. Naval Reserve and began his service on *Gilmer*. After leaving *Gilmer*, Brogger commanded USS *Sands* (DD 243/APD 13) from July 1943 until April 1944 and USS *Liddle* (DE 206/APD 60) from August 1944 until December 1944.

Lloyd Christian Brogger from the 1935 Naval Academy Yearbook *Annapolis Lucky Bag*.

Brogger's command of the *Liddle* was cut short by a kamikaze plane on December 7, 1944. While steaming in Ormoc Bay, Philippines, *Liddle* and other ships were attacked by several suicide planes. Two ships, USS *Ward* (DD-139) and USS *Mahan* (DD-364), were struck. *Liddle* then became the target of several planes, and she put up furious fire to protect herself. A Zero began a run on the *Liddle,* and according to *Liddle*'s official report, the ship opened fire with guns forward and port side batteries. The plane exploded in the air 30 feet from the port side of the ship. The entire port side of the ship and the weather decks were showered by fragments of the plane and shrapnel, causing several injuries. Shortly thereafter, another Zero crashed into the flying bridge and exploded, demolishing the bridge, CIC, radio room and captain's sea cabin (USS *Liddle*, 1944).

Casualties were heavy. According to *Liddle's* official report, the attack left six officers and 19 crew dead, two officers and nine crew missing, one officer and 21 crew wounded and transferred to USS *Mercy* (AH 8). Ten crew returned to ship with minor wounds. One of those listed as missing and eventually declared dead was Lt. Cmdr. Lloyd C. Brogger. His body was never found. A memorial grave marker for him was placed in the Manila American Cemetery in the Philippines.

Brogger was awarded the Silver Star Medal posthumously. Here is an excerpt from the citation:

> On 7 December 1944, the *LIDDLE* was attacked simultaneously by three enemy dive bombers. By his skillful maneuvering of his ship and effective gun fire Lieutenant Commander Brogger

succeeded in avoiding the first two planes which were shot down and crashed close aboard. The third plane succeeded in crashing into the bridge of the *LIDDLE* causing severe casualties. When last seen Lieutenant Commander Brogger was still at his battle station on the open bridge attempting to save his ship from damage. Lieutenant Commander Brogger's conduct and actions were in keeping with the highest traditions of the United States Naval Service.

USS *New Orleans*

The Coconut Log Bow

USS *New Orleans* (CA-32) in English waters, circa June 1934. Photographed by Wright & Logan, Southsea, England. Donation of Captain Joseph Finnegan, USN (Retired), 1970. NH 71787 Courtesy of Naval History & Heritage Command.

The Ship

USS *New Orleans* (CL/CA 32) was the lead cruiser in the New Orleans class, sometimes called "treaty cruisers" because they were the last to be built to the limiting standards of the Washington Naval Treaty of 1922. She was commissioned in April 1934. Originally classified as a light cruiser, she was reclassified as a heavy cruiser soon after being laid down in March 1931. Like the other six cruisers in her class, she saw extensive action in the Pacific campaigns.

After a shakedown cruise to northern Europe, *New Orleans* sailed from New York on July 5, 1934, to Panama, where she met USS *Houston* (CA 30), which was carrying President Roosevelt. She remained with *Houston* and the president on a cruise through the Panama Canal, then to Hawaii, and finally to Astoria, Oregon. From 1935 through the end of the decade, she operated in both Atlantic and Pacific waters. She joined the Hawaiian Detachment in late 1939.

New Orleans was moored at Pearl Harbor on December 7, 1941, with her engines under repair. When the Japanese attack began, shore power was cut. While engineers worked below deck by flashlight to raise steam, men on deck, breaking into the locked ammunition boxes, fought against enemy planes with rifles and pistols. The ship's guns, being aimed and fired manually without power, entered the action after ten minutes. Several crew members suffered wounds when a fragmentation bomb exploded close aboard.

A legend and a popular song of the late 1940s grew from the action on *New Orleans* that day. The story says that without power to operate the ammunition lifts, a bucket brigade was formed to bring the heavy shells up from below. According to testimony from the lieutenant in charge at the time and interviews with the crewmen involved, a chaplain, Lt. j.g. Howell Forgy, encouraged the men in the bucket brigade by patting them on the back and saying, "Praise the Lord and pass the ammunition." In May 1955, Forgy appeared on the American game show *I've Got a Secret* and told his story (Budanovic, 2017).

After convoy and screening duty, *New Orleans* sailed in January 1942 to San Francisco for repairs and installation of new radar and 20mm guns. After further escort duty, she returned to Pearl Harbor to join Task Force 11. With TF 11, she participated in the Battle of the Coral Sea, where she rescued 580 survivors from the sinking aircraft carrier *Lexington* (CV 2). *New Orleans* sailors dove overboard to rescue men in the water, and boats from the cruiser moved in close to the burning *Lexington*, in spite of the fire and shrapnel from explosions.

In June, *New Orleans* participated in the Battle of Midway, screening the carrier *Enterprise*, and in July and August she screened USS *Saratoga* (CV 3) in the Solomon Islands Campaign, fighting off intense air attacks at Guadalcanal. After *Saratoga* was torpedoed, *New Orleans* guarded her on her passage to Pearl Harbor. After returning to the Solomons, *New Orleans* fought in the November 30 Battle of Tassafaronga. A torpedo detonated her forward magazines, ripping off her bow and taking a fifth of the ship's length. The explosion killed 182 men. The severed bow punched several holes in the ship's port side hull as it passed, and it took heroic action to save her. According to James Linn, "The Damage Control Officer on the *New Orleans*, Lt. Cmdr. Hubert M. Hayter, and two of his men, Lt. Richard A. Haines and Ensign Andrew L. Forman, remained at their damage control posts despite the fact that it was filling up with toxic fumes." All three were asphyxiated by the fumes (Linn 2017). Hayter posthumously received the Navy Cross for his actions.

New Orleans was able to reach the harbor of Tulagi, a small Solomon Island, on December 1, and the crew, after camouflaging the ship to avoid air attacks, built a bow out of coconut logs. Eleven days later, they headed for Sydney, Australia, sailing backwards because of the nature of the rigged bow (Linn, 2017). On December 24, she arrived at Sydney, where a temporary stub bow was attached. In March 1943, she sailed to Puget Sound where she got a new bow and had all battle damage repaired.

In October, November and December, *New Orleans* was active at Wake, repulsing a Japanese torpedo plane attack, and in the Gilberts and the Marshals. On December 4, the new *Lexington* was torpedoed, and *New Orleans* guarded her on her passage to Pearl Harbor for repairs. Beginning in January 1944, she was active in the Marshalls, in the attack on the powerful Japanese base at Truk Island in the Carolines, and in the Marianas. During air strikes on Truk, U.S. warships circled the atoll attacking escaping Japanese ships and sinking a light cruiser, a destroyer, a trawler and a submarine chaser.

While supporting the Allied landings at Hollandia in April, one crewman was lost and another badly injured when a disabled plane from USS *Yorktown* flew into *New Orleans*' mainmast. The plane struck gun mounts as it fell and sprayed the ship with gas before exploding when it hit the ocean. *New Orleans* continued patrol and support of action until early May.

In June, while escorting the U.S. Fast Carrier Force (Task Force 58), *New Orleans* participated in the climactic Battle of the Philippine Sea. So dominant in numbers

USS *New Orleans* camouflaged at Tulagi, Solomon Islands, some days after she was torpedoed during the November 30, 1942, Battle of Tassafaronga. National Archives photo 80-G-216014.

and experience was American air power from the carrier group, the air-sea battle (June 19–20) was referred to as the Great Marianas Turkey Shoot. Naval aircraft and submarines sank three Japanese carriers and destroyed almost every enemy plane launched in those two days. *New Orleans* and other screening ships shot down the few planes that reached U.S. carriers. Japanese naval air power was virtually nonexistent afterwards.

From July through October 1944, *New Orleans* participated in campaigns at Saipan, Iwo Jima, the Palaus and Okinawa. In late October, she guarded the Fast Carrier Force in the Battle of Leyte Gulf. After participating in the attack against the Japanese Southern Force on October 24 and the attack on the Japanese Center Force, she was with Admiral Halsey as he chased the decoy Northern Force to Cape Engano. After making short work of the much smaller and weaker Japanese Northern Force, *New Orleans* and Halsey's Third Fleet returned to Leyte too late to engage what was left of the Japanese Center Force. Halsey's futile attempt to chase down Admiral Kurita, who was long gone, has been derisively called "Bull's Run," a reference to Halsey's nickname, Bull (Ray, 2021).

New Orleans sailed for Mare Island in December for overhaul and in late April provided artillery support for the long battle on Okinawa. She was in Subic Bay in August when hostilities ceased. From the end of August 1945 until January 1946, she worked in China, Korea and Japan evacuating Allied prisoners of war and carrying veterans home to San Francisco. After visiting her namesake city for ten days in February, she arrived at the Philadelphia Navy Yard in March. She was decommissioned in February 1947 and stayed in reserve until March 1959. She was sold for scrap in September of that year.

New Orleans received 17 Battle Stars for her service in World War II, making her one of the most decorated ships of the war.

The Poem

The deck log below was entered January 1, 1942, by Lt. J.H. Howard, USN. The poem is short, only 12 lines of six rhymed couplets. Howard writes the poem just three weeks after Pearl Harbor. Three weeks after *New Orleans*' crew fought Japanese planes with rifles and pistols. The ship is screening a convoy of troops to Palmyra and Johnston islands south of Hawaii along with USS *Reid* (DD 369) and USS *Conyngham* (DD 371), both of whom were also in Pearl on December 7.

The poem expresses a typical post–Pearl anger and swagger in lines four and five—the crew don't give a damn about Jap torpedoes and their guns are ready to right the wrongs. The ship is darkened, lit only by the full moon as it cuts the waves. Three engines supply enough power to make 18 knots. She is on a zigzag course, periodically changing direction and speed to confound enemy submarines. Choreographing dozens of ships spread out over ten square miles of ocean was a dizzying prospect, especially when the ships were running in radio silence and were darkened. And different countries had differing practices. The solution to the puzzle was a small device called a Zigzag Clock. Each ship in the convoy had one. The dance was planned out in detail ahead of time, and all the clocks were synchronized with the flagship. When the alarm rang on the clock, everyone made the same changes at the same time. The turns and speed changes were all prearranged.

Power on the ship is supplied by boilers one, two, five and six, and Howard speaks in typical American light-hearted slang when he says the boilers make the ship "[g]et up and git." The final two lines are reverent and show the standard American optimism after the dark days of Pearl Harbor. All hands are praying "[t]hat today's sun will bring a Happy New Year."

Here's the poem:

'Tis the first mid of forty-two,
NEW ORLEANS at sea and REID, too.
Also, screening is CONYNGHAM,
So for Jap torpedoes we don't give a damn.
Our guns are ready—wrongs will be righted!
With decks only by full moon lighted.
Three engines strain to make eighteen
From course seventy-one our zig-zags are seen.
To furnish the ship with "get up and git,"
Boilers one, two, five and six are lit.
And all hands join in this prayer
That today's sun will bring a Happy New Year.

J.H. Howard,
Lieutenant, U.S. Navy

The Poet

James Hampden Howard was born on November 8, 1908, in the District of Columbia to Charles Edward Nason Howard and Charlotte Agnes Small. It is small wonder that Howard chose a career in the military. His father and his brother both attained the rank of colonel in the U.S. Army, the latter being awarded a Silver Star for gallantry during actions in the Philippines during World War II.

Howard graduated from the Naval Academy at Annapolis in the Class of 1930. While at the academy, he captained the fencing team and was a national fencing champion. He married Phyllis Hammond on November 11, 1936, in Portsmouth, Virginia.

His first ship assignment took him to USS *Arkansas* (BB 33), and then to USS *Cincinnati* (CL 6), USS *Wyoming* (BB 32) and USS *Phelps* (DD 360). After postgraduate work in ordnance engineering, in 1939 he served on USS *Philips* (DD 498) before boarding USS *New Orleans* (CA 32). While aboard *New Orleans*, Howard participated in eight Pacific Theater Campaigns. During the Battle of Tassafaronga, when the bow of the ship was blown off, he played an important role in the heroic effort that saved the ship, entering dangerous areas that were flooding or filling with toxic gas. This was exactly 11 months after he wrote the midwatch poem above. He was awarded the Silver Star for his actions.

Midshipman James Hampden Howard from the 1930 Naval Academy Yearbook *Annapolis Lucky Bag*.

After the war, Howard commanded three vessels through the late 1940s into the early 1950s: USS *Merrick* (AKA 97), USS *Chukawan* (AO 100) and USS *Noble* (APA 218). He also served as Chief of Staff for Cruiser Division Two and in 1956 became commander of Transport Amphibious Squadron Two while aboard USS *Monrovia* (APA 31) (USS *Monrovia*, 1956). He retired from naval service in 1959 at the rank of rear admiral.

As a trained engineer, Howard authored *Electronic Information Displays for Management* (1966) and edited the book *Electronic Information Display in Management Information Systems* (1963). Also during the 1960s, he taught courses in computer science at American University and Northern Virginia Community College.

Howard died on November 12, 1998, in Alexandria, Virginia, and is buried at Arlington National Cemetery. Below is his citation for the Silver Star Medal.

> The President of the United States of America takes pleasure in presenting the Silver Star to Lieutenant Commander James Hampden Howard, United States Navy, for conspicuous gallantry and intrepidity in action while serving aboard the USS NEW ORLEANS (CA-32), during an engagement with enemy Japanese naval forces in the Solomon Islands Area, on the night of 30 November 1942. After his ship had been severely damaged by a terrific explosion, Lt. Commander Howard, with utter disregard for his own personal safety, entered gas-filled and flooding compartments and worked tirelessly to save his ship. His skill, courage, and outstanding devotion to duty were an inspiration to his men and were in keeping with the highest traditions of the United States Naval Service.

USS *Marblehead*

The Long Journey Home

USS *Marblehead* (CL-12) in harbor, circa the early 1930s. The location may be San Diego, California. Donation of Franklin Moran, 1967. NH 64633 Courtesy of Naval History & Heritage Command.

The Ship

USS *Marblehead* (CL 12), a scout cruiser (more lightly gunned and armored than the larger cruisers), was commissioned on September 8, 1924. After her shakedown cruise in the English Channel and the Mediterranean, she operated in Australia and Central America before moving to the Far East where she served in 1927 and 1928. For the next ten years, she operated in both the Atlantic and Pacific arenas. Then she was assigned to the Asiatic Fleet, operating out of the Philippines. When Japan attacked Pearl Harbor on December 7, 1941, she was anchored in Borneo.

In January 1942, *Marblehead* operated with the Netherlands and Australian Navies against enemy shipping in the East Indies. On February 4, she was swept into an adventure that would make her a legend in the chronicles of World War II survival. As she was steaming with a group of British, Dutch and Australian ships to intercept a Japanese convoy, she came under attack by waves of Japanese bombers. After avoiding damage from the first three waves, she took two direct hits and a near-miss off the port bow from enemy bombers in the fourth wave. She suffered a nine-foot hole in her hull and 34 compartments flooded (Topp, 2019). Arthur G. Robinson, who commanded the ship, claimed that at least 37 planes attacked them. There was no air cover at the time (Ritchie, 1942). *Marblehead* suffered extensive fires, listed to starboard, and began to settle by the bow. With her steering engines shot and her rudder frozen to hard port, she maintained speed and began careening in rapidly widening circles. Though the fires were brought under control, she counted 15 dead and 84 seriously wounded. According to Robinson, the crew "were called upon to work day and night in fuel oil, water and debris. They worked, ate, and—when they could find a place to lie down—slept in their oil-soaked clothing." Most of the sleeping compartments had been destroyed. Robinson manned the bridge for 60 hours without relief during the heroic effort to save the ship.

Commander Nicholas B. Van Bergen, who just a month earlier had written one of the deck log poems in this chapter and who became Executive Officer when Exec W.B. Goggins was seriously wounded by the first bomb, became a key force following the bombings. Captain Robinson said, "He was everywhere ... pulling men out of the oily water, rescuing wounded, reporting conditions to the bridge" (Ritchie, 1942). Van Bergen received the Navy Cross for his actions during the battle.

Steering entirely by varying the engine speeds on port and starboard, *Marblehead* made port at Tjilatjap two days and 400 miles later with a forward draft of 30 feet and an aft draft of 22 feet. "We'd tickle her with the left propeller," Robinson said, "and then with the right. And when we had her straight, we'd go full speed ahead" (Ritchie, 1942). Temporary repair could be made to the nine-foot hole in the hull, stanching the most serious flooding to keep her afloat, but they could not raise the stern to repair the steering. They were forced to leave their wounded crew members at the Dutch hospital under the care of Corydon M. Wassell, a Navy doctor from Little Rock, Arkansas, who would receive the Navy Cross for saving the most severely wounded from being captured by the Japanese and for shepherding them to safety in Australia. His heroics inspired a biographical novel by James Hilton the next year, *The Story of Dr. Wassell*, followed in 1944 by the Cecil B. DeMille movie by the same title, starring Gary Cooper.

After repairs at Tjilatjap, *Marblehead* narrowly escaped destruction when the tow line broke as she was being moved through the minefield protecting the harbor. Miraculously, the Dutch pilot was able to get her through. Still steering with her engines, she began an epic journey in search of permanent repairs. At Ceylon, she found the dry dock fully booked for the next month. The crew members were able to complete some repair to the steering engines using salvaged parts. Though the rudder had to be operated from the steering engine room instead of the bridge and had a limited range of motion, it was an advancement over using the engines to steer (Topp, 2019). On March 24, she arrived at Simonstown, South Africa, on the Cape of Good Hope, where she received repairs extensive enough to allow her to cross the South Atlantic to Recife, Brazil, before sailing for New York, where she arrived May 4, and entered dry dock for full repairs. Her journey home had covered 20,000 miles.

Marblehead put to sea again on October 15, 1942, operating in the South Atlantic until February 1944. She moved to the Mediterranean in July of that year and began preparations for Operation Anvil, the invasion of Southern France. She provided support bombardment for Allied assault troops in August before withdrawing to Corsica. She returned to the U.S. to perform training missions and was decommissioned in November 1945 and scrapped in February 1946.

She received two battle stars for her service in World War II.

Poem One

The following deck log was entered on January 1, 1941, by Ensign R.E. Fahnestock, USNR. The poem exhibits strong echoes of 19th-century poetry in its use of elevated language throughout, giving it a distinctive tone. Writing 11 months before Pearl Harbor, Fahnestock refers to "the war-wracked earth!" The poem includes a title, which is unusual in the deck logs, and consists of 44 lines, divided into four stanzas of varying lengths. The first three stanzas use a somewhat varied rhyme scheme—rhymed couplets with other rhymes interspersed. The fourth stanza is entirely rhymed couplets.

The ship rests in berth Cast-8 in Manila Bay secured by 270 feet of chain—"Two score fathoms of chain when added to five." The starboard anchor is at 30 feet depth—"A score of feet and ten below the sea." The poem opens with the ringing out of the old year in the Navy tradition at midnight of eight bells for the old year and eight for the new. The rest of the first stanza then waxes eloquent on the theme of time, the last line waking the new year "with the siren's shrill frenody." For that last word, "frenody," Fahnestock must have intended "threnody," a lament or requiem, especially since he refers to the bells as a "fit requiem" to the past year.

The second stanza offers a stark and sensual contrast between the peaceful mooring in Manila Bay and the war-wracked earth. Lovers reach out to each other with "parted lips, low sighs, soft parlance." But this "pagan reverence" is betrayed by "a year born in agony." The world in Manila Bay, Fahnestock says, seems to be "a world without hate," and the sounds that fill the night do not echo warfare and death or shriek of typhoon.

After stanza three centers the ship on bearings to various landmarks, stanza four attends to more of the usual deck log requirements. Power from boiler 12, a list of numerous ships and submarines—"sleek armed fish … ready to dive." Then, as in so many deck log poems, the young officer closes with a lament over what is lost in this late midwatch. On the nearby ships, he says, duty officers like himself are thinking of dancing and beer and muttering gloomily, "Happy New Year."

Here's the poem:

Nineteen forty-one begun
"Make eight bells on time," the O.D. said;
The echoes fit requiem to a year just now dead.
Yet, Muting the sorrow of time turned to memory,
Each double peal expanding in sound,
Thrust onward the earth in its breathless round.
Till the last stroke hails from eastward, time,
Suspended above, an imaginary line,
To wake the new year with the siren's shrill frenody.

Ashore parted lips, low sighs, soft parlance,
Betrays in the gloom man's pagan reverence
To a year born in agony from the war-wracked earth!
Yet in Manila Bay in berth Cast-8,
We seem to be anchored in a world without hate.
The night filled with sound but yet without strife,
No shriek of typhoon or of desecrated life.
Two score fathoms of chain when added to five,
Gives length and weight to the great iron jive,
Which holds us enchained within birth.

A score of feet and ten below the sea,
The starboard anchor embedded in the lea,
Of timbers, stark remainders of a Spanish man-of-war.
Bearing three naught five is South Breakwater light;
Naught seven four to where Michel's height,
Betrays through its windows the plume of a sub,
And naught two eight bears the A&N Club;
None of which were present on that tragic day of yore.

A light brown haze from boiler 12 shows power,
Steam for auxiliaries, machines used every hour.
About us in a circle, attentive to the belle,
Ford, Peary and Jones court the fair Isabel.
Eight sleek armed fish lie ready to dive,
Their sides showing phosphorous—almost alive;
Pike, Pickerel, Perch, Permit alongside the Tarpon,
Searaven, Seawolf, cruel Shark and Sealion.
While Pigeon and Bittern, nearby Napa and Heron,
Lie reverent beneath the proud flag on the Houston.
On Black Hawk and Pecos and Asheville nearby,
Are officers with the duty, even as I.

They're thinking as we are of dancing and beer,
And muttering gloomily
Happy New Year.
Here as an after thought I also might say,
That at zero hour we held searchlight display.
R.E. Fahnestock, Ensign, U.S. Naval Reserve

Poet One

Robert Eric Fahnestock was born on November 12, 1915, in Bournemouth, England, to Gibson Fahnestock and Valerie Elizabeth Windisch. His family featured prominently in American financial circles in the 19th and early 20th century. His great-grandfather, Harris C. Fahnestock, an investment banker, had a hand in many businesses and corporations that still exist in some form to date (e.g., Citigroup, Oppenheimer Holdings). The Fahnestocks loved yachting, and in 1902 Harris commissioned the building of *Shenandoah*, a three-masted schooner that sailed to the most glamorous places in the world. In fact, *Shenandoah* in all her 55-meter glory still sails today after a major refit. Chartering *Shenandoah* with her crew of 12 allows passengers to experience luxury reminiscent of the Victorian era, including listening to the playing of a Steinway grand piano in the ship's salon. Gibson Fahnestock also owned a yacht, *Shenandoah III,* that sported four masts.

The family spent time in the south of France during the 1920s. According to passport applications, this was for health reasons and for education of the children. Mrs. Fahnestock had contracted tuberculosis during the World War I years, an infection that would play a significant role in the family's life at the outbreak of World War II. According to newspaper reports, the family sailed around the world in 1930 and 1931 aboard *Shenandoah III*. Robert attended University of California, Berkeley, and joined the ranks of the U.S. Navy's Reserve Officers Training Program.

As war began to break out around the world, this wealthy family was about to experience tragic times. Robert's brother, Gibson Clarence, flew for the Royal Canadian Air Force and the RAF. In 1943, he joined the U.S. Army Air Corps, and in early 1944 while co-piloting a B-26 Marauder bomber, he was shot down and captured by the Germans. He spent time in Stalag Luft III, made famous by the movie *The Great Escape*, and survived a death march out of the camp when Russian armies got within a few miles in early 1945 (Dix Noonan, 2017).

Robert planned to formally announce his engagement and wedding to Charlotte Nathorst in late 1941. Charlotte was the daughter of General and Mrs. Carl E. Nathorst who lived in Manila, Philippines. The wedding was planned for December. Robert's mother and father arrived in Manila in late summer and looked forward to the upcoming festivities. Events of early December changed everything for these two families. On January 6, 1942, Robert's father and mother were forced into the Santo Tomas internment camp by the Japanese. According to Gibson Fanhnestock's testimony to a Congressional Committee in 1947, the conditions at the camp were horrific from the start.

Lack of food and "fearful overcrowding—30 to 60 in a room—the vermin-infested living quarters, the voracious mosquitoes, 750 women to 5 toilets, and the lack of medical care" led to his wife's flareup of a tubercular lesion. She began coughing up blood.

> My wife was allowed out of the confines of the camp on medical grounds, and as she was 90 percent deaf I was allowed out on a temporary pass to take care of her. But it was too late, and nothing could be done, and my beloved companion of 30 years passed away on June 30, 1942 [Fahnestock, 1947].

Gibson was eventually taken away with others to a work camp where he remained for a while until taken back to Santo Tomas. U.S. forces liberated the camp on February 3, 1945. At that time, he weighed only 105 pounds and was barely ambulatory due to beriberi.

Robert's fiancée, Charlotte Nathorst, and her parents suffered a different fate. The elderly General Nathorst, who had once been in charge of the Philippine Constabulary, was not put into an internment camp. However, in 1945 as U.S. forces began to take back Manila, the Japanese visited a series of atrocities upon the civilian population. A nurse to the general testified that he, his wife Lillian and their daughter Charlotte took shelter in a German club not far from their apartment. The Japanese threw grenades into the building and set it alight. Anyone who tried to escape was shot. The Nathorsts were never seen again by the nurse (Marbas, 1945). Newspapers around the U.S. reported their deaths.

Robert Fahnestock enlisted in 1939 and served on *Marblehead* during her epic voyage around the Cape as a watch and junior division officer. In December 1943, he took command of the landing ship USS *LST 491* and led *LST 491* during the D-Day landings of June 1944. After the war, he left active duty but remained in the Naval Reserve until retiring as a lieutenant commander in August 1959.

Fahnestock married Florence Annabel Degner in June 1948 and seems to have lived the rest of his life in relative obscurity compared to previous generations of his family. When his younger brother Herbert married Annette Francis Girton in 1938, the *Oakland Tribune* announced the wedding with the headline, "Socialite Heir Weds U.C. Girl: Herbert Fahnestock to Continue Studies; Shuns Wedding Trip." Herbert's comment about this choice: "[W]e want to live quietly so we can go on with our studies." A dearth of headlines about the Fahnestocks into the 1950s and '60s may indicate that the other children of Gibson Fahnestock wished the same.

Robert Eric Fahnestock died on January 8, 1980, in Los Angeles. He is buried in Woodlawn Cemetery in the Bronx, New York.

Poem Two

The following log was entered on January 1, 1942, by Lt. Cmdr. N.B. Van Bergen, USN. The poem is short, only 12 lines. But the structure is unusual, each line being long—all but one line spilling over the end of the line space—with the rhyme occurring internally in each long line. In the first line, "1942" rhymes with "its crew," and in the second line, "Timor Sea" with "Japanee." And so on until, after the 12 long lines, Van Bergen adds the average steam pressure and rpms before his signature.

The poem is unusual in another way. After the first line, a New Year wish that the ship will experience honest pride and success, everything else in the poem is standard deck log information. The ship is darkened. Van Bergen gives the course, speed, revolutions. He provides a quick list of the ships in column, then identifies the zigzag plan and the boilers that are online. The conditions of readiness come next, followed by a comment on the rain, the boilers and the final course plan.

Whereas most of the deck log poets take advantage of the New Year's opportunity to share various concerns about ship life, shore life and the world in general, Van Bergen seems satisfied simply to use the poetic license granted by the New Year's midwatch to communicate the bare essentials of the ship's condition. Van Bergen was more than the typical ensign or lieutenant j.g. who would normally be assigned duty for the New Year's midwatch. He was a lieutenant commander, an older and more experienced officer.

One month later, the ship experienced a cataclysmic attack that all but sank her. Van Bergen exercised all his courage and stamina to help save the ship. As a result of his heroic actions, he received a "battlefield promotion" and the Navy Cross. The vagaries of fate loomed in the shadows to push him to the edge and test his character. He passed the test with flying colors.

Here's the poem:

> This starts the year 1942—may it bring honest pride and success to this ship and its crew.
>
> Steaming, darkened, in the Timor Sea, with all eyes peeled for the Japanee.
>
> On course true and psc; 195 and 191 respectively.
>
> Our speed, for all these evolutions, is thirteen knots, one two one revolutions.
>
> The ships in column open order, with Langley guide and leading; then Holland, Marblehead (OTC) and Joffre, in that order proceeding.
>
> Preston and Parrott on either bow, screening as hard as they know how.
>
> The moon shines brightly in the heaven, so we use zig-zag number 7.
>
> Boilers 7 to 12 are on the line, the others out of commission at the present time.
>
> The ship's in the following conditions: Readiness Three, Yoke and Two for Ammunition.
>
> At one-o-five the rain began, the sleepers grabbed their beds and ran, and the ships abandoned the zig-zag plan.
>
> At 0130 by the Chief's own admission, boilers 1 to 6 were back in commission.
>
> At 232 it was sufficiently clear the courses of Plan #7 to steer.
>
> Average steam 265 Average rpm 116.4
>
> N.B. Van Bergen, Lieutenant Commander, U.S. Navy

Poet Two

Nicholas Bauer Van Bergen was born on May 27, 1899, to Edward August Van Bergen and Louise Bauer in San Francisco. Like the Fahnestock family described in the previous biography, the Van Bergens enjoyed wealth and notoriety that stemmed from their fathers' business acumen. Edward was often referred to as "Handsome Eddie" in the San Francisco newspapers' society pages. Louise Bauer was described as "a statuesque beauty, whose position in society was such" that her wedding to Edward "made history in San Francisco." "The Bauer–Van Bergen nuptials united two of the best known German-American families in California" (*San Francisco Examiner*, 1913).

Also like the Fahnestocks, the Van Bergens experienced a family tragedy that impacted the rest of their lives. Edward died at the young age of 47 in 1909 and left his fortune to his wife and two children Minna and Nicholas. Minna fell in love with Donald Jadwin, also an offspring of a wealthy family. They married in the summer of 1912, but the marriage struggled to match the high expectations that a highly touted society marriage created. Minna and Donald became estranged. Then on January 13, 1913, Donald arrived uninvited at a dinner party being held at the Van Bergen home. His manner led those present to believe that he came to reconcile with Minna. However, as he approached the table and reached around his wife for what all thought to be an embrace, he pulled out two pistols and shot her twice in the breast. He then stepped back and fired one shot into his own brain. Both Minna and Donald died from their wounds. Sitting next to Minna at that dinner table was her 13-year-old brother Nicholas Van Bergen.

Midshipman Nicholas Bauer Van Bergen from the 1921 Naval Academy Yearbook *Annapolis Lucky Bag*.

Nicholas received an appointment to the U.S. Naval Academy at Annapolis in 1917 and graduated in 1921. His entry in the Annapolis *Lucky Bag* states, "Here's hoping that Lady Luck will give you a better hand in the future than she has in the past" (U.S. Naval Academy, 1921). Whether that referred to his family tragedy is unknown. After receiving his commission as an ensign, he boarded USS *California* (BB 44). Battleships were the place to be for a newly minted Academy graduate.

After serving on *California*, Nicholas spent several years on destroyers, becoming Executive Officer aboard USS *Hovey* (DD 208). For a while in the mid–1930s, he was posted to the Naval ROTC at the University of California at Berkeley. Both Nicholas and Robert Eric Fahnestock, his future *Marblehead* shipmate, were associated with that program at about the same time. After another set of deployments on ships, Van Bergen spent time at the Department of the Navy in Washington, D.C. He got his first ship command in 1940, taking over USS *Monaghan* (DD 354) for a little over a year. Monaghan would later be lost with nearly all hands in Typhoon Cobra in 1944.

Van Bergen came aboard *Marblehead* as gunnery officer in late 1941 prior to the Japanese attack on the ship. His actions are well-documented in the ship's history above. He received his Navy Cross from Secretary of the Navy, Frank Knox. His final ship command began in August 1944 when, as a captain, he took over the attack transport ship USS *Clay* (APA 39). After leaving Clay in 1945, Van Bergen received a promotion to Rear Admiral and held a professorship at the University of Colorado for a brief period. Poor health led to his retirement. Some speculated that his health problems traced back to his experiences on the *Marblehead*.

Nicholas Bauer Van Bergan died at the Oak Knoll Naval Hospital in Oakland, California, on May 3, 1947. He was just a few weeks shy of his 48th birthday. He is buried at Cypress Lawn Memorial Park in Colma, California.

Poem Three

The following log was entered on January 1, 1944, by Lt. R.B.G. Creecy, USN. The copy preserved in the National Archives is the "rough log," in Creecy's own hand. It's clear that Creecy and Quartermaster D.E. White, and the navigator who approves the log, all took the opportunity to have a little fun. In the log heading that identifies the ship, Creecy wrote "Marble Maru," playing on the Japanese habit of using "Maru" in naming a ship; the word indicates great respect and love for the object. Just before Creecy signed the log, he added a parenthetical note that he had help writing the poem from D.E. White, Quartermaster 3rd Class. Below his signature, Creecy adds the complaint, "The Midwatch OOD Again." Then the Navigator, R.S. Gillette, who signs off on the log, joins in with, "Accepted but terrible poetry."

As Ensign Fahnestock did in the first *Marblehead* poem, Lt. Creecy provides a title for his work: simply "Happy New Year." The poem itself consists of 30 lines broken into nine stanzas of varying length, and the fun Creecy is having appears again in the way he sets the poem on the page. The placement of the stanzas and the varied indentation of lines is playful. The first stanza of the poem laments that sailing the South Atlantic is not as romantic as people think. Though the war will drag on for almost two more years, Creecy expresses the typical American optimism in stanza two when he hopes that 1944 will see the end of the war.

The rest of the poem, with one brief exception, provides standard deck log fare: boilers in use, ship's course, radar, conditions of readiness, speed. An exception comes in stanza seven, where Creecy's sense of humor re-surfaces: "'Happy New Year' the boatswain's mate said, / Some of the boys growled "we'll shoot you dead."

The convoy has been following a zigzag plan, but Creecy says the ship ceases the zigzag pattern and begins "[s]teaming as straight as the mythical crow" (as the crow flies). But the poem ends with a speed change and "Occasionally a few turns, less or more."

Here's the poem:

Happy New Year

Mid Watch—Oh we sail the South Atlantic,
Where the Fourth Fleet rules supreme;
But it's not so damn romantic
As some would have it seem.

We welcome in a New Year
That we hope will end the war,
So here's to all hands "Good Cheer,"
For Nineteen Forty-Four!

Steaming under boilers 12–11–10
Stop and think of that again
Also boilers 6–5-4
To generate steam more and more
Main engine in use to the fore
Cruisers aft; there is no more.

With the U.S.S. *Winslow*
On base course zero-nine-oh,
PSTC [Per Steering Compass] is one-one-three,
And 130 is PSC [Per Standard Compass].

Winslow guide, twenty-five hundred yards away,
Marblehead on form one-eight, they say.

Manned and searching, Radar One
Ship darkened for everyone.

Condition Two of Readiness
Material Condition "Yoke," I guess

0000 "Happy New Year" the boatswain's mate said,
Some of the boys growled "we'll shoot you dead"

Ceased zig-zag now on zero nine oh
Steaming as straight as the mythical crow

Changed speed to 13 knots (rpm 124)
Occasionally a few turns, less or more.

(Poetry with the assistance of
White, D.E., QM 3/c)
R.B.G. Creecy, Lieut. USN
The Mid Watch OOD Again

Poet Three

Midshipman Richard Bland Lee Creecy from the 1942 Naval Academy Yearbook *Annapolis Lucky Bag.*

Richard Bland Lee Creecy was born on June 16, 1920, to Donald Brooke Creecy and Clarissa Anne Balch in Baltimore. Donald, a Georgetown University Law School graduate, maintained a successful law practice in the Baltimore area. Richard attended the prestigious Gilman School before accepting an appointment to the U.S. Naval Academy at Annapolis. While there, he won the prestigious Trident Society Prize (a sword) for writing the best original paper on the U.S. Constitution. He graduated from the Academy in December 1941 (Class of 1942).

As a newly minted ensign, Richard reported for duty aboard USS *Tennessee* (BB 43) on January 4 but transferred to a hospital on January 31 suffering from "German Measles" (rubella). He returned to the ship on April 11. On September 1, he was detached from *Tennessee* and ordered aboard *Marblehead*. Creecy eventually attended flight school and became a Naval Aviator serving in various posts including on USS *Intrepid* (CVS 11) in the early 1960s. He retired at the rank of captain in 1966. In the mid–1940s, he married Lillian Edith Holgate, with whom he had four sons.

After retiring from the Navy, Creecy dedicated himself to promoting nuclear arms control. He served on the Arms Control and Disarmament Agency for over ten years. He also served as committee secretary at the SALT I talks and served as executive secretary of the U.S. delegation at SALT II meetings in Geneva. Capt. Creecy was a senior fellow of the Members of Congress for Peace Through Law and a member of the Arms Control Association.

Richard B.L. Creecy died at Bethesda, Maryland, on August 24, 1986. He is buried at Arlington National Cemetery in Arlington, Virginia.

Addendum

Creecy acknowledged the help of his quartermaster, D.E. White. Donald Eugene White was born in Dodge City, Kansas, on April 19, 1920. He lived in the Kansas-Missouri area for most of his life. His promotion in rate to Quartermaster

3rd Class came only a month before he assisted Creecy with the midwatch poem above. He attained the rank of Chief before leaving the Navy. White worked for Transcontinental & Western Airlines (TWA) for 43 years, which included time before and after World War II. He was manager of the reservation service office when he retired from the company. He died on November 8, 1990, and is buried at Leavenworth National Cemetery, Leavenworth, Kansas (*The Kansas City Star*, 1990).

USS *Russell*

A Highly Decorated Lady

An official Navy photograph of the USS *Russell* (DD 414) in 1939 or 1940, shortly after completion. NH 107278 Courtesy of Naval History & Heritage Command

The Ship

USS *Russell* (DD 414), one of the most decorated destroyers of World War II, was named after Rear Admiral John Henry Russell. When the ship was built, she was sponsored by the admiral's granddaughter and commissioned November 3, 1939. The war in Europe had broken out two months earlier. *Russell* operated on the Atlantic Neutrality Patrol, organized by President Roosevelt, in the Western Atlantic and Caribbean until the bombing of Pearl Harbor. Though Roosevelt declared the U.S. neutral in 1939, by 1941 Anglo-American collaboration would increase, and Fleet Patrols would become more aggressive (Hussey, 1991). When Pearl Harbor was bombed, *Russell* was sent to the Pacific where, in January 1942, she escorted reinforcements to Samoa, then joined Task Force 17, screening the carrier *Yorktown* during attacks on the Gilbert and Marshall Islands.

In February, *Russell* and TF 17 moved on Canton in the Phoenix Islands and then supported raids on Rabaul and Gasmata in New Guinea. During the Battle of the Coral Sea in May, she screened for the carrier *Yorktown*. When the carrier *Lexington* was heavily damaged and had to be abandoned, *Russell* joined her screen and circled as rescue ships evacuated personnel. At the Battle of Midway in early June, she again screened for *Yorktown* until the carrier was damaged by torpedo planes and had to be abandoned. *Russell* took aboard 492 survivors.

For the next two months, *Russell* performed training exercises before joining the campaign for Guadalcanal in August 1942. In October, she participated in the Battle of the Santa Cruz Islands, during which she joined rescue efforts for the carrier *Hornet*, taking aboard Rear Admiral George D. Murray, commander of Task Force 17. After rescue operations, she withdrew to Numea for repair of her damaged superstructure. From December 1942 through April 1943, she spent most of her time screening convoys.

After overhaul on the West Coast, she participated in the Aleutian Campaign. Then, following further brief escort duty, she supported the invasion of Tarawa in November and attacks on Kwajalein in early December. Throughout 1944, *Russell* was busy with escort duties and screening for various Pacific campaigns. In January 1945, she supported the invasion of Luzon. While screening outside Manila Bay on January 7, she participated in the sinking of the Japanese destroyer *Hinoki*. Under frequent attack from enemy aircraft, including kamikazes, and submarines, she spent the rest of the month screening, bombarding and escorting in the area. On January 10, with the task force in Lingayen Gulf, reports surfaced of small motor torpedo boats inflicting damage on transport ships in the early morning hours. According to the War Diary for that day, "another more desperate effort" was reported at 1300 when they spotted "swimmers under boxes carrying explosive charges." The destroyer *Smith* (DD 378) dropped depth charges in the area to eliminate the threat (USS *Russell*, 1945).

In April, *Russell* joined the battle for Okinawa, continuing escort, screening and patrol duty there into May. At the end of that month, she returned to the U.S. for a yard overhaul. She was still in Seattle when the war ended. She was decommissioned on November 15. In September 1947, she was sold for scrap.

Russell earned 16 battle stars for her service in World War II.

Poem One

The crew of USS *Russell* left three poems describing their wartime experience. The log below was entered on January 1, 1941, by Lt. L.S. Pancake, USN. The poem consists of 30 lines of rhymed couplets with no stanza breaks. Pearl Harbor is 11 months and one week in the future. *Russell* has been serving in the Neutrality Patrol off the East Coast for the past year and will do so for the rest of 1941. She is currently moored in the Philadelphia Navy Yard on the Delaware River. Steam and water are being supplied from the pier, and in the perpetual complaint by deck log poets, Pancake says, "Likewise comes juice, but not any beer."

For the next ten lines, Pancake details the ships of Squadron 2 that accompany *Russell*. He salts the list with comments about the Senior Officer's snarl, the crew's nightly nap, and a tongue-in-cheek comparison of USS *Allegheny* to one of the great actors of the time, Lon Chaney, probably Lon Chaney Jr., best known for his role as the Wolf Man in 1941. After asserting that he is peeved by crewmen returning from leave, the final six lines of the poem register three of the returnees and comment on their business ashore or aboard.

There is a deep poignancy in reading this poem, with the simplicity of its pre-war tone and its relaxed humor. Less than a year into the war, Lt. Pancake will be killed in action.

Here's the poem:

Moored starboard side to U.S.S. HUGHES,
With manila lines in lieu of thews,
Both ships are resting beside pier three,
And of snow and ice are wholly free.
We float in the dirty Delaware,
And all aboard are well aware,
That at the Philadelphia Navy Yard
We are resting from the neutrality guard.
No steam nor water is being made,
But they come aboard in a steady parade,
Through lines connected to the pier.
Likewise comes juice, but not any beer.
Squadron 2 is here less the WALKE and O'BRIEN,
But conspicuously absent is the ORION.
THE SOPA [Senior Officer Present Afloat] in the ALBEMARLE,
At the following ships has a right to snarl:
The CIMARRON which resembles a raft,
And looms o'er a bevy of smaller craft.
On the CURTIS, O. INGRAM and BELKNAP,
The crew are taking their nightly nap.
Present likewise is the ALLEGHANY,
Whose appearance reminds one of Lon Chaney.
Some of the boys came back from leave,
A fact which causes me to peeve.
McGASKILL, Gunner's Mate two pieces [two pieces: Second Class]
Is back from visiting his nieces.
HICKS, J.A., Seaman First Class,
Over the brow was seen to pass.
While Fireman Second F.W. BOWER,
Is back to generate more power.

L.S. Pancake,
Lieutenant, U.S. Navy

The Poet

Lee Sylvester Pancake was born on April 24, 1907, to George Washington Pancake and Alvina Catherine Canfield. He earned an appointment to the U.S. Naval Academy at Annapolis, where he was known for his ability to stay calm in any situation.

He graduated from the Academy in 1931. Navy registries indicate that he served on a variety of ships prior to 1940, when he came to serve on *Russell* as Engineering Officer. The ships he served on were USS *Aaron Ward* (DD 132), USS *Evans* (DD 78), USS *Oklahoma* (BB 37), USS *Augusta* (CA 31) and USS *Mindanao* (PR 8).

In December 1938, Pancake became engaged to Sara Ann Schaidt. Schaidt was educated at Duke University and the Cours de civilization française de La Sorbonne. They married on February 21, 1939, in the chapel at the Naval Academy at Annapolis.

On August 16, 1942, Pancake received orders to transfer to USS *Morris* (DD 417) for duty as Engineering Officer for Destroyer Division Two. That transfer sealed his fate. On October 26, 1942, during the Battle of Santa Cruz Islands, *Morris* was under attack by Japanese planes dropping bombs and torpedoes, as well as strafing the ship. Lt. Cmdr. Pancake climbed up to *Morris'* gun director to assist in tracking the aircraft when he was hit by a single round from one of the planes. He died almost instantly. He was buried at sea and was awarded the Navy Cross posthumously for his actions.

His Navy Cross citation reads:

> The President of the United States of America takes pride in presenting the Navy Cross (posthumously) to Lt. Cmdr. Lee Sylvester Pancake (NSN: 0–70263), United States Navy, for extraordinary heroism and distinguished service in the line of his profession as Engineering Officer of Destroyer Squadron TWO, during the operations against enemy Japanese forces off the Santa Cruz Islands, on 26 October 1942. When hostile planes launched a vicious raid against the task force to which his group was attached, Lt. Cmdr. Pancake, with cool courage and utter disregard for his own personal safety, unhesitatingly volunteered to go aloft to the director platform. There, although perilously exposed to violent attack by low-flying enemy strafers, he rendered valuable assistance in the spotting of Japanese aircraft until he was killed. His conspicuous initiative and unyielding devotion to duty were in keeping with the highest traditions of the United States Naval Service. He gallantly gave his life for his country.

Poem Two

The log below was entered on January 1, 1942, three weeks after Pearl Harbor, by Ensign W.H. Bargeloh, USNR. The poem is short, only 16 lines of rhymed couplets. *Russell* has just been assigned to the Pacific after working for two years in the Neutrality Patrol off the East Coast. Bargeloh does not wander far from the standard expectations of a naval deck log, and other than a passing nod to the ship's condition of readiness, there is no mention of the war.

Russell is moored at San Diego, and line six of the poem makes a tongue-in-cheek allusion to the practice of censoring communications during the war. He shares the ship's condition of readiness, the boilers in use, and location of the Senior Officer Present Afloat, and then names the ships that share the harbor with them. Line 14 echoes the standard lament of the poor OOD (Officer of the Deck) on duty for New Year's Eve. Referring to three of *Russell*'s sister ships, he says, "No doubt their crews are ashore on a lark." He closes with a mention of the busy yard craft around them.

Here's the poem:

Moored with starboard anchor chain to buoy Number Twenty,
To keep us afloat, six fathoms seem plenty.
San Diego, California, is our location now,
But we'll tell not a soul (Censor, take a bow!)
All hands are now feeling comparatively free,
Because the *Russell* for a change, has set Condition III,
Boiler Number two for auxiliary use simmers,
Not a light do we show—not even our dimmers.
The *Trenton* is with us, just across the way,
Board her may be found the SOPA [Senior Officer Present Afloat]
Our sisters, the *Hughes*, the *Walke*, and the *Sims*,
Are also here with us, shipshape and trim.
The *Dent*, *Talbot*, and *Kilty* loom shadowy and dark;
No doubt their crews are ashore on a lark
The *Yorktown* and *Richmond* nearby lie,
As various harbor craft passeth by.

W.H. Bargeloh,
Ensign, D-V(G), U.S.N.R.

Poet Two

William Henry Bargeloh, Jr., was born on August 17, 1915, to William Henry Bargeloh, Sr., and Anna Lee Armstrong in Parkersburg, West Virginia. William Sr. operated Bargeloh Groceries in Parkersburg for many years. William Jr. graduated from Parkersburg High School in 1933 in the college preparatory program and then earned his bachelor's degree at West Virginia University. For a time after college graduation, he worked for Monongahela West Penn Public Service Company, which was a short line–trolley system in Parkersburg and the surrounding area.

Bargeloh received his commission as an ensign in February 1941 after attending the USNR Midshipman's School in New York. He married Elizabeth Leanora Acker in Charleston, West Virginia, a week after the Pearl Harbor attack. Acker was working at the Interstate Commerce Commission and attending classes at Georgetown University (*The Evening Star*, 1942).

At the end of World War II, Bargeloh became the Executive Officer of the V-12 Navy College Training Program at Emery and Henry College in Emery, Virginia. In 1946, he was made head of the Navigation Department at the NROTC program at Pennsylvania State College. After promotion to lieutenant commander, he boarded

USS *Weiss* (APD 135) to serve as its captain. He eventually rose to the rank of commander and in the early 1960s served for a time as Operations Officer at the Fleet Training Group at Guantanamo Bay, Cuba. He retired from the Naval Reserve in August 1962.

William H. Bargeloh, Jr., died on September 1, 1978, and is buried in Mount Olivet Cemetery in Parkersburg, West Virginia.

Poem Three

The log below was entered on January 1, 1945, by Lt. j.g. L.C. Feldmann, USNR. The poem consists of 28 lines of rhymed couplets, which are steeped in references to the war. *Russell* is en route to the attack on Luzon as part of Rear Admiral Edward Barbey's Task Force 78, the Northern Attack Force. As Feldmann provides the required information for a deck log (boilers, speed, other ships present, course, formation, condition of readiness), he intersperses frequent images of the conflict in which they are engaged. They are steaming to "keep up the fight" and to "speed the setting of the 'Rising Sun.'" He mentions "the outer guard" and says they are on "[a] collision course to meet the foe." They keep rolling so they can keep their date with the enemy. He claims that their disposition is sure to confuse "the Nips." The ships are darkened to conceal the might of Admiral Barbey's force.

The final two lines ring with American determination to finish the fight: "Thus starts the log on this New Year's Day / As we steam to westward, let come what may."

Here's the poem:

Under boiler one we are steaming tonight
From Aitape, New Guinea, to keep up the fight.
Destination—Lingayen Gulf, Luzon
To speed the setting of the "Rising Sun."
With Task Group seven eight point one we ride
The BLUE RIDGE Sopus [Senior US Officer Present] and fleet guide.
Then there is the JENKINS, she's Comscreen [Commander, Screen]
Among the outer guard she rates supreme.
Present also are other ships galore
As listed in OP [Operational Priority] ten three—forty four.
Course true and gyro—320
A collision course to meet the foe.
Course 318 magnetic sail
Should Sperry's Gyro Compass fail.
Station ninety one fifty, we are patrolling
Our speed ten knots, yet we just keep rolling.
Formation speed is only eight
But we'll be sure to keep our date.
In disposition Charlie two we cruise,
The Nips I'm sure, it will confuse.
Condition of readiness three we keep
As we patrol along in our sea-going jeep.

For any trouble that might be met
Condition Baker we have set.
The ship is darkened throughout the night
To conceal the extent of Barbey's might.
Thus starts the log on this New Year's Day
As we steam to westward, let come what may.

L.C. Feldmann, Lieut. (j.g.), USNR

Poet Three

Lilburn Charles Feldmann was born on May 12, 1917, to "Guy" Guido George Feldmann and Sophia L. Koch in New Franklin, Missouri. He graduated from New Franklin High School in 1935 and from Central College in Fayette, Missouri, in 1939. According to his draft registration, Feldmann worked for the National Youth Administration in Jefferson City, Missouri, a New Deal works program that provided employment and educational benefits to individuals ages 18 to 25. He was an avid basketball player and played the trumpet while in college. In the 1940s, he and his brother had a dance band in Marthasville, Missouri, called the Melody Masters (*Indiana Gazette*, 2000).

Like many men his age, he enlisted in the Navy and spent some time as an enlisted man before attending Midshipman's training in Chicago. He received his commission as an ensign on November 14, 1942, and reported aboard *Russell* in February 1943. He eventually became *Russell*'s first lieutenant and Damage Control Officer. By mid–1945, he had risen to the rank of lieutenant.

After the war, on June 5, 1946, Lilburn married Sara May Contrucci, a registered nurse he met while serving in Philadelphia. He earned a master's degree from the University of Missouri in 1947. He worked as a CPA for the Devereaux Foundation until his retirement in 1999. He died on February 11, 2000, in Bryn Mawr, Pennsylvania. He is buried in the cemetery of Saint Bernard of Clairvaux Roman Catholic Church in Indiana, Pennsylvania.

USS *North Carolina*

"Showboat"

USS *North Carolina* (BB 55) at sea off New York City, June 3, 1946. Photographed from a Naval Air Station, New York, aircraft. NH 97267 Courtesy of the Naval History & Heritage Command.

The Ship

USS *North Carolina* (BB 55) was commissioned on April 9, 1941. She was the first new battleship to join the fleet in nearly two decades. She received so much attention in the buildup to her commissioning as a new, modern battleship that she was given the nickname "Showboat." After a shakedown cruise in the Caribbean, she performed intensive training exercises and then sailed to the Pacific in June 1942. She joined the drive across the Pacific, supporting the landings on Guadalcanal and

Tulagi in early August and engaging in the Battle of the Eastern Solomon Islands later that month. While protecting the carrier *Enterprise* there, *North Carolina* shot down between seven and fourteen planes in an eight-minute engagement. She lost one man to strafing during the fight.

Continuing to support the landings at Guadalcanal in the following weeks, she was twice attacked by submarines, and on September 15, while sailing with the carrier *Hornet*, she took a torpedo to her port side. According to the war report, the torpedo passed astern of USS *Mustin* (DD 413), which radioed warning to *North Carolina*. The battleship turned right full rudder attempting to avoid the hit, but the torpedo struck 20 feet below the waterline. The explosion caused a water column to rise to the level of the stacks and washed one man overboard. The ship immediately developed a five-and-a-half–degree list to port, which was quickly corrected by counter-flooding. In all, the ship lost five crewmen to the explosion, but after damage control righted the ship, she continued her mission (USS *North Carolina*, 1942).

North Carolina spent much of 1943 screening fast carriers and in September began preparations for the Gilbert Islands campaign. She spent ten days in November providing heavy bombardment of Makin, Tarawa and Abemama. Then in December, she supported the invasion of the Marshall Islands, the bombardment of Nauru and the attack on Kavieng, New Ireland. In January 1944, she joined Admiral Mitscher's Fast Carrier Strike Force 58. In February, she participated in campaigns in the Caroline Islands and the Marianas. In March and April, she joined attacks on Palau, Woleai, Hollandia, Truk and Ponape before heading to Pearl Harbor for repairs.

In June, *North Carolina* returned to the Marianas and provided protection to carriers as well as heavy bombardment in the assault on Saipan. On June 19, in what came to be known as the Great Marianas Turkey Shoot, she joined the Battle of the Philippine Sea and shot down one of two Japanese planes that penetrated the air defense. She continued support of the campaign in the Marianas until the end of June, then returned to Puget Sound for overhaul. After rejoining the carrier group in November, she was immediately confronted by Typhoon Cobra before finishing the month supporting the Leyte Campaign.

She screened carriers in December 1944 and January 1945 for assaults throughout the Philippines, Formosa and the Ryukus, then provided bombardment for the assault on Iwo Jima in February. In April, she supported the assault on Okinawa. On April 6, after fighting off three kamikazes, she took a five-inch round of friendly fire that killed three men and wounded 44. After overhaul at Pearl Harbor, she participated in the bombardment of the Japanese home islands.

After the Japanese surrender, *North Carolina* participated in occupation duty until September, then returned to Boston in October. After overhaul in New York, she participated in exercises and carried Naval Academy midshipmen in a summer training cruise. She was decommissioned in 1947. After being struck from the Navy list in 1960, she was transferred to the people of North Carolina in

1961. In April 1962, she was dedicated as a war memorial at Wilmington, North Carolina.

She received 12 battle stars for her service in World War II.

Poem One

The following log was entered on January 1, 1942, by Lt. A.G. Ward, U.S.N. *North Carolina* was still involved in training in the Atlantic. The poem is not long, 16 lines of rhymed couplets, and Lt. Ward sticks pretty close to the information expected in a Navy deck log. The ship is sailing into the New Year with clear weather on course 344; USS *Washington* (BB 56), the second North Carolina Class battleship (commissioned a month after *North Carolina*), is leading the formation while *North Carolina* brings up the rear. Line three of the poem hints at the typical complaint by deck log poets that the sailors on the bridge are not having any New Year's fun. Boilers three through six provide power for a speed of 12 knots.

Ward gives the ship's material condition and condition of readiness and says the ship is protected from Japanese and German subs by USS *Hogan* (DMS 6) and USS *Stansbury* (DD 180). After giving the ship's course, he wraps up the poem with relief that the end of his watch has come and a wish for a Happy New Year.

Here's the poem:

The beginning of a New Year, all bright and clear,
Course 344; Washington ahead, we in the rear,
The watch on the bridge hasn't any kicks,
Boilers in use three, four, five and six.
Our speed from these, with more in store,
Only twelve knots, not a bit more.
Ship has been set in condition red Yoke,
Never at sea do we intend to joke.
Protected from subs of the Japs or Germany,
By those faithful destroyers, HOGAN and STANSBURY.
In the AA battery condition three,
As it should be, when at sea.
One thing neglected, to be added too,
By psc [per standard compass], ship's head three four two.
With this the end of the first watch of the year,
To my relief, a Happy New Year.

A.G. Ward,
Lieutenant, U.S. Navy

Poet One

Alfred Gustave "Corky" Ward was born on November 29, 1908, to Benjamin Edward Ward and Helen Scott Toulmin in Mobile, Alabama. After attending Barton Academy in Mobile, he enrolled at the U.S. Naval Academy in 1928. He served as editor-in-chief of the Annapolis *Lucky Bag* in his senior year. Ward acquired the nickname "Corky" while at the Academy and it apparently followed him throughout his career. A commission as ensign followed his graduation from the Academy in 1932. A few years later, he earned a Master of Science degree in electrical engineering from Massachusetts Institute of Technology.

Ward's first assignments were aboard USS *Northampton* (CA 26) and USS *Perry* (DD 340). While stationed on *Northampton*, he married Winona Elizabeth Viereck on March 9, 1937, in Washington state. As conditions for a second world war loomed, he boarded USS *North Carolina* (BB 55) and distinguished himself as a gunnery officer. Twice he earned Bronze Star Medals with "V" device for his actions during the war. After World War II, he commanded USS *Hollister* (DD 788) and began a series of commands of Destroyer Forces in both the Pacific and Atlantic. He rose to the rank of rear admiral in 1957 and vice admiral in 1961 as he approached what was likely to be his best-known command.

In 1962, Vice Admiral Ward played a significant role in the Cuban Missile Crisis. As tensions between America and the USSR grew, it became known that Cuba had received nuclear weapons from the Soviets. The U.S. perceived this as a significant security threat, and President Kennedy and his advisors weighed several options, including an invasion of Cuba. The president decided that a blockade or quarantine of Cuba was the best option. As Commander of the Second Fleet (Atlantic), Ward led the naval forces enforcing this escalation of responses. Those who knew Ward believed that he was the right person for the job. One admiral colleague was quoted as saying, "Corky is a quiet, positive guy who does things in an easy way.... Problems don't excite him" (*Fort Worth Star-Telegram*, 1962). During the crisis, Ward was told that at least one ship heading toward Cuba had missiles in her hold (Allen, 2012). The blockade and political negotiations avoided a nuclear conflagration.

Midshipman Alfred Gustave "Corky" Ward from the 1932 Naval Academy Yearbook *Annapolis Lucky Bag*.

Ward went on to serve as Deputy Chief of Naval Operations and U.S. Representative to the NATO Military Committee. He retired as a full admiral in 1968. After retirement, he served as the fifth headmaster of the Severn School in Maryland, a boarding school that had close connections to the Academy in Annapolis.

Admiral Alfred Gustave Ward died

on April 3, 1982, and is buried in the U.S. Naval Academy Cemetery in Annapolis, Maryland.

Poem Two

The following log was entered on January 1, 1945, by Lt. j.g. F.A. Gates, USNR. From the time Lt. Ward had written his New Year's Day 1942 poem, the ship had spent two and a half years in the Pacific engaging in almost every major campaign. At the time of writing this poem, *North Carolina* was screening carriers for various strikes in the East China Sea. The poem is long—68 lines divided into 17 stanzas and consisting of rhymed couplets throughout. Gates' tone is light-hearted and informal, at times droll or ironic. The opening lines set the tone with stoic resignation: "Forty-four is gone—here's forty-five. / What a helluva place to see it arrive." With the second stanza, he establishes his self-deprecating humor. His ambition is to "log this watch in the best Navy tradition, / Which, so they tell me, calls for verse, / So here I go, for better or worse."

The third stanza takes a humorous swipe at the navigator (who will have to sign off on the deck log) for drinking tea instead of coffee, saying it's a Russian habit. Stanza four exhibits typical 1940s slang with the phrase "hep to the jive" and refers to a potential Japanese ship as a "skunk." With stanza five, Gates initiates the standard content for a Navy deck log, which carries through the rest of the poem. They are in Task Force 38.3, and the carrier *Essex* (CV 9) is the guide ship (the ship from which all other ships calculate their position). The tone is informal, slangy, creative. The stanza ends with an interesting turn of phrase. He mentions "our fleet, 3-Williamized." The Third Fleet was formed in 1943 under the command of Admiral William Halsey. The next year, the Fifth Fleet was formed under the command of Admiral Raymond Spruance from the ships of the Third Fleet. Halsey and Spruance alternated command of the fleet for major operations—designated Third Fleet when under Halsey and Fifth Fleet when under Spruance. When either staff was not in command, they planned the next operation. Gates seems to be saying that the fleet is currently "Williamized" under Halsey as Third Fleet.

Stanza seven begins the usual listing of ships in the formation. He calls the carriers "flat-tops" and seems to address a phantom audience when he says that the carriers are "queens of the ocean to you." In stanza eight, he notes that the battleships *North Carolina* and *Washington* are together in the formation, as they were in Lt. Ward's poem three years earlier. Stanza nine ends with a creative rhyme when Gates pairs *Preston* with *molestin'*. Stanza ten follows with a little humor at the expense of the helmsman, accusing him of being asleep at the wheel, and another great pairing of rhyme words: *rumpus* and *compass*.

After commenting on speed and propeller revolutions in stanza 11, Gates adds indirectly in stanza 12 the typical complaint about lack of New Year's celebrations, saying the ship is darkened and adding a parenthetical comment: "On New Year's Eve? Some joke!" The stanza ends with what may be a mistyped word, when he says that the ship is in Condition of Readiness Three and "On the twenties you'll find *navy* a man." (Italics added.) It seems likely Gates meant to say that on the 20mm guns there was *nary* a man, since Condition Three would require only one-third to one-half of the crew to be on watch. All eight boilers are providing top speed, thanks to the "black gang toilers." The term "black gang," referring to the crew manning the boilers, is a holdover from when early ships were powered by coal.

At 0358, planes are launched from the carrier *Essex*, and Gates considers the move with droll American humor: "They'll hit the Japs, and we'll watch the fun." The poem's final line, while commenting on the weather, seems to play on the old adage on the month of March: "In like a lion, out like a lamb." Gates claims, "Like a lamb doth FORTY-FIVE come in!"

Here's the poem:

Forty-four is gone—here's forty-five.
What a helluva place to see it arrive,
The Captain is in his shack, and all the watch is alert,
The uniform today is with hats—and with shirts.

But let's get along with my one ambition—
To log this watch in the best Navy tradition,
Which, so they tell me, calls for verse,
So here I go, for better or worse.

Now the watch is drinking coffee—
The Navigator, tea.
That's the way in Russia
But it's not for me.

The *North Carolina* (BB55),
Is still in the Navy, hep to the jive,
Afloat with Admiral Halsey's Fleet
Hoping for a skunk to meet.

Our task force is numbered 38.3
With Essex guide and O.T.C. [Officer in Tactical Command]
38.1 and 2 comprise
The rest of our fleet, 3-Williamized.

5 Roger is our disposition.
Right now we're passing through position,
130°T from the guide we bear—
Four thousand yards from here to there,

With *Essex*, *Langley*, *Ticonderoga*
and *San Jacinto* we fear no bogie
They're our flat-tops, queens of the ocean to you.
But to us—just the guys on circle two.

While at three and a half thousand, out away,
There's the *Flint*, *Vincennes*, *Miami*, *Santa Fe*
And *Biloxi*, our cruisers—not to shun
The *North Carolina* and the *Washington*.

Seventeen cans have a helluva time
Chasing the subs on circle nine.

Three of them, the *Cotten*, *Prichett*, and *Preston*,
Are picketing for what may be a molestin'!

295°T&pgc [True & per gyro compass], is base course. But I'll not guarantee.
What the helmsman is heading, for when a look I steal
I usually find him asleep at the wheel.
(But I did hear him say, midst the din and the rumpus,
"checking 276 per steering compass")

16 knots is standard speed
107 rpm we need. [rpm—revolutions per minute]
But the tanks are waiting! There's fuel we must burn!
Steam 25 knots—use 178 turns!

We're in material condition "Red Yoke"—
Darkened. (On New Year's Eve? Some joke!)
Condition of readiness is three (Nan).
On the twenties you'll find navy a man. ["navy"—nary]

On the line are all eight boilers
Top speed from our black gang toilers!
(26.5 knots can be done)
Engineering condition 31.

In condition 8 are the planes.
Radio 2, which means we must refrain
From chipping, kicking, and squawking too much.
Radar condition 5 (no guard, or such)

At zero zero twenty-five
Course was changed to 305,
Speed, to 22. Tell me, how
Will we manage to use our fuel up now?

The *Essex* launched at fifty-eight past three.
Our truck lights enabled them to see.
Their pilots are training for what is to come.
They'll hit the Japs, and we'll watch the fun!

The weather is cool, the moon is bright.
Clouds fill half of the sky tonight.
The sea is calm, there's a little wind.
Like a lamb doth FORTY-FIVE come in!

F.A. Gates,
Lt (j.g.), USNR

Poet Two

Floyd Albert "Duke" Gates was born on August 6, 1918, to Louis Henry Gates and Margaret Metcalfe Farnsworth in Joliet, Illinois. He participated in both football and basketball during his time at Joliet High School, earning all-conference honors in football and playing on the state championship basketball team. After graduating in 1938, he enrolled at Lake Forest College and majored in education. Over his four years at LFC, Gates earned nine varsity letters in three different sports.

According to his entry in the Lake Forest Sports Hall of Fame, he was a top scorer in basketball and football and one of the top hitters in baseball. He captained the football team during his senior year (Forester Athletic Hall).

Gates joined the Navy after graduation in 1942 and received his commission as an ensign. Most of his World War II service was aboard *North Carolina,* where he manned one of the ship's fire control system's gun directors. In August 1944, Gates married Jocelyn Bonnie McAlister.

After the war, he was a district manager for Mobil Oil and owned his own business in Wisconsin until retiring in 1981. He died in Green Bay, Wisconsin, on May 30, 1997, and is buried in Forest Home Cemetery, Greenville, Michigan.

USS *Aylwin*

Surviving the Hurricane

USS *Aylwin* (DD-355) underway at sea, circa the 1930s. Collection of Vice Admiral George C. Dyer, USN (Retired). NH 77066 Courtesy of the Naval History & Heritage Command.

The Ship

USS *Aylwin* (DD 355) was a Farragut-class destroyer commissioned on March 1, 1935. Pre–World War II, she carried out missions to Europe, the Gulf of Mexico, the west coast of the U.S. and around the Hawaiian Islands. *Aylwin* almost did not make it into World War II: On March 17, 1941, while on night maneuvers, her sister ship USS *Farragut* (DD 348) nearly sliced off her bow in a collision. USS *Turkey* (AM 13) towed *Aylwin*, stern-first, back to port for repairs.

On December 7, 1941, *Aylwin* was moored in Pearl Harbor when the Japanese attacked. Even though only at half-strength, she got underway and steamed out of the harbor, as per her instructions, with all guns firing. Ensign Stanley B. Caplan, a veteran of only eight months at sea, assumed command along with three other ensigns with even less sailing experience. As *Aylwin* left the harbor, Lt. Cmdr. R.H. Rodgers, her captain, along with the ship's other senior officers, trailed her in a motor launch hoping to get aboard. Even though Rodgers was spotted by the crew, the commander of Destroyer Squadron One refused to allow the ship to slow down. Caplan followed orders to clear the harbor and patrol at speed, leaving *Aylwin*'s captain in the ship's wake. Lt. Cmdr. Rodgers was able to board USS *Chew* (DD 106) and assist her operations until being able to get back aboard *Aylwin* the following day. His after-action report had high praise for Caplan and the other three ensigns who skillfully operated the ship under difficult conditions.

Aylwin went on to participate in many of the best-known operations in the Pacific, including the Battle of the Coral Sea, Midway, the Aleutians Campaign, Battle of the Philippine Sea, the capture and occupation of Saipan and Guam, Iwo Jima and Okinawa. On December 18, 1944, she had a harrowing encounter with Typhoon Cobra that nearly led to her loss. As the early morning storm increased in intensity, *Aylwin* developed steering problems and experienced significant loss of stability in the large swells. At 1050, according to the official war report, she "commenced shifting fuel oil and crew to starboard to anticipate next course." At 1100, under full hurricane conditions, she "rolled 70 degrees to port and stayed there for at least 15 seconds" (*Aylwin*, 1944). After the ship righted, the helm attempted to bring her to the designated heading with no success. Only by backing the ship could they get her back on course. However, shortly thereafter, *Aylwin* lost rudder control and she swung off course again, listing 70 degrees for a second time for about 15 seconds. She "only righted to 60 degrees after that bad roll and then staying between 30 and 60 degrees for about 20 minutes" (USS *Aylwin*, 1944). Eventually she sailed out of the storm, battered and bruised but still afloat. She lost two crewmen washed overboard and suffered considerable damage above and below the waterline.

In early August 1945, *Aylwin* was sent to look for survivors of USS *Indianapolis* (CA 35), which had carried components of the atomic bomb dropped on Hiroshima to Tinian Island in the Northern Marianas. As the *Indianapolis* was heading to Leyte, in the Philippines, on July 30, she was hit by Japanese torpedoes. According to *Aylwin*'s official report on August 4, the ship "sighted several bodies, life jackets, and debris. During the morning, the medical officer identified three bodies and gave them burial while the ship recovered two life rafts" (USS *Aylwin*, 1945). Other ships also recovered bodies and debris as well as survivors of the *Indianapolis*' sinking. In one of the tragic ironies of wartime, nearly two-thirds of *Indianapolis*' crew perished just a couple of weeks prior to the cessation of hostilities.

Aylwin earned 13 battle stars for her participation in the Pacific Theater.

Poem One

The following deck log was entered by Lt. F.J. Foley on January 1, 1942, while *Aylwin* was running as part of a convoy escort. The poem is relatively short, 17 lines, with 16 lines of rhymed couplets and one unrhymed line. The first 14 lines describe in some detail the condition of the ship, and the last three lines offer a personal observation by Foley, commenting obliquely on the broader situation of America's entry into the war three weeks earlier.

In the opening lines, Foley reports *Aylwin*'s course according to the gyro compass and standard compass and mentions that there are "six other ships" sailing with them. She is making 16 knots with power supplied by the forward boilers. A destroyer ("a can") and a cruiser are escorting the convoy. Lines seven and eight exhibit Foley's creativity in rhyming as he pairs "cruiser" with "lose 'er." *Aylwin* is participating in Task Group 15.7, transporting evacuees from the Hawaiian Islands to San Francisco, in "the land most like heaven." The ships of the convoy are blacked out. The escorts are in Material Condition Three, with half the guns manned and the crew on alert, and the convoy is following a zigzag plan. Foley's sense of humor appears again in line 14 while commenting on the zigzag with a touch of sarcasm: "And we all turn together,—that is, some of us do." Perhaps some of the ships were having trouble keeping their zigzag clocks synchronized.

The last three lines turn to Foley's personal feelings about his situation. Though he does not directly mention the Pearl Harbor attack, it has left bitterness in its wake. After saying that they have just ushered in the New Year, he lashes out at the enemy in the last two lines: "Oh what a year it's gonna be," he claims, "With the Yellow Japs wiped off the sea." The lines clearly express Foley's bitterness in the stereotypical reference to the Japanese people, but they also feature the brassy self-confidence and optimism of a young American officer, an optimism found in many of the young poets of the New Year's deck logs. In his mind, it will take only a year to wipe them off the sea. The American sailors will soon realize that the challenge is much greater than they believed, and they will endure four long years of grinding warfare.

Here's the poem:

Steaming on course zero five five true,
With six other ships heading that way, too.
We're checking five five pgc. [per gyro compass],
On the standard compass, four six, we see.
Making sixteen knots, one fifty-six turns.
In the forward boilers, the fire burns.
Along with us are a can and a cruiser;
Herding a convoy to be sure we don't lose 'er.
We make up Task Group fifteen point seven,
Bringing evacuees to the land most like heaven.
Our ships are all darkened as the convoy we skirt
With half our guns manned, the crews all alert.
The zig zag we follow is Plan 42.

And we all turn together,—that is, some of us do.
At zero zero zero zero, we ushered in the brand new year.
Oh what a year it's gonna be,
With the Yellow Japs wiped off the sea.

F.J. FOLEY,
Lieutenant, U.S. Navy

The Poet

Francis Joseph Foley was born on May 28, 1910, in East Orange, New Jersey. He graduated from Jamaica High School in New York and went on to Annapolis for his college training. He graduated from the Naval Academy in 1931. Apparently short in stature, Foley nonetheless excelled in "the sweet science" (boxing), earning the nickname "Kid." After his graduation he served on USS *Trenton* (CL 11) and USS *Flusser* (DD 368). During his time in the Navy, Foley commanded three ships: USS *Lansdowne* (DD 486) 1943–1944; USS *Gainard* (DD 706) 1944–1946, and USS *Rolette* (AKA 99) 1955–1956. During his time commanding the *Gainard*, the ship served on picket duty for the invasion of Okinawa. His actions earned him the Navy Cross. The official citation reads in part as follows:

Midshipman Francis Joseph Foley from the 1931 Naval Academy Yearbook *Annapolis Lucky Bag.*

> When the GAINARD was subjected to numerous attacks by enemy suicide planes, Commander Foley directed his ship in shooting down four hostile planes and further assisted in the destruction of one and repelled twenty other aircraft without sustaining damage to either personnel or material aboard his vessel. In addition, he directed the combat air patrol under his command in shooting down twenty-two enemy planes. His leadership, courage and devotion to duty were in keeping with the highest traditions of the United States Naval Service.

Prior to commanding USS *Rolette*, Foley served as head of the Mathematics Department at the U.S. Naval Academy. He retired from the Navy at the rank of captain. He died on April 7, 1982, and is buried beside his wife Rita Downs Foley at Arlington National Cemetery.

Poem Two

The following deck log was entered by Lt. j.g. J.H. Wessells, Jr., USNR, on

January 1, 1945. The world had endured the ravages of war for three long years. The Battle of Leyte Gulf in the Philippines, one of history's largest naval battles, had decimated the Japanese navy just two months earlier, with great loss of American ships and lives. Light was finally visible at the end of the long dark tunnel. The *Aylwin* is docked at Ulithi, a previously unknown atoll of very small islands with a tiny population and no ports or facilities, surrounding one of the world's largest lagoons; it had been miraculously transformed during the month of October 1944 into a major forward staging area, a complete floating base with immense repair and supply capabilities and floating dry docks powerful enough to hoist battleships out of the water. The Japanese had abandoned Ulithi, thinking it too far from any functioning port to be of any use to their enemies. They must have been shocked to see its transformation.

The *Aylwin* is tied up alongside USS *Markab* (AD 21), a destroyer tender that would leave the following month to prepare landing craft for the invasion of Japan. Wessells says that *Markab* is "crapped out," a phrase that in military slang typically meant sleeping on duty, but here may mean simply that the ship is shut down. Wessells says the same thing about the USS *Griswold* (DE 7) a few lines later. He demonstrates his adroitness with rhyme in the next passage, which describes the lines securing *Markab,* by rhyming "after" with "abaft her" (further aft). And his sense of humor—an element common to almost all the wartime deck log poems—sneaks in when he claims *Markab* is tied so snugly because "we are taking no chance / On the wind grinding coral in the seat of our pants."

USS *Griswold*, an Evarts-class destroyer, along with several merchantmen are also at Ulithi. Various yard craft (small craft used to support ship operations, such as tugs and security boats) are busy day and night. Lines 13 and 14 of Wessells' poem are typical of the alphabet soup of abbreviations that often appear in deck logs: "With TBS handy, old SOPA sits wary, / It's COMSERVRON 10 on his throne in the PRAIRIE." TBS stood for "Talk Between Ships," a high-frequency connection that allowed ships in combat operations to communicate with each other. "Old SOPA" is the Senior Officer Present Afloat, who has established his command center on the *Prairie*, a destroyer tender that remained at Ulithi until the end of the war. The SOPA in this case is COMSERVRON 10, the Commander of Service Squadron 10. Service Squadrons supported fleet combat units, creating temporary forward combat bases that could supply combat ships close to conflict areas. Ulithi was such a forward combat base.

The ship is in material condition of readiness three, and she is in material condition of readiness Baker, a condition of air tightness set in port when an attack is likely. Boiler four is supplying power. The typical strand of wry American humor and the constant refrain lamenting the lack of female companionship and alcohol appears when Wessells claims it is "just like the usual watch, / No whistles, no sirens, no women, no scotch."

Though most of Wessells' poem serves the standard needs of a Navy deck log, the first line and the final four lines encapsulate the human aspirations that burn through so many of the deck log poems. The opening line seems to bemoan that the "start of the new year is just like the old," while the closing lines speak to the hope that the end is near: "But we're hoping this year will for sure be the last, / That soon we will fire the last five inch blast, / And that next New Year's Eve this old log relates / We all stood our mid-watch at home in the States." Though the war in the Pacific would drag on for eight more months, Wessells eventually got his wish. The deck logs written on January 1, 1946, were the first poems posted in peacetime since New Year's Day 1941.

Here's the poem:

Well, the start of the new year is just like the old,
Starboard side to the MARKAB, crapped out, I am told.
She sags at the springs, both forwards and after,
From bow and from quarter, with a wire abaft her,
And one through the bullnose, we are taking no chance,
On the wind grinding coral in the seat of our pants.
The GRISWALD is to port, all shiny and bright,
But she's crapped out too, so that is all right.
We're all at Ulithi, the place you can meet
The best and the sourest ships in the fleet.
Some merchantmen too, and chugging through spray,
Are various yard craft, all night and all day.
With TBS [talk between ships] handy, old SOPA sits wary,
It's ComServRon 10 on his throne in the PRAIRIE.
The ship's in condition of readiness three
Which means that we're sleeping off yesterday's spree,
But Baker is set, so whatever you're thinking,
We aren't in any great danger of sinking.
Boiler four is in use and auxiliaries humming,
While the watch lays its plans for the next mornings' bumming.
By and large, it is just like the usual watch,
No whistles, no sirens, no women, no scotch,
But we're hoping this year will for sure be the last,
That soon we will fire the last five inch blast,
And that next New Years Eve this old log relates
We all stood our mid-watch at home in the states.

J.H. WESSELLS, Jr.,
Lt.(j.g.), U.S.N.R.

The Poet

John Howard Wessells, Jr., was born in Hackensack, New Jersey, on July 4, 1917, to John Howard Wessells and Elenora Mildred French. A 1940 Census record from Denver, Colorado, showed Wessells as a student at the University of Colorado–Denver working as an apprentice "door sash man" in a local lumber mill. He majored in journalism at UCD.

Wessells entered U.S. Naval service in April 1942 and served as Communications

Officer aboard USS *Aylwin*. His final promotion in the Navy occurred on August 1, 1945, when he was made a lieutenant. After the war, Wessells met Frances Anne Davies while both were singing in the choir at an Episcopal church they attended; they married a year later and journeyed to Virginia. One of Wessells' sons, Stephen, after reading his father's *Aylwin* poem, shared it with his mother, who at the time of writing this book was still doing well at age 101.

According to Stephen, John and Frances converted a surplus munitions carrier into a "sort of covered wagon" and traveled east with little notion of what they would do. They ended up in Virginia with John taking on positions as a reporter for the *Lynchburg Daily Advance* and then the *Richmond Times Dispatch*. Covering the political scene eventually led Wessells to participate in Virginia politics by working at the State Department of Commerce and Agriculture and being an aide and speechwriter for two governors, Albertis S. Harrison, Jr., and Miles A. Godwin, Jr. (emails, September 14 and 15, 2020, and March 25, 2021). After leaving government, he became executive assistant to the vice-president and general manager of Virginia Blue Cross and Blue Shield. During this time, Frances Wessells became well-known for her dancing and dance instruction. She studied with Hanya Holm, one of the icons of modern dance in the U.S. Frances also distinguished herself as an educator, spending many years at the University of Richmond and Virginia Commonwealth University.

Wessells resurrected his woodworking skills later in life, according to Stephen, and was apparently handy at all manner of tasks, such as toy assembly and making accessories for Halloween costumes. He enjoyed reading Western novels like those of Zane Grey and published his own book, *The Bank of Virginia: A History*, in 1973. Like most veterans of the war, he never spoke much of his experiences. He died on April 21, 1988, and is buried in Grace Episcopal Church Cemetery, Goochland, Virginia.

USS *Casco*

God Keep Our Ship

USS *Casco* (AVP-12) running trials off Vashon Island in Puget Sound, Washington, on March 3, 1943, upon completion of battle damage repairs. US National Archives photo # 80-G-455262.

The Ship

USS *Casco* (AVP 12), a Barnegat-class small seaplane tender, was commissioned on December 27, 1941. Her first year of service found her patrolling the waters of the Pacific Northwest, servicing seaplanes. Based at Cold Bay, Alaska, she operated out of Dutch Harbor, Chernofski Harbor, Kodiak and Nazan Bay.

On August 30, 1942, while anchored in Nazan Bay, *Casco* sighted a submarine periscope and two torpedo wakes heading in her direction. The first torpedo missed forward by about 50 yards and ran up onto a beach. It was later salvaged by explosive experts. The second torpedo hit *Casco* about eight feet below the waterline on the starboard side and exploded, killing five crewmen and wounding 20. According to *Casco*'s commander, the ship lost power and began to list slightly, and in his words, "The 5"/38 cal. opened fire under manual control and fired an embarrassing barrage of five shots in the direction the submarine was last seen." The crew released the anchor chains and managed to beach the ship to prevent sinking. The *Casco* was fortunate that the torpedo did not start fires due to the presence of large amounts of aviation fuel.

The next day, the submarine that torpedoed *Casco* was spotted by an airplane that dropped a depth bomb on it, causing damage. While the sub made a valiant effort to repair and flee the area, USS *Reid* (DD 369) was directed to the sub's location. After two depth charge attacks, the sub surfaced and received a punishing gun barrage from *Reid*, sending it to the bottom. *Reid* reported seeing 17 survivors in the 50-degree water but was only able to rescue five Japanese enlisted submariners. *Casco* received a message from *Reid*, according to an action report: "Got the sub that got you. Have five survivors for proof."

After repair, *Casco* spent 1943 supporting U.S. Army actions in the Aleutians, including the invasion of Attu. In 1944, she sailed southwest to the Marshall Islands, where she completed her wartime duties by servicing both seaplane and motor patrol boat squadrons. After the war, in 1949, the Navy loaned her to the U.S. Coast Guard, and she served as USCGC *Casco* (WAVP 370) and high-endurance cutter (WHEC 370) until 1969, when she was given back to the Navy and was sunk as a target in the North Atlantic Ocean.

Casco earned three battle stars for her World War II service.

The crew of *Casco* left three poems, the first written on January 1, 1942, three weeks after Pearl Harbor; the second written on January 1, 1945, eight months before the end of the war, and the third written on January 1, 1946, four months after the Japanese surrender.

Poem One

Ensign W.P. Hodnett, Jr., posted the following deck log on January 1, 1942. Though the poem is written in rhyming couplets, it is difficult to recognize it as a poem because Hodnett wrote it as a paragraph, without marking the line breaks at the points of rhyme. Slash marks have been inserted in the copy below to indicate the line breaks so that readers can have a better sense of what Hodnett was attempting. The poem represents an expression of the first day of the first year of America's war with Japan. Three weeks after Pearl Harbor, Ensign Hodnett describes the emotional reaction to the "date which will live in infamy."

As he writes, *Casco* is anchored in Puget Sound, Washington. The opening lines claim that 1941 is a year of "treachery, war, hell, and tears." Hodnett uses a striking image of a "peace loving world aflame with hate." The bulk of the lines that follow supply all the required technical information on the condition of the ship. She is tied on her port side in Berth 5-D with "stout 5/8-inch wires" and is receiving all services from the dock. He lists the ships that are moored across from *Casco,* including USS *Maryland*, whose Commander is the Senior Officer Present Afloat. At 0326 hours, G.T. Foster, MM2c (Mechanics Mate Second Class), returns from shore patrol.

Midshipman William Philip Hodnett, Jr., from the 1940 Naval Academy Yearbook *Annapolis Lucky Bag*.

In the final nine lines of the poem, Hodnett shifts both the tone of his words and the rhyme scheme of the work. He expresses a heartfelt hope that would have been shared by all: joy and happiness "in the coming year of hardship and trials." Then he abandons his earlier rhymed couplets and writes five rhymed lines that offer the clarion call to battle. The words he uses to create rhyme in those closing lines reveal his powerful sense of mission: Our cause is *right*. It is a worthy *fight*. With unity and *might*, "we'll give them a hell of a *fight*." And the final line echoes the closing of the quintessential American Christmas poem "The Night Before Christmas": "Now—happy New Year to all, and good night." As in other deck log poems, there is a certain pathos in the young ensign's clarion call, for he will not survive the war.

Here is the poem:

Eight bells knell the passing of a memorable year. / One of treachery, war, hell, and tears. / Into a peace loving world aflame with hate, / steps the babe, 1942, tyranny to abate. / "Happy New Year to All" is his ironic greeting / to the CASCO and crew at our first meeting, / where in Puget Sound Navy Yard, Bremerton, Washington, we're moored, / Port side to Berth 5-D, with standard lines we're secured. / All are stout 5/8" wire, keeping us pinned, / to prevent our being moved by tide and wind. / Services we're receiving around the clock, / steam and electricity from the dock. / Fresh and salt water, and a telephone too, / are considered essential for ship and crew. / Along with the CASCO, we've plenty of might / U.S.S. COLORADO, U.S.S. TENNESSEE, and HMS WARSPITE. / The U.S.S. MARYLAND is secured across the way, / her ComBatShips is our SOPA. / Various yard and district craft too, here repose, / bringing the list of ships present to a close. / 0326 Foster, G.T., MM2c has returned from duty as shore patrol. / In the Bremerton area, he has helped to keep matters under control. / And now, the end, the first watch of the New Year, / our utmost wishes, simple, but clear. / May joy and happiness in abundance be ours, / in the coming year of hardships and trials. / Now that we've finally decided we're right, / may we increase our efforts in this worthy fight. / And God give us unity, and in unity, might, / for whatever comes, we'll give them a hell of a fight. / Now—"Happy New Year to All," and goodnight.

W.P. Hodnett, Jr.,
Ensign, U.S. Navy

The Poet

William Philip Hodnett, Jr., was born on November 27, 1918, to parents William P. Hodnett and Myrtle Rose Hubbard in Martinsville, Virginia. His father owned a local grocery store in Martinsville in the early 1920s. By the 1930 Census, William, Jr., and his father were living with a relative, Callie M. Hodnett, in Martinsville. By the 1940 Census, Hodnett was living in Annapolis, Maryland, as a Naval Academy Midshipman.

The 1940 Academy yearbook, *Lucky Bag*, published the following for the graduating senior:

> A true Virginian, Bill's neatness made him most desirable as a roommate. His happiest moments were spent in participating in arguments, regardless of the subject. Athletic activities included wrestling, football, and baseball; and in sports, as in all things, he was ever a good worker. Bill's troubles with the Academic as well as the Executive Department were several: his main weakness being—"Parlez-vous francais?" Little difficulty was experienced with the fairer sex, except an occasional encounter with those above the Mason-Dixon line. Here's wishing you the best, Bill, you will make your own breaks.

Upon graduation, Hodnett spent time on USS *Colorado* (BB 45) before being transferred to *Casco* in late 1941. He was married on February 19, 1943, to Ruth Evangeline Hanson at the Church of the Epiphany (Episcopal) in Seattle. Hanson was then a nurse at the Bremerton Naval Hospital.

Over the next year, Hodnett was promoted to lieutenant commander and boarded USS *Cooper* (DD 695) as its Executive Officer for her launching and shakedown. *Cooper* eventually began screening carriers during the fight to retake the Philippines. In what became known as the Battle of Ormoc Bay, *Cooper* and several other destroyers attacked Japanese ships attempting to land reinforcements. The ensuing melee reportedly involved surface vessels, submarines, aircraft, mines and shore batteries.

At approximately 0017 on December 3, 1944, *Cooper* was hit amidships by what its commander believed was a large Japanese torpedo. She immediately took a 45-degree list to starboard, broke in two, and sank within minutes. Ten officers and 161 crewmen were lost, including Lt. Cmdr. Hodnett. His body was never recovered (USS *Cooper*, 1944).

Hodnett was posthumously awarded the Bronze Star. He insisted that the crew wear their life jackets while at their battle stations. Many of the crew who survived believed that his attention to this detail saved their lives.

A commemoration plaque for Hodnett can be found at Manila American Cemetery and Memorial (Tablets of the Missing) in the Philippines (Hodnett).

Poem Two

The following deck log was entered on January 1, 1945, by Lt. j.g. J.F. Roohan, USNR. He writes a short poem in rhyming couplets separated into seven verses, offering a very different appearance from Hodnett's poem. Interestingly, he further divides each line in the poem in half with a dash, reminiscent of 19th-century American poet Emily Dickinson. The ship is anchored in Kossol Passage, a reef that lies between Palau and Kayangel Island in the Philippine Sea, in Berth V-2 in 13 fathoms of water with 75 fathoms of chain on the starboard side. Stanza three gives the ship's location using position beacons D and E. The ship is in readiness Condition Three, with half the guns manned and material condition Baker (medium level of air tightness), and Roohan offers the pervasive complaint by young sailors in the New Year's deck logs: the absence of alcohol. Stanza five offers a touch of humor in its reference to the Senior Officer Present Afloat (SOPA) and his dog, who are on the USS *Argonne* (AS 10).

The final two stanzas reflect a sentiment found in so many of the deck log verses, the hope for victory with a touch of humor. It is late in the war, New Year's Day 1945. Victory in Europe will be achieved four months later. Victory over Japan will come in eight. Roohan cannot know this with any certainty, though victory is in sight. "We still have a helluva war to fight—this year we hope to win." And the emperor of Japan will be really angry, he says, when we sink his ships and give him back the Kossol reef.

Here is the poem:

> Anchored in Kossol Passage—of all the places to be
> In berth V-2—Isles of Palau—too far from home to suit me
>
> Thirteen fathoms of water—unless you measure the rain
> The starboard anchor is holding us here—with 75 fathoms of chain
>
> Beacon "D" bears 340—if it means anything to you
> Beacon "E" bears 318—the bearings of course are true
>
> The ship is in condition three—condition Baker integrity
> No whiskey—no gin—but the water is free to the whole ships company
>
> In the ARGONNE lives Sopa—there also lives his dog.
> If you want to know what ships are here—just go look in her log
>
> We rang the old year out tonight—we rang the New Year in
> We still have a helluva war to fight—this year we hope to win
>
> The Emperor is going to be mad—when we've sunk all his ships
> I'll bet it would make him madder still—if we gave Kossol back to the Nips
>
> J. F. Roohan
> Lieut. (j.g.), U.S.N.R.

Poet Two

James Francis Roohan, Jr., was born on November 22, 1920, in Philadelphia to parents James F. Roohan and Sarah Barnholt. Prior to his birth, his father served in the U.S. Army Medical Corps as a physician. Credited with four campaigns in France during World War I, he attained the rank of major. By 1925, the Roohans moved to Saratoga Springs, New York, where the elder James practiced medicine.

James, Jr., graduated from Michigan State College (now University) with a bachelor's degree in Hotel Management in 1942. He later enlisted in the Navy and attended the Midshipman's School at the University of Notre Dame, receiving his commission as an ensign in 1943. His service spanned World War II, Korea and Vietnam. During his nearly 30 years in the Navy, he served on 11 ships and commanded four, including USS *LSM* 398, USS *English* (DD 696) and USS *Knudson* (APD 101). He also held a staff position for the Chief of Naval Operations. He retired from the Navy in July 1969 at the rank of commander.

Roohan was also apparently an excellent billiards player. According to his obituary,

> In 1967, he represented the Navy in the U.S. Open Pocket Billiard Championship tournament. In addition, he was the New York Athletic Club pocket billiard, English snooker and handicap three cushion champion for several years. He represented the United States, in 1977, at the International Snooker matches in England. Jim took particular pride in having defeated Minnesota Fats not just once, but twice [James Francis Roohan].

In 1958, while serving as Executive Officer (XO) on USS *Arneb* (AKA 56), Roohan became somewhat of a mentor to adventurer-writer Richard Pape on an expedition to Antarctica (part of Operation Deep Freeze IV). Jimmy, as Pape called him, provided valuable insight into the life and hazards of Antarctic life. For example, regarding leopard seals, Roohan warned, "Watch out for them ... take no chances, because if you run your fastest on the ice, the leopard seal will overtake you. It's damned fast" (Pape, 1960).

In 1979, Roohan married Sun Hi Han of Seoul, Korea. In 1999, he was invested a knight in the papal Equestrian Order of the Holy Sepulchre of Jerusalem by Roger Cardinal Mahony. James Francis Roohan, Jr., died on August 18, 2004, in La Jolla, California.

Poem Three

The following poem was posted in the January 1, 1946, deck log by Boatswain's Mate First Class (BM1) Louis Claire Templeton. World War II had ended four months before the poem was written. The joy and relief that victory brought, as well as the pain and grief over all the suffering and death, was still fresh. Yet in Templeton's short and simple poem, there is no hint that the long purgatory of the war ever happened. Twelve lines of rhymed couplets offer the most basic information on the ship's condition and position. The poem closes with a brief blessing.

In reading this poem, written so soon after the end of the war, it is hard not to think of the statement heard so often from the children of survivors: "He never talked about it." The families of Midwatch poets never knew their fathers had written the poems. Their refrain was always the same. These men said almost nothing about their experiences in the war. So it should not be a surprise that the first Midwatch poem of 1946 on USS *Casco* would say nothing.

Perhaps if looked at closely, that final blessing might at least hint at the solace sought by those survivors: "God keep our ship in Subic Bay; / Far, far from home on New Year's Day."

Here's the poem:

Anchored as before in Subic Bay
Watching the old year pass away
Seventy-five fathoms on the starboard chain
Hold's us safe amist the rain.
Seventeen fathoms at berth 206,
The following bearings give us the fix.
Three four four on the beacon to port
The one on the left that looks like a fort.
One zero zero on the starboard light
That gleams out bright, in dark of night.
God keep our ship in Subic Bay;
Far, far from home on New Year's Day.

L.C. TEMPLETON
Bos'n U.S.N.

Poet Three

Louis Claire Templeton was born in Savanna, Oklahoma, on September 1, 1913, to James Francis Robinson Templeton and Dorthea Lewis. The Templetons lived in the Savanna area into the 1930s. Louis enlisted in the Navy in 1931 and completed his basic training in San Diego. In the late 1930s, he was posted to USS *Oklahoma* (BB 37).

While on *Oklahoma* on December 7, 1941, Templeton figured prominently in an incident recounted in Stephen Bower Young's book *Trapped at Pearl Harbor: Escape from the Battleship USS* Oklahoma. Templeton, highest-ranking enlisted sailor in the Division 4 crew, manned Gun Turret 4. Young described him as a short, profane and pugnacious sailor of the "old school" Navy. He seemed to get along very well with Ensign Herbert F. Rommel, the Division 4 commander. According to Young, Rommel was prim, proper and prissy, making him and Templeton the embodiment of the stereotypical odd couple. When three Japanese torpedoes hit *Oklahoma* and she began to list, many men in lower decks attempted to retreat to upper decks due to fear of capsizing. Rommel ordered the men below in the mistaken notion that they would be safer there than on the upper decks. During a heated exchange between Rommel and the fleeing sailors, Templeton pulled a .45 side arm, pointed it at them and ordered them in colorful language to go below. They did so, not wishing to argue with the business end of a .45. Rommel and Templeton went topside promising to come back and apprise the men of the situation. *Oklahoma* did capsize, trapping many men—including those whom Rommel had ordered below. A number of them were pulled out through the bottom of the *Oklahoma*'s hull the next day. Some never got off the ship. Young recounts that, years later, Rommel said that he always regretted not telling those men to abandon ship (Young, 2013).

Templeton stayed in the Navy until 1958 when he retired at the rank of Chief Warrant Officer 2 (CW2). In addition to serving on *Oklahoma*, he was also assigned to USS *Idaho* (BB 42), USS *Progress* (AMc 98), USS *San Francisco* (CA 38), USS *Casco* (AVP 12), USS *Caliente* (AU 53) and USS *Prescott* (PCS 1423).

In 1980, the advice columnist, Dear Abby, asked her readers where they were on December 7, 1941, when they learned the news of Pearl Harbor. One of the responses published by Dear Abby was by Templeton: "I was a first-class petty officer aboard the USS *Oklahoma* at Pearl Harbor. Abby, 445 of my mates were killed on that ship, so I have no trouble remembering where I was." At the time, Dear Abby's column was estimated to have tens of millions of readers.

Templeton married Loretta Wermes on June 16, 1945, in Chicago. He died on June 29, 1993, in San Diego, California. He was buried at Fort Rosecrans National Cemetery, San Diego.

USS *Allen*

The Old Girl

USS *Allen* (DD 66) off Pearl Harbor, Oahu, Hawaii, December 17, 1942. NH 103524 Courtesy of the Naval History & Heritage Command.

The Ship

USS *Allen* (DD 66) was a Sampson-class destroyer with a long and checkered history. It could almost be said that she was snakebit from the start. Commissioned on January 24, 1917, she patrolled the coast of the U.S. and the West Indies. In the early hours of May 1, 1917, while escorting USS *Connecticut* (BB 18), *Allen* collided with USS *Duncan* (DD 46) off the coast of Virginia. Even with the evasive action ordered by the OOD, *Allen*'s stern was crushed, and *Duncan* was disabled. *Allen* managed to tow *Duncan* to Philadelphia for repair. As if the collision at sea were not bad enough, while on blocks during repairs, *Allen*'s port block gave way. She crashed once again into the *Duncan*, injuring two of *Allen*'s crew and killing one *Duncan* crew member. This bizarre accident was a harbinger of things to come.

In what was becoming an all too frequent occurrence, the *Allen* was steaming up the East River in New York on May 26, 1917, when she lost steering and was grounded. Two tugs unseated her and towed her to repair the leaks caused by the grounding. She finally set out for Saint-Nazaire, France, in late June. Her first European patrol found her sighting a German submarine during an escort operation. She opened fire, but the shell burst above her own bow, causing minor damage but no injuries. Then on September 12, *Allen* tangled with an underwater object. A blade on her starboard propeller was bent and required repair. She managed to avoid any additional damage until November 2 when she collided with a dock and suffered propeller damage again. She suffered damage one final time during World War I when on October 30, 1918, as she escorted the British steamship *Mauratania* (sister ship of the famous *Lusitania*), a storm caused her hull plating to buckle.

During World War I, *Allen* had at least ten encounters with suspected German submarines. In some cases, she fired guns and in others dropped depth charges. Post-war analysis did not verify any "kills," although she may have caused damage to at least one sub. She likely experienced more damage to herself through misadventure than she caused the enemy.

After the war, she continued East Coast patrol duty until June 22, 1922, when she was decommissioned and placed in the reserve fleet. *Allen* was recommissioned on June 23, 1925, and served as a training vessel until being returned to the Reserve Fleet in 1928. With world tensions rising, she was recommissioned on August 23, 1940.

After a short time on the East Coast of the U.S., *Allen* sailed to the Pacific, where she remained until the end of World War II. She was moored in Pearl Harbor on December 7, 1941, and her men claimed to have played a role in the downing of three Japanese aircraft. Afterwards, *Allen* spent most of her time based in the Hawaiian Islands serving as a target ship while helping to train U.S. submarine crews.

In September 1945, captained by J.C. Tyler, Jr. (writer of the midwatch poem below), *Allen* sailed east through the Panama Canal to Philadelphia, where she was decommissioned on October 15, 1945. She was later sold for scrap. She was considered to be the longest-serving destroyer on the Naval Register when she was sold. She earned one battle star for her service.

The Poem

The deck log below was entered on January 1, 1943, by Lt. j.g. J.C. Tyler, Jr. The poem consists of 16 lines of rhymed couplets and a seventeenth line that seems to have been an afterthought concerning steam pressure and engine speed. Those first

16 lines do a masterful job of working all the technical information into a regular rhythm and rhyme scheme. The ship is steaming alone, not part of a convoy or group, on its way back to Pearl Harbor, presumably from participation in training exercises. Tyler fondly refers to the age of the destroyer in line two, where he gives the speed as 14 knots and says, "not bad for an old girl." The ship is in material condition of readiness AFIRM, in which she is prepared for action by making closures watertight. When giving the ship's course, he comments that they require magnetic steering rather than gyro steering, indicating that the seas were too rough for the gyro to be accurate. A bit later they are cruising at 15 knots with boilers one and two lit, and the gyro is okay for steering because the seas have calmed.

The second half of the poem turns from technical details to Tyler's observations about the ship and the war. As they approach Oahu, he offers the typical sailor's plaintive regret about being on duty on New Year's Eve. America has been fighting in the war for one full year, what Tyler calls a "troublesome" year, and there is some pathos in the fact that they are sailing into Pearl Harbor, where *Allen* was moored one year earlier during the surprise attack that caused such destruction and loss of life. He is proud that the *Allen* has done her work well, but he looks to the future, where there is "work to do." His sense of pride carries forward into a pledge that *Allen* "will always come thru," no matter what the situation, no matter what condition of readiness has been called. He closes the poem with a bold claim that the ship will "do e'en better" in the coming year.

Here's the poem:

Steaming singly, we are returning to Pearl,
Making 14 knots, not bad for an old girl.
AFIRM 7 completed, on 248 true,
Steering 238 magnetic, the gyro won't do.
Main engines in compound, standard speed 15,
Boilers 1 & 2 lighted, producing the steam.
The gyro's O.K. now—result of calm sea,
But compare we must—220 p.s.c. [per standard compass]
Approaching Oahu, Makapuu to the right,
What a place for a sailor on New Year's night!
The old year its troublesome course has run
And the *ALLEN*'s completed her jobs—"well done."
But let's look ahead, where there's work to do
And pledge that our ship will always come thru—
Whether it's EASY or UNIT or an AFIRM to sea.
She'll do it e'en better in 1943.
Average steam 240, average RPM [propeller revolutions per minute] 245

J. C. Tyler, Jr.,
Lt.(j.g.)., D-V(G)., U.S. Naval Reserve

The Poet

Joseph Curtis Tyler, Jr., was born on May 11, 1916, to Joseph C. Tyler, Sr., and Annette Oudin Tyler in Spokane, Washington. Joseph, Sr., was a prominent businessman and Annette was considered a socialite with a talent for acting.

Tyler had a lifelong love of being on the water, according to his son Curtis. By the time his family moved to Berkeley, California, he was honing his skills for ocean sailing. After graduating from high school at the young age of 15, he took a train to New York City and shipped out on MS *Santa Maria,* running cargo between New York and Central and South America. *Santa Maria* was acquired by the U.S. Navy in 1940 and designated USS *Barnett* (APA 5). He also spent time on MS *Santa Elena.* After being at sea for three years, Tyler returned to California and enrolled at the University of California at Berkeley. He joined the Naval ROTC and won special awards in astronomy and celestial navigation.

In the summer of 1936, at the age of 20, Tyler boarded USS *New York* (BB 34) as a midshipman on a training cruise from California to Hawaii. While en route, the crew of the old battleship engaged in navigation drills, gunnery practice and other tasks that the nascent sailors would need in the wake of December 7, 1941.

According to Tyler's son, Joseph and his shipmates took a guided tour of the Dole Pineapple Cannery at Iwilei. Seventeen year old Thelma Weeks, a recent graduate of Oahu College, aka Punahou School, was their guide. Joseph exclaimed, "It was then and there that I truly met the girl of my dreams." Joseph and Thelma fell in love.

Joseph wanted to leave school (Berkeley) and return to the islands to be with the girl of his dreams. His parents had other ideas, taking him on a six-month visit to Europe, during which they hoped he would reconsider moving to Hawaii. But letters between Joseph and Thelma strengthened their resolve to be together, and eventually he moved to Hawaii where the two were engaged to be married. As Curtis put it,

> Mom and Dad became engaged in front of the Halekulani Hotel on the sands of Waikiki Beach with Diamond Head in the background.
>
> On 6 August 1938, they were married in Parke Chapel at St. Andrews Cathedral in Queen Emma Square.... Dad's parents, his grandmother and sister were all in attendance, as were Thelma's family and many of her Punahou classmates and close friends [email, April 10, 2020].

On May 15, 1941, Tyler received his commission as an ensign in the Naval Reserve and was assigned a duty station at Naval Station Pearl Harbor adjacent to the Fleet Landing. With no married housing available, he commuted from Manoa to Pearl in an old 1932 two-door convertible Chevrolet with a rumble seat. When new married housing construction was completed in the fall of 1941 on Halawa Drive, the Tylers were amazed to be assigned to a home a few doors down from Captain Charles Momsen (later Admiral Momsen, the inventor of the Momsen Lung) and just down the street from Admiral Husband Kimmel, Commander-in-Chief of the U.S. Pacific Fleet.

Curtis Tyler tells the following story regarding his father's entry into World War II at Pearl Harbor:

> Just before 0800 on Sunday, 7 December 1941, Dad and Thelma, along with their 2 house guests, her mother and brother (a Navy Seabee), awoke to the sound of planes flying, diving

> low overhead and in close proximity. Why is the Army Air Corps training on a Sunday AM, grumbled the groggy Seabee … that is, until he saw the red circles under the wings; "It's the Japs," he shouted!
>
> Everyone ran out of the house, piled into the '32 Chevy convertible, and headed east. Shortly thereafter, a Zero started strafing Halwa Drive, and Dad pulled into Capt. Momsen's covered, but open, garage, as bullets shattered the pavement.
>
> Thelma and her mother were dropped off and took shelter in the cane fields to the north and below of Admiral Kimmel's home, Dad and his brother-in-law headed downhill and gained access thru the Makalapa Gate, then reported to their duty stations. As fate would have it the 22-year-old boot ensign was assigned to set up the recently-completed Bloch Arena and to take command of the Fleet Landing where many of the wounded and dead casualties were off-loaded and taken to the Arena [email, April 10, 2020].

Tyler spent the rest of the war at sea. Over this time, he commanded three vessels: USS *Peridot* (PYc 18), USS *Azurlite* (PY 22) and USS *Allen* (DD 66). He was in command of the latter as she sailed through the Panama Canal to the Philadelphia Naval Shipyard to be sold for scrap. According to Curtis, Thelma joined Joseph in Philadelphia for a time, and then they headed back to Hawaii.

Tyler managed operations of American Factors in the Kona district of West Hawaii in the 1950s and into the 1960s. American Factors, founded in the mid–19th century, was once considered one of the Big Five companies in the Territory of Hawaii. During his time at American Factors, Joseph made many contacts with first-generation Kona coffee farmers, and his interest in improving coffee processing facilities grew. A short trip to Central America to study coffee production with famed agronomist Dr. Y. Baron Goto contributed more to Tyler's conviction that coffee processing in the Kona district could be made more efficient, leading to enhanced production and marketing. He even developed a small family business in which roasted Kona beans from the factory were loaded into small burlap sacks and sewn shut to resemble the actual 100-pound sacks that were sold to retailers. The small sacks were sold at local stores and waterfront tourist shops.

Tyler retired from American Factors in 1962 and began working for the International Basic Economy Corporation (IBEC) headquartered at 30 Rockefeller Center in New York City. IBEC was a private business that promoted expanding less-developed economies around the world to create higher productivity and eventually mutually advantageous trade arrangements. His position focused on housing and food production.

Tyler retired again in the late 1970s and returned to Kona with his wife. As his son Curtis put it,

> [H]e daily weeded, pruned and fertilized the 2 small family coffee farms originally planted in 1894 by Mom's grandfather, whose father (Henry Weeks), a young shipwright, had emigrated to Hilo HI from Plymouth GB. In 1830, he was granted 18 acres of land from ruling monarch, King Kamehameha II, on which he planted and grew some of the first coffee on Hawaii Island [email, August 11, 2021].

Curtis Tyler followed his father into the Navy and related his experience of attending OCS at Newport Naval Base in Rhode Island. His father was in the audience when Curtis was commissioned, using "the very dress sword Dad had worn during WWII." In January 1969, Curtis reported on board USS *Maury* (AGS 16) in Pearl Harbor (email, April 10, 2020).

Joseph Curtis Tyler, Jr., passed away in Kealakekua, Hawaii, December 19, 2004. He is buried in the Christ Church Episcopal Cemetery Kealakekua, Hawaii, USA.

USS *Colorado*

A Tale of Endurance

USS *Colorado* (BB 45) in the mid- or late 1930s, after the addition of machine gun positions on her foremast top. Airplanes on her catapults are Vought O3U-3 Corsairs. NH 55275 Courtesy of Naval History & Heritage Command.

The Ship

USS *Colorado* (BB 45), the third Navy ship of that name, was the lead ship of the Colorado class of battleships. She was commissioned on August 23, 1923, and made her maiden voyage to various points in Europe. From 1924 to 1941, she operated with the battle fleet in the Pacific, participating in a variety of exercises and ceremonies.

In March 1933, she helped with earthquake relief at Long Beach, California. While serving as a training ship for NROTC students in the summer of 1937, she participated in the search for Amelia Earhart, rendezvousing with the Coast Guard Cutter *Itasca* and launching her seaplanes to search the Phoenix Islands.

From January to June 1941, *Colorado* participated in exercises and war games in Hawaii, then returned to Puget Sound Navy Yard for overhaul. She was there when Pearl Harbor was attacked on December 7. Starting at the end of March 1942, she conducted training maneuvers on the West Coast and patrolled off San Francisco with USS *Maryland* (BB 46). She returned to Pearl Harbor in August and operated in the Fiji Islands and New Hebrides from November 1942 until September 1943. In October 1943, she provided pre-invasion bombardment and fire support for the invasion of Tarawa. After a second overhaul on the West Coast, in January 1944 she provided pre-invasion bombardment and fire support for the invasions of Kwajalein and Eniwetok. Then it was back to the Navy Yard at Puget for a third overhaul.

In June and July 1944, *Colorado* supported the invasions of Saipan, Guam and Tinian. On July 24 at 0740, after *Colorado* had bombarded Tinian Town and the surrounding area, well-hidden shore batteries in the bluffs behind the town began pummeling the battleship and USS *Norman Scott* (DD 690), the destroyer supporting her. According to that day's war diary, the first two minutes of the battle were devasting for the ships. *Colorado* began taking hits immediately from shore fire described as rapid and extremely accurate. Reports of damage, fires and casualties poured in. A shell struck below the bridge, disabling a 5" gun mount, killing and wounding the gun crew. On the bridge, the captain, navigator, communications officer and signal officer were wounded, along with quartermasters and those standing watch (USS *Colorado*, 1944).

Colorado immediately swung away to increase the range for the shore batteries. According to the Report of Operations, more fires were reported as the casualties mounted. At 0750, more shell hits, fires, and personnel casualties were reported. Two minutes later, the ship's main batteries recommenced firing. Severe casualties were reported on the forecastle. At 0755, the decision was made to retire from range of shore batteries. The crew made what repairs it could and continued to provide fire against shore batteries until 1600 that afternoon. The final sentence in the report narrative says, "The ship sustained twenty-two (22) direct hits with extensive fragmentation damage both to material and personnel." They suffered 43 dead and 198 wounded (USS *Colorado*, 1944). The destroyer *Norman Scott* also endured significant damage: 22 dead, including the captain, and 50 wounded (National History and Heritage Command, no date).

Colorado continued supporting the operation until August 3, when she left for repairs on the West Coast. While supporting the Leyte Gulf Campaign in late November, she was hit by two kamikazes on the 27th. The first, carrying a bomb, struck the port side above the disbursing office, killing and wounding crew there. The second plane crashed close aboard on the port side, disintegrating in a high order explosion. The ship suffered 19 men killed and 72 wounded from the two hits, while receiving only moderate damage to the structure (USS *Colorado*, 1944).

She bombarded Mindoro in mid–December, then headed to Manus Island for repairs. According to the ship's action report, while supporting operations at Lingayen Gulf on January 9, 1945, a five-inch 38 caliber round from another U.S. ship hit her superstructure, killing six officers and 14 enlisted men and wounding 51. At the same time, the ship was hit by many 40mm and 20mm rounds. The officers killed included the air defense officer, a gun battery control officer and the navigator. The report describes the resulting situation: "As this ship has only one Air Defense Station, this unfortunate hit practically wiped out our key air defense personnel and seriously affected the ship's combat efficiency..." (USS *Colorado*, 1945). *Colorado* supplied fire support at Okinawa until May 22, and in August she supported the occupation of Japan, covering airborne landings at Atsugi Airfield, Tokyo, on August 27.

After returning to Seattle in October for Navy Day celebrations, *Colorado* was assigned to "Magic Carpet" duty, making three trips to Pearl Harbor and transporting 6357 veterans home. She was taken out of commission in January 1947 and sold for scrap in July 1959.

Several parts of the ship were repurposed in museums and memorials. Her bell is at the University Memorial Center at the University of Colorado. One of her five-inch deck guns resides at the Museum of History and Industry in Seattle. Six more of her guns were placed aboard the cruiser USS *Olympia* (C 6) when it became a museum in 1957. Other guns and remnants have been preserved in various places in the state of Colorado.

Colorado received seven battle stars for her service in World War II.

The Poem

The following deck log was entered by Lt. j.g. L.B. Garrison, USNR, on January 1, 1943. The log consists of 32 lines of rhymed couplets divided into eight four-line stanzas, followed by a short prose paragraph describing the makeup of Task Force 65. At the time of the writing, *Colorado* was part of a group operating in the Fiji Islands to prevent further Japanese expansion in the Pacific. Lt. Garrison surely has his tongue firmly in his cheek when he censors his own profanity in lines three and five when referring to the Japanese: "(censored)." Garrison refers indirectly to Pearl Harbor, calling it the "stab in the back."

The second stanza exhibits the typical American confidence and swagger seen in so many deck log poems. He claims the U.S. will clear the Japanese "out of the whole SoPac" (Southern Pacific), and he boasts that "those Sons of Heaven" and "those filthy bums" will abandon ship when they see the *Colorado* coming.

The ship is in the Tomba Ko Nandi anchorage at Viti Levu, the largest of the Fiji Islands, moored in line with the battleships USS *New Mexico* (BB 40) and USS *Maryland* (BB 46) in 11 fathoms of water. Garrison locates *Colorado* precisely, using bearings from four beacons and Malolo Peak. She is in Condition of Readiness Three and in Material Condition of Readiness "Yoke." In other words, she is ready for battle but not in imminent danger. The Senior Officer Present Afloat, who is aboard *New Mexico,* is the commander of battleships in the Pacific.

The final two stanzas name several other ships of various types moored with the battleships, including two minesweepers and the net-laying ship USS *Catalpa* (AN 10). Garrison breaks the last line of the poem into three parts on three different lines in a light-hearted *adieu*. "That's all the dope ... 'Relieve the Watch' ... Good-night."

Here's the poem:

On the old COLORADO, we welcome '43,
  Ready to strike from the Isles of Fiji.
Just awaiting a chance at those (censored) Nips,
  To give 'em a look at some fighting ships.

We'll teach those (censored) to stab in the back,
  As we clear them out of the whole SoPac. [SoPac—South Pacific]
And those Sons of Heaven—Why those filthy bums,
  Will be yelling "Abandon Ship—Here the COLORADO comes."

We're moored to the buoy in Berth #49,
  With NEW MEXICO and MARYLAND moored in line.
At Tomba Ko Nandi, Viti Levu,
  And Beacon "A" bearing Oh-Three-Five-Point-Two.

The water just under is eleven fathoms deep,
  While bearing two-five-seven is Malolo Peak.
We're in the islands known as Fiji,
  And bearing one-four-four is Beacon "C."

Away at Oh-nine-eight-point-five is Beacon "B,"
  And at one-seven-six-point-five is Beacon "D."
Boiler number four is steaming for aid,
  Number one stands by, but her fires are laid.

Ship is in Condition of Readiness "Three,"
  Protecting ourselves and the old KANKAKEE.
Modified Battle Cruising Watch at midnight awoke,
  To find all doors and hatches in Condition "Yoke."

S.O.P.A. in NEW MEXICO is ComBatPac [Commander Battleships Pacific],
  BatDiv III [Battleship Division III] will be complete when IDAHO gets back.
Also, here's the HULL, FARRAGUT, and CASTOR,
  And of the two minesweepers, the PREBLE is faster.

YMS-94 is the other sweeper,
  And in troubles with the nets, the CATALPA is our keeper.
The other two ships are the HAMMONDSPORT and WRIGHT,
  That's all the dope
                    "Relieve the Watch"
                                        Good-night.

Organization of Task Force 65 as follows: Rear Admiral C.P. Mason, U.S.N., in NASSAU, ALTAMAHA; ComBatDiv 4 in MARYLAND, COLORADO;

ComDesRon 12, WOODWORTH, LANDSDOWNE, LARDNER, BUCHANAN, GRAYSON and MACALLA. Task Force 65 in South Pacific Force, Pacific Fleet.

L.B. Garrison
Lieut. (j.g.), U.S.N.R.

The Poet

Lionel Burton Garrison was born on July 5, 1917, in Estill, Kentucky, to Edward Austin Garrison and Mabel Clara Reynolds. Edward worked as a drilling contractor in the oil fields. He died in 1922 of Bright's Disease at the young age of 28. The 1930 Census showed Lionel and his younger siblings, brother Donald Vincent and sister Mildred Louise, as wards of the Masonic Widows and Orphans home in Louisville. For a time, Mabel also resided at the Masonic home, but she returned to Eastern Kentucky and remarried. The Garrison children would join her at home in Rogers, Kentucky, on weekends and holidays. Donald eventually became a dentist and practiced in Kentucky and Ohio, while Mildred married and settled in California (Lionel Burton Garrison).

Lionel graduated from Lees College, now Lees College campus of Hazard Technical and Community College, in Jackson, Kentucky. He then attended U.S. Army Flight School and received his pilot's license but requested to withdraw before he was commissioned a flight officer due to pressure from Mabel, who was worried for his life. Her warning proved prophetic when all but one of his fellow flight classmates were killed in action during the war. Lionel received his midshipman's officer training in 1941 at the United States Navy Reserve Midshipmen's School at Northwestern University in Evanston, Illinois. While there, he met Martha C. Janssen, and they were married in September 1941 in Seattle. Lionel had been assigned to USS *Colorado* (BB-45), which was homeported in Pearl Harbor. Lionel served as gunnery officer on *Colorado,* assigned to duty in charge of forward mounts, including the massive 16-inch guns. He remained on the ship for the entirety of the war and was on board while she was anchored in Tokyo Harbor on the day of the formal Japanese surrender in September 1945. After the war, he requested a transfer to the regular Navy, but was denied due to force reductions. He left active duty in 1946, retiring from the Naval Reserve in 1962 at the rank of commander (Victor Crowe, email, November 15, 2021).

Lionel and Martha stayed together for more than 69 years and had four children, Lionel, Jr., Edward, Martha and Joanna. After the war, the Garrisons moved around the country while Lionel held positions in several businesses. In 1947, he worked for Snap-On Tools, based out of Kenosha, Wisconsin. In 1952, he worked for Ashland Oil and Refining in Ashland, Kentucky, before moving to Buffalo, New York, to work for Frontier Oil. By 1956, he was living in Huntington, West Virginia. According to city directories, he held a position in sales.

By the early 1960s, the Garrisons had moved to St. Croix, U.S. Virgin Islands, where Lionel worked with Carib Gas Company. Later in the 1960s, he started a business with other partners that sold Dow Silicone roofing products. The business, which became known as Rooftops, still operates as of this writing (Lionel Burton Garrison).

After retirement, Lionel moved back to the mainland U.S. and spent many hours with organizations such as Shriners International helping children in need and their families, particularly those who required assistance getting to medical care facilities. "Lionel doted on his family and loved corresponding via letters and emails. Though he suffered from various physical ailments, his sharp mind never deteriorated. He died on January 13, 2011, in Columbus, North Carolina, at the age of 93" (Victor Crowe, email, November 15, 2021).

USS *Murphy*

The Luck of the Irish

A mid–1942 overhead view of the USS *Murphy* (DD-603) underway. The ship is seen, as commissioned, with Measure MS12 (mod) camouflage scheme. National Archives Photo from Navsource.org - 0560317.

The Ship

The career of the USS *Murphy* (DD 603), a Benson-class destroyer, would put a Hollywood version of World War II to shame. She was commissioned on July 27, 1942, and participated in some of the landmark battles in the European, African, Middle Eastern Campaign. The ship was visually distinctive because, as *Murphy* officer John Keating wrote, "for the 'luck of the Irish,' … Bethlehem's shipbuilders welded a large green shamrock to her aft smokestack, making her 'one of the best known of all Atlantic destroyers'" (USS *Murphy*, 2016). As it happens, *Murphy* would need all the luck the Irish could offer and more.

After her shakedown cruise, *Murphy* joined the ranks of ships participating in Operation Torch, the invasion of French North Africa. While providing fire support

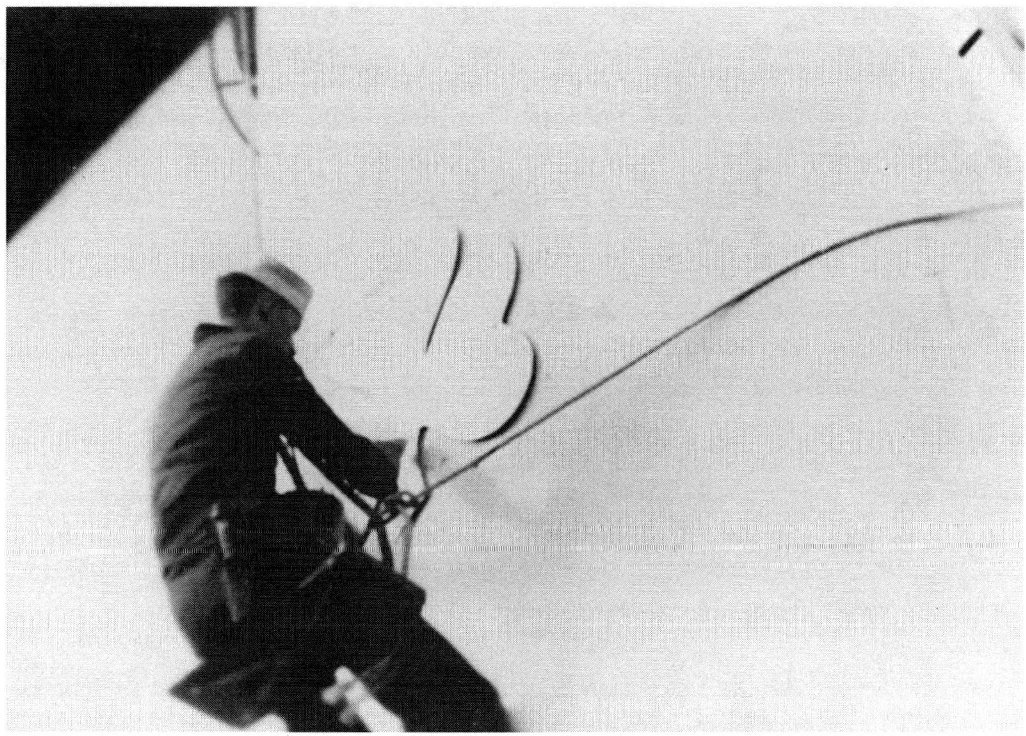

A *Murphy* crew member touches up the shamrock on the ship's bow while awaiting the arrival of King Ibn Saud of Saudi Arabia on board for transporting to Great Bitter Lake near Cairo, Egypt, for a meeting with President Franklin D. Roosevelt in February 1945. NH 84732 Courtesy of Naval History & Heritage Command.

off Port Blondin, *Murphy* was hit in her after engine room by a barrage of shore battery fire, killing three and wounding 25. The men effected emergency repairs and continued to participate in the operation. Two days later, she repelled an air attack in the Battle of Casablanca. She was soon en route to Boston for full repair.

Murphy escorted convoys to Panama and across the Atlantic to Casablanca until, in July 1943, she supported the landings of Patton's U.S. Seventh Army and Gen. Bernard L. Montgomery's British Eighth Army in Sicily. During the landing, *Murphy* and other destroyers were called on to provide artillery support, at one point firing on a column of German tanks approaching the beach. Their interdiction forced the column to turn back. Over the following days, the troops and the ships supporting them came under frequent attack by German planes. *Murphy* sustained minor damage, with one man wounded; she narrowly missed a direct hit when a bomb exploded just yards away. *Murphy* remained off the coast of Italy, supporting the invasion and regularly fending off attacks by German aircraft through August. While escorting transports to Palermo, she was again attacked and managed to down two aircraft in the skirmishes.

In September, *Murphy* returned to the U.S. and joined Task Force 69, assigned to escort convoys across the North Atlantic. On October 21, 1943, Convoy UT-4, which included one troop transport, two tankers, two cargo ships and 13 freighters carrying 46,455 troops to Europe, left New York. The luck of the Irish faced its toughest test on the first night at sea. Lt. Thaddeus R. Beal, the Officer of the Deck (OOD), manned the bridge with Lt. William R. Gordon, a signalman, a quartermaster, the helmsman and two lookouts. The ships were blacked out, and the night was pitch dark. The *Murphy*'s radar reported a strange blip, and Albert Murdaugh, commander of the destroyer division aboard the *Nelson* (DD 623), ordered Beal to divert a suspected submarine away from the convoy. *Murphy*'s commander, Leonard W. Bailey, entered the bridge and ordered *Murphy* to come right, intending "to divert the stranger to starboard'" (USS *Murphy*, 2016).

What *Murphy* was seeing on radar was actually a tanker, SS *Bulkoil*, which had been part of an earlier convoy and had lost power in one of her boilers. She was heading back to New York for repair. *Bulkoil* had no radar on board, only a limited sound system for detecting torpedoes. Her officers, convinced that *Murphy* was a German U-boat, took evasive action. In the black of the night, the two ships collided, and *Bulkoil* sliced off the bow of *Murphy* just aft of the bridge, nearly half of the ship. Within minutes, the severed forward section, including the bridge and the forward smokestack, capsized and sank, taking 35 officers and men to their deaths. Amazingly, *Murphy*'s crew, securing hatches and doors, dousing fires and plugging leaks in the bulkhead, saved the aft section from sinking.

According to the account of Fredric E. Sheller, Yeo2c, USNR, who was in the forward section when *Murphy* was struck, seawater began pouring into the Combat Information Center (CIC) where he was stationed. He and several other crewmen climbed toward the deck of the sinking bow through a galley whose overhead was now a bulkhead due to the capsizing. Sheller scrambled onto the side of gun mount number two and took off his shoes, socks and shirt. As the forward section of the ship began sinking, he leapt off the gun mount and grabbed a lifeline, spotting a light near the bow. It was the captain and several others standing near the port anchor. Sheller joined the group, and the skipper said, "Well, boys. Looks like we're going to have to get out of here" (Sheller, 2019).

They went into the water and swam away from the pull of the sinking ship. They were soon able to attach themselves to a lifeboat full of other survivors. Eventually, USS *Glennon* (DD 620) picked them up. Three other survivors were picked up by USS *Jeffers* (DD 621). The rescued survivors, totaling a little over a hundred men, were ultimately transferred to a Coast Guard cutter, USCG *Cartigan*, who returned them to New York, escorted by USS *Mentor* (PYc-37). Approximately 100 *Murphy* crewmen remained on the damaged aft two-thirds of the ship. Deck logs from *Glennon* indicated that those rescued included Captain Bailey, 12 officers (including the OOD, T.R. Beal, the author of the deck log verse below) and 95 men (USS *Glennon*, 1943).

The aft two-thirds of *Murphy*, including the shamrock on her remaining smokestack and what was left of the luck it gave her, was towed back to New York,

Line shows the location of the collision with the SS *Bulkoil*. National Archives Photo from Navsource.org – 0560317.

stern-first. Over the next seven months of reconstruction, she was fitted with a new bow so that she could fight another day. The photo above marks the point at which *Murphy* was split in the collision.

In June 1944, *Murphy* patrolled off Omaha Beach during the D-Day invasion; she was posted to screen the area from German subs and torpedo boats. She engaged shore batteries in gun battle and repelled numerous torpedo attacks by U-boats. A month later, in the Mediterranean, she participated in Operation Dragoon, the invasion of Southern France at Provence, then sailed back to the U.S. for overhaul.

After fighting so fiercely and suffering great damage and loss of life, the crew of *Murphy* enjoyed a very different experience later that year. *Murphy* joined a convoy in Norfolk, Virginia, to escort USS *Quincy* (CL 71), carrying President Roosevelt to the Middle East for the Malta Conference with Prime Minister Churchill and then to a subsequent meeting (the Yalta Conference) with both Churchill and Marshall Stalin. After these conferences, Roosevelt dispatched *Murphy* to pick up Saudi King Ibn Saud and bring him to Great Bitter Lake, Egypt, for yet another meeting. *Murphy be*came the first U.S. warship to enter the harbor at Jeddah after being the first American warship to transit the Suez Canal since World War I.

What awaited the *Murphy* crew must have been mesmerizing. The king's advance party arrived to survey the guest accommodations aboard ship. Finding them below the king's standards, the Foreign Minister told the U.S. emissary, Marine Colonel William Eddy, that the king could not possibly live in such quarters. Negotiations led to the pitching of royal tents on the *Murphy* deck. But according to an article by Peter Carlson, there were further complications:

> The king customarily traveled with an entourage of 200, including wives, slaves, cooks, aides, a ceremonial coffee server and the royal astrologer. Colonel Eddy informed the minister that

Commodore, Destroyer Squadron 17 (upper right with glasses), and senior officers of USS *Murphy* (DD-603) (all unidentified) with Saudi Arabia's King Ibn Saud and his brother during the journey from Jidda, Mecca, to meet with President Roosevelt in February 1945. NH 84742 Courtesy of Naval History & Heritage Command.

> the ship couldn't possibly accommodate so many guests, and they somehow managed to whittle the entourage down to a mere forty-two [Carlson, Peter].

The next day, when the king arrived, he brought with him tents, carpets, the royal throne and several dozen sheep. The sheep were intended to be slaughtered and fed to the entire crew. The king was graciously thanked but assured that the rules required the crew to eat the chow provided on board. He was allowed to bring just enough sheep for his entourage. They were corralled between the depth charge racks on the stern. Several pictures show sheep "grazing" on the deck of *Murphy* awaiting their fate (Carlson, Peter).

According to Carlson, while sailing for two days to the rendezvous with the *Quincy*,

> [t]he sailors entertained their royal guest by firing cannons and machine guns and detonating depth charges. The king loved it. "First I am a warrior," he said, "then I am a king."
>
> The king also ate his first slice of apple pie a la mode, which he loved, and watched his first movie, a documentary about aircraft carriers. He enjoyed the film but told Eddy that he wouldn't permit his subjects to watch movies because they would "distract them from their religious duties" [Carlson, Peter].

King Ibn Saud's entourage on the USS *Murphy* deck. Note carpets on deck and portable throne just in front of gun turret. NH 94741 Courtesy of Naval History & Heritage Command.

After dropping off her royal passengers, *Murphy* returned to the U.S. and engaged in anti-submarine duty in the Atlantic until July 1945, when she headed to the Pacific. She arrived in September, about the time Japan formally surrendered, and she remained in the Pacific on occupation duty until November. Then she headed home to be placed in the Reserve Force. She was decommissioned on March 9, 1946, and struck from Navy rolls in 1970. She was sold for scrap in October 1972.

Murphy received four battle stars for her participation in World War II.

But this is not the end of *Murphy*'s story. In 2002, diver Dan Crowell and his team verified that a large piece of ship they found 75 miles off the coast of New Jersey in 260 feet of water was the bow of *Murphy*. This discovery was one of the subjects of a Military Channel documentary series, *Quest for Sunken Warships*.

The Poem

Below is the deck log in verse posted by Lt. j.g. Thaddeus R. Beal, on January 1, 1943. Beal writes 38 lines of rhyming couplets in a driving rhythm that echoes the well-known "The Tyger" (1794) by English poet William Blake. That poem would have been well-known to a Yale grad like Beal. It opens with the lines "Tyger Tyger burning bright / In the forests of the night." And just as Blake evokes the strength

On *Murphy*'s fantail, an Arabian servant prepares a sheep for the king's dinner while other sheep graze on the steel deck. NH 195499 Courtesy of Naval History & Heritage Command.

and majesty of the Tyger, so Beal's rhythm, like the thrumming of a ship's engines, evokes the strength and majesty of the destroyers escorting the convoy.

The ship is sailing in the Caribbean under Operating Plan 142. She has just left Jamaica and expects to see Panama the next day. The convoy consists of seven destroyers and eight transports moving in two columns. All is going smoothly, with "Zig Zag plan not yet alive." As Beal says a bit later, "German subs have gone away, / Leaving flying fish to play." He expects the journey to be a straight shot and calls it a "[h]igh speed convoy" at 15 knots, with the anti-submarine screen doing a couple of knots more. They are an hour from moonrise, with possible rough seas ahead: "Squalls may make 'Mint Jelly' sour."

The poem's final 14 lines offer a very human, personal touch. Beal imagines a winter scene: "Back at home near fireside glow, / Outside whirls of flaky snow." Family and friends will shed a tear for their loved ones in uniform looking to another war-torn year. The men of *Murphy* will push forward. Beal hears an accordion playing on board and thinks of the Shamrock on the smokestack. He refers to a ship's mascot, "Fedala Murphy bull dog hound" in her hammock. Beal looks forward to the next day, going to the Stranger's Club, an iconic bar that operated from the 1920s to the 1970s in Colon, Panama.

The men of the *Murphy* are leaving 1942: "Sailing through the Sapphire blue, /

Hoping that in '43 / Broadway's bright lights we may see." The war would grind on for two and a half more years, but Beal's American optimism is strong at the birth of the new year.

Here's the poem:

Steaming with Task Group 39.
Through the Caribbean's brine,
Under Op-Plan [Operating Plan] one-forty two,
Tomorrow Panama in view,
Murphy screening at Dog Four,
And with six destroyers more.
Transports eight in columns two,
Pixies many, Germans few.
Course is South plus twenty-five,
Zig Zag plan not yet alive,
High speed convoy knots fifteen,
Two knots more for A/S [Anti-Submarine] screen.
Jamaica left in clouds astern,
A straight run without a turn,
Moonrise due within the hour,
Squalls may make "Mint Jelly" sour.
Task group Boss is Coman, "Plug,"
Convoy call is "Waterbug."
"Big Boy" runs the mad "Bull Pen,"
J.L. Holloway tells us when,
German subs have gone away,
Leaving flying fish to play.
Back at home near fireside glow,
Outside whirls of flaky snow,
They greet another war-torn year,
Shed for us a longing tear,
We perspiring push along,
Accordion squeezing out a song,
Shamrock on our after stack
May produce some extra "flak"
In her hammock sleeping sound,
Fedala Murphy bull dog hound,
One day more the Stranger's Club,
The escort back some freighter tub.
Thus we part from '42,
Sailing through the Sapphire blue,
Hoping that in '43
Broadway's bright lights we may see.

T.R. Beal Lt.(j.g.),
USNR

The Poet

Thaddeus Reynolds Beal, Jr., was born in New York on March 22, 1917, to Thaddeus Reynolds Beal, Sr., and Alice Louise Dresel. His father was well-known as the president and general manager of the Central Hudson Gas & Electric Corporation, a company that continues to operate in 2021.

Thaddeus, Jr., graduated from the Hotchkiss School in Lakeville, Connecticut, in 1935. His entry in the yearbook indicated that he was something of a Renaissance Man, active in a wide variety of school activities, including several sports, drama club and glee club.

After high school, Beal attended and graduated from Yale, then began the study of law at Harvard before receiving a commission in the U.S. Naval Reserve. He spent five years in the USNR, eventually attaining the rank of lieutenant commander. He was OOD on the fateful night when *Murphy* collided with the *Bulkoil*. The luck of the Irish must have been with him, as it is a miracle that anyone on the bridge survived. He also spent time as Operations Officer for Destroyer Squadron 61 (DESRON 61) aboard the flagship USS *DeHaven* (DD 727).

During 1944, Beal's engagement to Navy Officer Lt. j.g. Katharine Putnam was announced in *The New York Times*. The two were married later that year.

After his Navy service, Beal was associated with the law firm of Herrick, Smith, Donald, Farley and Ketchum of Boston as associate and later as partner. He was president and chief executive officer of Harvard Trust Company of Cambridge, Massachusetts, and was active in business and community organizations in the greater Boston area as trustee, Cambridge Savings Bank and Boston Personal Property Trust, director of Middlesex Mutual Insurance Company, member of Cambridge Redevelopment Authority, and trustee of Radcliffe College. One of Beal's most visible positions was as Undersecretary of the Army during the Nixon administration under Secretary Melvin R. Laird.

According to his *New York Times* obituary, Beal died while riding his bicycle in Lyme, New Hampshire, on May 2, 1981, at the age of 64. He is buried in the Mount Auburn Cemetery, Cambridge, Massachusetts (*New York Times*, 1981). After reading Beal's midwatch verse, his son George (who along with his other surviving siblings had no knowledge that Beal had written it) said his father always had an interest in poetry, usually of a humorous nature (personal communication, June 9, 2020). Beal's daughter Alice spoke of her mother's Naval service and added that neither her father nor mother talked much about their time in the Navy (personal communication, June 11, 2020).

USS *Washington*

Not Just Any Man Overboard

USS *Washington* (BB 56) running post-overhaul trials in Puget Sound, Washington, on September 10, 1945. National Archives Photo 19-N-89065.

The Ship

USS *Washington* (BB 56), a North Carolina-class fast battleship, was commissioned on May 15, 1941, at the Philadelphia Naval Shipyard. During her initial activity, she provided a training platform on the East Coast. On May 25, 1942, *Washington* joined Task Force 39 as the flagship of Rear Admiral John W. Wilcox. The Atlantic

Fleet detached *Washington* to the British Fleet to protect convoys re-supplying Russia. And on May 27, she became involved in one of the most unusual events in U.S. Naval history.

According to *Washington*'s official report, while sailing in moderately heavy seas with fog and intermittent rain and snow, at 1031 the "Man Overboard" alarm sounded. USS *Tuscaloosa* (CA 37) dropped life buoys, and destroyers raced to the location to search for the crewman. A crewman on one ship said he saw someone struggling to swim in the rough waters. Another reported that the man was bald-headed (USS *Washington*, 1942). According to Richard J. Bauman, in a 2018 *Naval History Magazine* article, another eyewitness saw someone floating face-down in the water. A muster of the crew found no one to be missing, as did a second muster. When a report of the incident was taken to Admiral Wilcox's quarters, he was not there. Several crewmen later described seeing the admiral looking confused or possibly ill just before the incident. The final report found that Admiral Wilcox fell or was washed overboard through no fault of anyone on the crew. Some suspected that he had a heart attack before falling over the side. By 1228, the search for Wilcox was discontinued. This was the only time that a U.S. Navy admiral perished by falling over the side of a U.S. Navy ship (Bauman, 2018).

For the next four months, *Washington* operated with the British Home Fleet out of Scapa Flow in the Orkney Islands, providing security for convoys heading to Murmansk. On May 1, the *Washington* was in another unusual and very tight situation after the battleship HMS *King George V* collided with the destroyer HMS *Punjabi*, slicing her in half just in front of *Washington*. *Washington* had to steam between the two sections of the sinking destroyer while the destroyer's depth charges began exploding beneath *Washington*. Explosions threw water over *Washington*'s forecastle and shook the entire ship, but caused only minor damage.

In July 1942, *Washington* sailed back to the U.S. for refit before being deployed to the Pacific Theater. From November 12 to 15, 1942, she participated in the Naval Battle of Guadalcanal, crucial to the U.S. maintaining a foothold in the Solomon Islands. Two things of note about this battle. First, on November 13, two of the three U.S. admirals killed in action during World War II fell. Rear Admiral Daniel J. Callaghan died when the bridge of his flagship USS *San Francisco* (CA 38) was hit by enemy fire, and Rear Admiral Norman Scott died when the bridge of his ship, USS *Atlanta* (CL 51), was hit by friendly fire from USS *San Francisco*.

Second, *Washington* engaged with the Japanese battleship *Kirishima* in the first head-to-head battleship conflict of the war. *Kirishima*, several cruisers and nine destroyers steamed near Savo Island intent on shelling U.S. Marines on Guadalcanal and clearing the way to reinforce Japanese troops on the island. *Washington*, the battleship *South Dakota* and four destroyers sailed toward *Kirishima*'s group after seeing it on radar. It was nearly midnight on November 14 when the Japanese attacked the four screening U.S. destroyers, sinking two within ten minutes and putting the other two out of commission. Later, *South Dakota* drew the Japanese attention and was mercilessly shelled by many of the IJN ships, taking over 20 hits and losing her ability to effectively retaliate. At the same time, *Washington* slipped closer to the IJN ships undetected and at fairly close range for her 16" guns opened fire on the *Kirishima*. Battle damage reports differ, but all agree that *Washington* scored several hits on *Kirishima* with her big guns and many more with her smaller 5" guns. A few hours later, *Kirishima* capsized and sank.

After this action, *Washington* continued to be active in most of the significant Pacific Theater campaigns, including the Marianas, Luzon, Leyte, Palau, Iwo Jima and Okinawa. Like most of the other newer U.S. battleships, she joined the fast carrier groups that inexorably pressed westward across the Pacific toward Japan. During this time, she was assigned to Task Force 34. During the Battle of Leyte Gulf in the Philippines, TF 34 was intended to guard the San Bernardino Strait and help the 7th Fleet protect the Leyte landings. However, though Admiral Halsey did designate Task Force 34, he committed a major tactical error when he declined to assign the task force to its intended duty. When the Japanese sent their Northern Force carrier group as a decoy to lure Halsey's 3rd Fleet away from Leyte, Halsey took the bait and steamed north after them, taking with him *Washington* and the other ships of TF 34.

Halsey's move allowed the Japanese Center Force—composed of four large battleships, six heavy cruisers, two light cruisers and 11 destroyers—to steam through the San Bernardino Strait and threaten the Leyte landing forces, encountering only a small American force of six escort carriers (smaller, slower and more vulnerable than their larger cousins), three destroyers and four destroyer escorts. This confrontation led to one of the most heroic stands of the Pacific War by U.S. ships: The Battle Off Samar. When it became clear that Task Force 34 was not guarding the San Bernardino Strait, Pacific Fleet Commander Chester Nimitz sent a message to Halsey. The message was to read, "Where is, repeat, where is Task Force Thirty Four?" However, wartime messages included a great deal of padding to reduce enemy decryption. In this case, the added phrase "The world wonders," which would typically be stripped off by the receiving operator, remained. Halsey saw, "Where is, repeat, where is Task Force Thirty Four? The world wonders." Feeling slighted, his temper erupted. He threw his hat to the deck, vented his anger and sulked, taking precious time away from a response. A version of TF 34 was eventually formed to chase down crippled Japanese ships near Leyte, too late to take on the massive battleships that decimated and sank two destroyers, a destroyer escort and one of the escort carriers.

Who knows what the history of USS *Washington* would have been had Task Force 34 remained to defend San Bernardino Strait? Glory and victory against the Japanese Center Force off Samar? A victory that would have destroyed the Japanese fleet? Or would she have suffered loss and destruction at the hands of Japan's larger ships?

After the war, *Washington* moved to the Reserve Fleet, but was sold for scrap on May 24, 1961. She earned 13 battle stars for her service in World War II.

The Poem

Lt. P.E. McArthur, writing the New Year's deck log entry on *Washington* for 1943, offers one of the most ambitious attempts in all the World War II deck logs. It is a parody of one of the best-known and most-loved poems in American literature: Edgar Allan Poe's "The Raven," published in January 1845, 98 years to the month before McArthur penned his poem. Poe was made famous with the publication of "The Raven," but Lt. McArthur has remained in obscurity. Until now.

Poe's "Raven" was a long poem, 108 lines divided into 18 stanzas. It is memorable for its long, musical lines, its strong pounding rhythm, its repetition and its internal rhyme in line after line. The result is an incantatory rhythm that reinforces the supernatural atmosphere of the poem. Here is the first stanza of "The Raven":

> Once upon a midnight dreary, while I pondered, weak and weary,
> Over many a quaint and curious volume of forgotten lore—
> While I nodded, nearly napping, suddenly there came a tapping,
> As of someone gently rapping, rapping at my chamber door.
> "'Tis some visitor," I muttered, "tapping at my chamber door—
> Only this and nothing more."

McArthur's parody is shorter than the original, only seven stanzas. The first two are the closest to Poe in style and structure. His opening line is an almost word-for-word repetition of Poe's. McArthur changes only one word: "Once upon a midnight dreary, while I *slumbered* weak and weary." The rest of the stanza offers a close imitation of Poe, repeating much of Poe's imagery, with a sly and humorous twist in the next-to-last line, in which he is called to his four-hour midwatch. Here is McArthur's first stanza:

> Once upon a midnight dreary, while I slumbered, weak and weary,
> Dreaming of such far-off places as New York and good old Philly,
> Suddenly there came a tapping, and someone opened up my chamber door,
> "Tis a visitor," I muttered as he uttered—"Twelve to four."
> Only that, and nothing more.

McArthur's second stanza again begins with a line written by Poe: "Presently my soul grew stronger, hesitating then no longer." And here again he displays his humor, describing his struggle with sleep as he is "groping blindly in the darkness." His foggy brain and perhaps his impatience appear humorously in the line that follows, which imitates Poe's internal rhyme: "Then while I nodded, nearly napping, someone near me began yapping."

The middle three stanzas of McArthur's poem include the technical requirements of the ship's docking situation, location, depth, active boilers and ship's condition. *Washington* is moored in Dumbea Bay, tied to a buoy in Berth 32, in nine and a half fathoms of water. Checking his charts, McArthur finds they are near the French port of Numea in New Caledonia. In stanza five, he says they blow the tubes. Boiler tubes accumulate sooty deposits, especially when moored for any length of time, and need to be cleaned periodically for best efficiency. A soot blower installed in the boiler used a jet of hot steam to clean the boiler tubes. Power is supplied by boiler number three. The ship is in Condition of Readiness III and Material Condition Yoke. They are moored in port, but they are uneasy, and stand ready to fight at a moment's notice. McArthur notes "the grim, gaunt, ghastly outline of the warships in repose," with all lights out.

In the final two stanzas of McArthur's poem, he is able to recreate the rhyme and rhythm of Poe while giving a long list of the 26 ships anchored in the harbor. He ends the poem, his watch nearly over, yearning for the arrival of his replacement—the "four to eighter." The final lines echo the opening while quoting directly a line from Poe: "Is that you rapping at my door?" he asks, hoping to be relieved of duty, then closes in disappointment, "Tis the wind and nothing more."

McArthur's poem is unusual in another way. It is January 1, 1943. America has been fighting for a year, but McArthur makes no direct reference to the war. It appears only indirectly in the material conditions of the ship. And perhaps in his perception of the grim, gaunt and ghastly outlines of the warships. And the line that follows, "Darkness there and nothing more!"

Here is the poem:

Once upon a midnight dreary, while I slumbered, weak and weary,
Dreaming of such far-off places as New York and good old Philly,
Suddenly there came a tapping, and someone opened up my chamber door,
"Tis a visitor," I muttered as he uttered—"Twelve to four."
Only that, and nothing more.

Presently my soul grew stronger; hesitating then no longer,
Groping blindly through the darkness, to the quarterdeck I wandered,
Then while I nodded, nearly napping, someone near me began yapping,
All about the boats and people somehow caught off on the shore,
And leaving me, said nothing more!

Soon I sat engaged in guessing what all that was he had to say,
Then, distinctly, I remembered, 'T'was all about Dumbea Bay.
Moored there, are we, with the starboard chain, to a buoy in berth #32,
In nine and one-half fathoms of water—a deep blue,
Black now, and not so blue!

Desolate, yet not unsettled, are the shores around about,
For close by is Port Noumea, of French fame throughout,
And from my books I gather, and according to our charts,
'Tis part of New Caledonia, this barren, foreign port,
Here now—but we shall part!

Methought the air grew denser, oh yes, they're blowing tubes,
Boiler number three is in use for the auxiliary lubes,
Condition III, condition Yoke, and not a light does show,
From the grim, gaunt, ghastly outline, of the warships in repose,
Darkness there and nothing more!

Though the darkness is unbroken and the stillness gives no token,
'Tis said the following ships are here about:
NORTH CAROLINA, INDIANA, SAN JUAN, BALCH, AND DIXIE, and;
CRESCENT CITY, RUSSELL, GRAYSON; PRESIDENT ADAMS, HAYES, and JACKSON,
And from the flagbridge—even more!

HUNTER LIGGETT, DUNLAP, GRIDLEY; FRAZIER, LARDNER and the WHITNEY;
WEST POINT, LASSEN, LANDSDOWNE, SHASTA; MAURY, HUGHES and TALAMANCA;
And now the watch is nearly over; with the ARGONNE and SARATOGA,
So come you four to eighter, "Is that you rapping at my door?"
'Tis the wind and nothing more.

P.E. McArthur,
Lieutenant, USN

The Poet

Paul Enoch McArthur was born to Thomas Braidwood McArthur and Eveline Cordelia Paine on November 18, 1916, near Cincinnati. Thomas supported his family for many years as a ticket agent at Cincinnati's Union Station. The family spent much of Paul's early life in nearby Norwood. He demonstrated leadership qualities during his time as a Norwood High School student, serving as senior class president. His yearbook entry cited his executive abilities as one of his most valuable assets. His most admired person was Teddy Roosevelt.

After graduation from Norwood, McArthur attended the U.S. Naval Academy, graduating in the Class of 1940. His Annapolis *Lucky Bag* entry indicated that he had a strong interest in golf by his participation for three years on the team.

Midshipman Paul Enoch McArthur from the 1940 Naval Academy Yearbook *Annapolis Lucky Bag*.

McArthur's commissioning as an ensign sent him to USS *Maryland* (BB 46) for a brief deployment before he became a plank owner (a member of a ship's commissioning crew) of USS *Washington* in 1941. He remained there through at least part of 1943. At the same time, McArthur's older brother, Arthur Paine McArthur, served in the U.S. Marine Corps, eventually rising to the rank of lieutenant colonel and at one point being deployed to Guadalcanal. It is likely that the brothers served on and off the coast of that island at the same time. McArthur continued to serve in the Navy until his retirement in November 1976 at the rank of commander.

In 1946, Lt. Cmdr. McArthur became a minor celebrity in newspapers from coast to coast: He reportedly proposed to Nancy Lou Brinckman (formerly Nancy Lou Muck), an actress who appeared in 20 movies from 1941 through 1947. Brinckman's roles were mostly uncredited, but her credits included movies starring Kane Richmond and the Bowery Boys. A chronicle of Brinckman's career in modeling and theater during the 1940s appears in hundreds of newspapers. When word of McArthur's proposal became public, articles began to appear in newspapers touting his relationship to General Douglas MacArthur. Depending on the newspaper, Paul McArthur was described as "grand-nephew," "distant cousin" or "kin" to the five-star Army general. To lend credibility to this claim, most papers misspelled McArthur's name as "MacArthur." But in fact, Paul E. McArthur was not related to Douglas MacArthur at all. Apparently, Brinckman's publicity people conjured up the relationship to draw upon the popularity of the five-star general. Brinckman and McArthur married in 1946 and had one child. Nancy Brinckman McArthur died in 1985. Paul died in Las Vegas in 2010. His remains are interred at the United States Naval Academy Cemetery at Annapolis.

USS *Buchanan*

The Scrapperoos

USS *Buchanan* (DD-484) off the Mare Island Navy Yard, California, after overhaul on June 19, 1944. The ship is painted in camouflage Measure 31 Design 3d. NH 97772 Courtesy of the Naval History & Heritage Command.

The Ship

USS *Buchanan* (DD 484), one of the most decorated U.S. ships in World War II, was a Gleaves-class destroyer commissioned on March 21, 1942. She was the second U.S. destroyer named after 19th-century naval officer Franklin Buchanan. The first

Buchanan (DD 131) served from 1919 to 1941, when she and ultimately 50 other ships were transferred to the Royal Navy under a "Destroyers-for-Bases" agreement; she was renamed *Campbeltown* to honor towns in England and in Florida. The second *Buchanan* was sponsored by the great-granddaughter of the ship's namesake.

Buchanan shipped to the Pacific Fleet in May 1942 and was active at Guadalcanal and Tulagi. She rescued many survivors from several ships sunk at the Battle of Savo Island. She continued to be active in Pacific campaigns. In November 1942, she was damaged by friendly fire at the Naval Battle of Guadalcanal, suffering the loss of five crewmen and withdrawing from the action.

In early 1943, *Buchanan* was assigned to escort duty. She joined Task Force 15, and in April of that year, while screening, she ran aground off the southern coast of Guadalcanal and had to jettison heavy equipment and ammunition to be pulled off the reef. After repairs, she joined the New Georgia Campaign in the Solomon Islands in June and July. During the Battle of Kolombangara, she collided with USS *Woodworth* (DD 460) and again had to retire from action. After repairs, she was assigned to convoy duty and in November participated in the Treasury-Bougainville campaign. In January 1944, as part of Task Force 38, while going to the rescue of the torpedoed oiler USS *Cache* (AO 67), *Buchanan* hunted down and sank a Japanese submarine.

In February, while supporting the Bismarck Archipelago operations off the coast of New Guinea, *Buchanan*, along with the destroyers USS *Farenholt* (DD 491), USS *Woodworth* (DD 460), USS *Lardner* (DD 487) and USS *Lansdowne* (DD 486), penetrated the archipelago and attacked Rabaul. During the attacks, *Buchanan* and *Farenholt* were hit by shore battery fire. The engagements earned the destroyer group the nickname "Simpson's Solomons Scrappers," later simply "Scrapperoos," after their commander, Commodore Roger W. Simpson (Destroyer History Foundation). Following that action, *Buchanan* returned to the U.S. for overhaul at Mare Island, California.

Later that year, *Buchanan* returned to the Pacific and participated in the Mariana and Palau Islands campaign. In mid–December 1944, she participated in the striking of Luzon Island in the Philippines. On December 18, she suffered heavy damage in Typhoon Cobra, Halsey's Typhoon. The day before, several screening vessels had attempted to refuel, but the sea and wind were increasing, and attempts failed. According to *Buchanan*'s War Diary for December 18 and 19, the ships rendezvoused early that morning to again attempt fueling, but conditions worsened. At 0730, refueling was cancelled.

Now most of *Buchanan*'s tanks were empty, giving her very little ballast for stability. The course which the fleet was ordered to take put the Force 12 wind (Hurricane level on the Beaufort Scale) broadside to the ships. As conditions continued to deteriorate, *Buchanan* experienced power failures and flooding. Visibility was zero. USS *Monterey* (CVL 26) reported that all planes on her hangar deck were on fire. *Buchanan* began rolling dangerously, up to 54 degrees, and struggled to hold her course. At one point, with most of her pumps out from flooding, all hands were ordered to the starboard side to counteract listing. The crew used axes to punch holes in the 20mm machine gun shields, where water had collected and was contributing to the listing. Using maximum power, the ship was finally able to change course, "and with the wind almost dead astern commenced running before the wind."

An hour later, the fleet was ordered to the course *Buchanan* had taken, "and this fact alone prevented us from becoming separated." By 1400 hours, visibility was improved to three miles and the wind was down to 45 knots, and *Buchanan* joined a handful of ships, "[a]ll other screen vessels having become separated." The ship had sustained extensive damage to its electrical systems. The next morning when she pulled alongside USS *Caliente* (AO 53) to refuel, being down to nine percent fuel and having very little ballast for stability, handling was difficult. After refueling to 65 percent, *Buchanan* spent the rest of the day passing pilots and mail between ships (USS *Buchanan*, 1944). She was then ordered to Ulithi for repairs. After repairs, she returned to the Luzon operation.

From February to August 1945, *Buchanan* participated in campaigns against Iwo Jima, Okinawa and Third Fleet operations against Japan. On September 1, she transported Admirals Nimitz and Halsey from Tokyo Bay to Yokohama for a meeting with General MacArthur. According to the War Diary for September 1–3, 1945, after the meeting with MacArthur, *Buchanan* transported Nimitz and Halsey to the USS *Benevolence* (AH 13), which carried evacuated Allied prisoners of war, where the admirals made an official call. The next day, *Buchanan* transported MacArthur to USS *Missouri* (BB 63) for the signing of the surrender, anchoring close aboard *Missouri* during the ceremonies. Following the ceremonies, she returned MacArthur to Yokohama (USS *Buchanan*, 1945).

She remained on occupation duty until October, then returned to San Francisco and finally to Charleston, South Carolina, where she was decommissioned and put in reserve in May 1946. She was recommissioned in December 1948 and in March 1949 sailed for Golcuk, Turkey, where she was turned over to the Turkish Navy. She served there as TCG *Gelibolu* (D 346) until being retired in 1976.

Buchanan received the Presidential Unit Citation and 16 battle stars for her service in World War II.

The Poem

The following deck log was entered on January 1, 1944, by Lt. j.g. A.G. Keeshan, Jr., USNR. The poem consists of 24 lines of rhymed couplets, broken into four six-line stanzas, and exhibits a regular waltz-like rhythm. The war has been grinding on for two full years, but Keeshan is not discouraged. Rather, he exhibits the typical confidence and irreverence of many of the young deck log writers. He opens the poem "Exactly at midnight" while *Buchanan* is moored with three other destroyers—*Farenholt* (DD 491), *Lardener* (DD 487) and *Lansdowne* (DD 486) at the island of Bougainville in the Northern Solomons.

Keeshan calls the commander of the destroyer squadron an "old cuss." The ships have been in an echelon (stairstep) formation in case of attack. Keeshan gives the ship's course and a speed of 15 knots, though he says they could go much faster because boilers two and four are ready to go. They are in Condition of Readiness One, which is General Quarters with all hands at battle stations, because they don't want "to get caught with our pants at half mast." At the stroke of midnight, they ring the traditional Navy 16 bells for New Year—eight for the old year and eight for the new. The squadron commander orders the ships to turn 180 degrees, and they "search" northwest for two hours and then northeast for two more.

As Keeshan's watch draws to a close, he complains that the radar has been active but has not produced any enemy targets. At 0358 hours, they are ordered to turn southeast, and Keeshan closes with "Thus endeth this mid-watch—the first of the year, / We'll catch some the next time, if they'll only come near."

Here is the poem:

Time: Exactly at midnight. Place: Bougainville Isle,
Four ships are in line, that is, most of the while,
There's the *Farenholt*, *Lardener*, the *Landsdowne* and us,
Led by C.D.S. Twelve [Commander Destroyer Squad Twelve] who's in charge, the old cuss,
To strike for an echelon not so far back
Should a Japanese task force attempt an attack.

Course is one thirty five, and by check can be seen
That by standard [compass] it is just a hundred thirteen.
Speed's set at fifteen, but we're good for much more,
For on ten minute's notice are cans [boilers] two and four.
"Condition of Readiness One" has been passed
For we'd hate to get caught with our pants at half mast.

After ringing eight bells for the year we've been thru
We proceeded to ring eight bells for the New.
C.D.S. at this time orders "Turn, if you please,
Exactly one hundred and eighty degrees."
To the northwest we searched for two hours at least
Then formed into column and headed northeast.

Though radar was active, announcing each pip,
Not a one of these contacts produced us a Nip.
So at three fifty eight, the man with the flag
Yells by phone "Turn southeast, and eight-four don't lag."
Thus endeth this mid-watch—the first of the year,
We'll catch some the next time, if they'll only come near.

A.G. Keeshan, Jr.
Lt. (j.g.), D-V(G), USNR

The Poet

Alfred George Keeshan, Jr., was born on March 17, 1918, in Larchmont, New York, to Alfred G. Keeshan, Sr., and May C. Byrnes. The Keeshan family had a long history of working in the hat-making industry. Alfred, Jr.'s, grandfather John, was the Midwest representative for the Stetson hat company while living in St. Louis. Alfred, Sr., followed in his father's footsteps and spent his career in management of several hat-making companies on the East Coast. During World War II, the Quartermaster General of the War Department appointed Alfred, Sr., as a consultant, requiring him to spend considerable time in Washington, D.C. (*Hartford Courant* 1942).

Keeshan, Jr., attended two prestigious Connecticut schools during his childhood and adolescence, the Brunswick School and Cheshire Academy. He also attended Yale University. He entered military service in 1942 and served on both *Buchanan* and USS *Massey* (DD 778). By late 1944, he had attained the rank of lieutenant.

The May 15, 1949, edition of the *New York Times* announced the engagement of Keeshan to Barbara Bigelow, a member of *Life* magazine's editorial staff. They married later that year. In January 1958, the family experienced a tragedy when Alfred G. Keeshan III drowned in an accident at a private pond in Rye, New York (*The Daily Item*, 1958).

Keeshan and his father served the Larchmont Yacht Club over the course of many years in positions such as chairman of the race committee. Keeshan, Jr., died at the age of 55 in Connecticut on February 9, 1974. He is buried in Elm Grove Cemetery in Mystic, Connecticut (Keeshan, Alfred G.).

USS *Texas*

Engage Until Neutralized

USS *Texas* (BB 35) underway off Norfolk, Virginia, on March 15, 1943, with her main battery gun turrets trained to port. National Archives Photo 80-G-63542.

The Ship

USS *Texas* (BB 35) was a New York–class battleship commissioned on March 12, 1914. In May, before she had time to perform a standard shakedown cruise, she was sent to Vera Cruz, Mexico, to support American troops occupying the city during the "Tampico Incident." For the next couple of years, she maintained a schedule of training and tactical drills until the U.S. entry into World War I in April 1917. Shortly after completing scheduled repairs at the New York Navy Yard in September of that year, the ship ran aground during the midwatch of April 27 off Block Island, Rhode Island. After three days of fruitless effort by her crew to lighten the ship to refloat her, six tugs pulled her loose, but the damage to the hull required extensive repairs. She crossed the Atlantic in February 1918 and joined the Sixth Battle Squadron of Britain's Grand Fleet. From that time until the end of the war, she performed convoy missions and other escort duties. She was present at the surrender of the German Fleet to the Grand Fleet in November 1918.

From 1919 to 1937, *Texas* alternated duties in the Atlantic and Pacific. In January 1928, she transported President Calvin Coolidge to Havana for the Pan-American Conference. During the inter-war period, she became a testing ground for several innovations. According to Peter Suciu, she was the first U.S. battleship to launch an aircraft—a British Sopwith Camel—in March 1919. In the mid–1920s, she became the first U.S. battleship to mount anti-aircraft guns and the first U.S. ship to control gunfire with directors and range keepers (Suciu, 2021). In late 1938 or early 1939, *Texas* became the flagship of the newly organized Atlantic Squadron. Following the outbreak of war in Europe in September 1939, she served briefly in the West Indies and then in May 1941 began operating in President Roosevelt's Neutrality Patrol on the East Coast, making three extended cruises into the North Atlantic.

When news of the Pearl Harbor attack came, *Texas* was in Casco Bay, Maine. From January to October 1942, she operated in convoy duty in the Atlantic. Then in October and November, she supported the landings in North Africa in Operation Torch. During those operations, a young journalist named Walter Cronkite was covering the war from the battleship and even flew off the ship in one of her Kingfisher aircraft (Suciu, 2021).

Through 1943 and early 1944, *Texas* carried out convoy escort duty between New York and Europe. Then beginning on June 6, 1944, she provided heavy arms bombardment for two weeks supporting the Normandy landings. According to the National World War II Museum, on June 25 *Texas* and the battleship *Arkansas* (BB 33), with three destroyers, exchanged fire with German Battery Hamburg at the town of Cherbourg in support of the Seventh Army Corps. Her orders were to engage the batteries until neutralized. Located six miles east of the city and reinforced by thick concrete casements, Hamburg was the most powerful German battery in the Cherbourg area. The range of the Hamburg guns was nearly twice that of the American battleships. The opening salvo was fired by *Arkansas*, and what followed was a three-hour battle involving seven ships and multiple shore batteries. *Texas* was repeatedly straddled by near-misses as she rapidly returned fire and maneuvered to avoid being hit. Under crossfire from two batteries, the ship's luck ran out when a 280mm shell hit just below the navigation bridge and exploded (National World War II History Museum).

The deck of the pilot house "peeled up as if it were tin" from the explosion, which killed the helmsman and wounded 13 others. *Texas* continued to fire her 14-inch guns, which ignited a fire on the fantail and blew 40mm ammunition from its racks.

Marines threw the ammo overboard as sailors extinguished the fire. The ship's guns finally scored a direct hit on one of the Hamburgs, destroying it. Then just a few minutes before *Texas* was ordered to retire from the conflict, "a 240mm shell was found in the bunk of the ship's clerk, Warrant Officer M.A. Clark." The exact time the unexploded shell struck, tearing a large hole in the hull, was unknown. It had likely been there for some time during the commotion of battle. The crew covered it with mattresses and left it where it was (National World War II History Museum). The shell was later defused and presented to the ship as a lucky charm. German shells had straddled and near-missed the ship over 65 times during the three-hour conflict.

In July and August, *Texas* supported the invasion of Southern France in the Mediterranean, then returned to New York in September for repairs and replacement of the barrels on her main battery. She then moved to the Pacific Theater and spent Christmas at Pearl Harbor before steaming to Ulithi Atoll. In February 1945, she provided heavy bombardment supporting the invasion of Iwo Jima, then moved on to Okinawa, where she remained for two months, again providing pre-invasion bombardment and fire support for the troop landings. She repelled numerous aerial attacks, including kamikazes, without suffering serious damage.

In May, the ship retired to Leyte Gulf and was there when the Japanese surrendered. From September to December, she participated in Operation Magic Carpet, bringing troops home to the West Coast. She returned to the East Coast in February 1946, eventually ending up in Baltimore, where she remained until 1948. She was then moved to San Jacinto State Park in Texas and decommissioned. She was given to the state of Texas and stricken from the register in April. The battleship museum has been in operation since that time.

She earned five battle stars for her service in World War II.

The Poem

The deck log below was entered on January 1, 1944, by Lt. R.P. Axten. The poem consists of 26 lines of rhymed couplets, with the last four lines rhyming together to form a concluding farewell. Axten manages the rhythm and rhyme scheme skillfully, making the poem an enjoyable read.

As Axten writes the poem, *Texas* is on escort duty with convoy UT-6 during a round trip mission between New York and the British Isles. The operation lasted from December 29 to January 23. The poem's first eight lines lay out the organization of the convoy and escort ships, and the alphabet soup can be confusing. The Commodore (officer in command of the convoy) is on board the transport ship USS *Dorothea L. Dix*, and *Texas* is in the guide position and carries the Senior Officer Present Afloat, who is Commander of Task Force 60 (CTF 60), the escort group protecting the convoy. The destroyer USS *Davison* (DD 618), commanding the destroyer squadron, leads the screening group.

Lines nine through 16 of the poem offer much of the usual technical information expected in a deck log. Six boilers provide power, and the guys in the engine room—"the black gang"—are happy. The ship is blacked out. Condition of Readiness is "Three-Sugar," and the Material Condition is set at "Yoke." Axten gives the ship's course, speed and propeller revolutions. In lines 21 through 24, the reader senses his delight that at 0100 the clocks were set 30 minutes ahead, meaning he will get to bed a half-hour early.

The final four lines reflect the steadfast optimism and determination seen in all the deck logs. Unlike the rhyming couplets through the rest of the poem, Axten heightens the emphasis by creating a four-line unit of rhymes that echo two of the most common themes repeated in so many deck log verses. First, he asserts that there is no New Year's celebration on board the ship—"no dancing, imbibing, or revelry here"—and that everyone is hard at his task. And second, the ship's company joins their loved ones "in a prayer sincere, / For a happy, successful, victorious New Year." The progress toward victory in 1944 would be slow and grueling.

Here's the poem:

Steaming in convoy UT dash six
With Commodore sailing in DOROTHEA DIX.
The TEXAS is guide in the five-one position
And the convoy's aligned in a shipshape condition.
Commanding the escort with vigor and drive
Is CTF 60, known as Com Bat Div [Commander Battleship Div] Five.
Up ahead in the DAVISON, Com Des Ron [Commander Destroyer Squad] Fifteen
Exercises command over all of the screen.
Six boilers in all are merrily steaming,
Our progress is sure and the black gang is beaming.
To lessen the chances of Nazi attack,
The ship, like the night, is reassuringly black.
The "Three Sugar" condition watch crews are alert;
That condition "Yoke's" set I can truly assert.
Our course from true North is zero eight four,
Our speed is fifteen, no less and no more.
Fifteen for us is nine-four revolutions,
Sufficient for all but extreme evolutions.
At zero one hundred the clocks went ahead
Thirty minutes, and so we'll be sooner abed.
Our Captain has wished us the best of the season,
A sentiment all hands return with good reason.
There's no dancing, imbibing or revelry here,
We're right on the job but we're all of good cheer
And we join with our loved ones in a prayer sincere,
For a happy, successful, victorious New Year.

R.P. Axten,
Lieut. U.S.N.R.

The Poet

Richard Phillips Axten was born on June 9, 1915, to John Axten and Anne Cobb Phillips in New York City. John and Anne emigrated to the U.S. from England several years prior to Richard's birth. Richard's grandfather, Thomas Phillips, reportedly served as a bodyguard for Queen Alexandra, the consort of King Edward VII. John Axten became J.P. Morgan, Jr.'s, private secretary, which led to many Atlantic crossings for the Axten family while on business trips with Morgan. Richard, who made 38 Atlantic crossings during his life, told his family about a trip as a toddler during which he sat on Morgan's lap on deck inhaling his cigar smoke during rough seas that kept the rest of the family below decks (Negri, 2004). Indeed, passenger records show Richard and Morgan on a voyage from New York to Liverpool when Axten was younger than two years old.

Axten graduated from Harvard in 1937 as a fine arts major with an eye toward working in public relations. His first job after graduation was as a laborer in a steel mill. He believed that he needed to know all levels of a business before he represented it. In fact, his work with many European immigrants in the mill sensitized him to the plight of the thousands fleeing the increasingly aggressive Hitler regime, culminating in Axten's enlistment in the U.S. Navy in 1940. On April 19, 1941, he married Caroline Wilson, a Wellesley College graduate who was an editor for the *Readers Digest* Cleveland office. After their wedding, J.P. Morgan, Jr., told them to visit his warehouse in New York City and pick out any furniture stored there for their home (Negri, 2004).

Axten served on USS *Texas* as a gunnery officer during the Normandy invasion in 1944 and the Iwo Jima and Okinawa campaigns in the Pacific Theater in 1945. He rose to the rank of lieutenant commander in 1945.

After the war, Axten joined the public relations firm of Earl Newsome and Company and later became public relations director for Alexander Smith & Sons, a well-known carpet manufacturer. In 1955, he joined Raytheon Manufacturing, which later became a major U.S. Department of Defense contractor. After holding vice-president of Public Relations and Secretary positions at Raytheon, Axten retired in 1980. He died on June 20, 2004, in Needham Corner, Massachusetts, and is buried in Woodlawn Cemetery in Wellesley.

USS *Lansdowne*

The Lucky L

USS *Lansdowne* (DD 486). National Archives Photo 80-G-339352.

The Ship

USS *Lansdowne* (DD 486) was a Gleaves-class destroyer commissioned on April 29, 1942. She was named after Lt. Cmdr. Zachary Lansdowne, victim of a Navy dirigible crash in 1925. The *Lansdowne*'s first captain, Lt. Cmdr. William R. Smedberg III, received Lansdowne's Annapolis class ring from Lansdowne's widow on commissioning day: Years after the fatal crash, an Ohio woman found it while weeding her garden. The widow wrote to Smedberg, "It is with deep pleasure and satisfaction that I present the ring to the ship that bears Commander Lansdowne's name. I am sure that he would have wanted this done and that the two symbols of his beloved navy life—his class ring and a ship named in his memory should thus be united" (Wright, 1973).

Lansdowne spent her early months in the Atlantic Theater escorting convoys and carrying out anti-submarine duties. On July 3 and July 13, 1942, she engaged two

German U-boats resulting in "probable sinking" of both. In August, she entered the Pacific Theater where she remained throughout the war.

In September 1942, *Lansdowne* served as a screening vessel for carrier operations during the battle for Guadalcanal. On September 15, *Lansdowne*'s watch noticed a huge explosion on USS *Wasp* (CV 7), and the destroyer steamed toward the carrier at flank speed. At 1450, a "torpedo wake passed directly beneath the bow of the *Lansdowne* and passed under almost her entire length." She immediately changed course to locate the enemy submarine. Under new orders, at 1507 she moved alongside *Wasp* and began evacuating crew members. She took aboard 40 officers and 405 men. The order to scuttle *Wasp* came to *Lansdowne,* and between 1908 and 2011 hours, she fired five separate torpedoes in an attempt to sink the carrier. According to the official report, only the second, fourth and fifth torpedoes exploded, but that was enough to send *Wasp* to her watery grave (USS *Lansdowne*, 1942).

Through the rest of the war, *Lansdowne* participated in actions in the Aleutians, Marianas, Bougainville, Tinian and Okinawa. She escorted several Japanese dignitaries to Tokyo Bay for the formal signing ceremonies of Japan's surrender. After the war, *Lansdowne* was decommissioned to the Atlantic Reserve Fleet until 1949, when she entered service for the Turkish Navy until 1973.

Lansdowne's crew often referred to her as "The Lucky L" due to her ability to dodge many close-aboard hazards and because she had no official casualties during her World War II service. She earned 12 battle stars for her actions in World War II.

Poem One

The following deck log was entered on January 1, 1944, by Lt. R.C. Inghram, USNR. The poem consists of 28 lines of rhymed couplets divided into two stanzas. As the poem opens, *Lansdowne* is patrolling with three other ships off Bougainville and Torokina in the Solomon Islands. Typical of many of the deck log poets, Inghram begins by mourning the lack of alcohol: "We greet the New Year, without any booze."

Lansdowne had been active escorting ships and landing troops in the area in late 1943. The Americans had overwhelmed a smaller Japanese force in taking Bougainville, the largest island of the Solomon chain, in early November; this included the Naval Battle of Empress Augusta Bay, referred to in line six of the poem. The ship would continue an active role in bombardment, supporting landings at Bougainville, Torokina and Green Island in early 1944.

Lansdowne is escorting a group of LSTs (tank-landing ships), which Inghram calls "Love Sugar Tares," large landing craft that off-loaded vehicles (including tanks) and troops directly onto the beaches. She is accompanied by three other ships from "Squadron Douze" (Twelve). The odds for Japanese success, according to Inghram, will soon decrease, "[o]nce these Love Sugar Tares get to Point Torokina." *Lansdowne* is steering course three one five, powered by two boilers, with two more at ready. Inghram complains about the slow speed of 15 knots, which he says is "all that they mote us," using an archaic Medieval form of "might" meaning "allow" here.

The crew is on high alert, searching the skies and the ocean beneath them for enemy threats. They are at modified General Quarters (Condition II) and maximum watertight integrity (AFIRM). "A bogey! A bogey!" sighted above them creates momentary excitement, but "he shows IFF," meaning "Identification Friend or Foe." Another typical theme of the deck log poems, the absence of women, appears when Inghram says that the soundman, while "sending out pings down below," is "dreaming of a redhead named Flo."

Inghram flashes the customary American cockiness when he says, "The Japs know we're here, yet they stay in Rabaul, / 'Cause with Ole DesRon 12, they have learned not to fool." Rabaul was at that time a major Japanese base, and Inghram's bragging has some basis in fact. Destroyer Squadron 12 (DesRon 12) had a strong battle record, beginning at Guadalcanal in 1942. After their attack on Rabaul, they would be known as "The Scrapperoos."

In the poem's final lines, Inghram admits to being bored during a watch that included little action. He ends with a tongue-in-cheek expression of anger at his replacement for being 15 minutes late. He threatens to send the Quartermaster after the laggard, but the relief arrives, and Inghram ends by saying "[T]hat's how we started our 'Happy New Year.'"

Here's the poem:

'Tis the virgin hour of forty four,
As the Lansdowne patrols off a foreign shore,
With three other ships of Squadron "Douze" [Twelve],
We greet the New Year, without any booze,
We faithfully guard with all skill we can muster
Echelon Fifteen, for Empress Augusta [Empress Augusta Bay].
'For we know the Nips chances are gonna get leaner
Once these Love Sugar Tares get to Point Torokina.
At the moment we're steering on course three one five
Keeping station on "Malta"—(Oh Lord how we strive!)
We've got two kettles [boilers] on, and two on short notice,
Yet a slow 15 knots is all that they mote [allow] us.
Our gadgets are searching the skies right and left,
A bogey! A bogey! Now he shows IFF [Identification Friend or Foe]
The QC [standard sonar system] is sending out pings down below
While the soundman is dreaming of a redhead named Flo.
We're ready for action—Condition II and AFIRM
(After eighteen long months, how those words make me squirm!)
The Japs know we're here, yet they stay in Rabaul,
'Cause with Ole DesRon [Destroyer Squadron] 12, they have learned not to fool.
This watch has seemed endless! Most midwatches do,
The bogies were missing, the chances were few.
We "Turned nine" at 3:30 and again about four,
So now you might say our behind is before.

Say where's my relief? Its now four fifteen.
Quartermaster! Go get him, 'ere I start venting splean.
Ah! Here he comes now as G.Q. hovers near,
And that's how we started our "Happy New Year."
R. C. INGHRAM,
Lieutenant D-V(G), U.S.N.R.

Poet One

Richard Curtis Inghram was born in Chicago on December 18, 1915, to Curtis Inghram and Harriet Madge Gatton. The Inghrams moved to a farm near Burlington, Iowa, during Richard's early years. Richard attended New London High School, Burlington Community College, the University of Iowa and then midshipmen's school at Northwestern University. Commissioned as an ensign, he boarded USS *Chenango* (AO 31) before she was converted to an escort carrier (CVE 28). Inghram next boarded USS *Lansdowne* until late 1944. His posting after leaving the *Lansdowne* is unknown; however, in 1946, he was awarded a Purple Heart and received a medical discharge at the rank of lieutenant commander.

Inghram's family took seriously the desire to serve their country. In May 1946, he married Ensign Mary E. Becker, who served in the Navy Nursing Corps. Two of his brothers became aviators and also served during World War II. Robert Inghram joined the Army Air Corps in 1942 only to be shot down over the English Channel and captured by the Germans. He spent the rest of the war in Luft Stalag III and reportedly worked on all three tunnels made famous in the book and later movie *The Great Escape* (Richard Curtis Inghram). Benjamin Inghram became a Naval aviator and served on USS *Bennington* (CV 20). In February 1945, he was shot down while on a raid near Tokyo and was never recovered. The spirit of service in the Richard Inghram family persisted with his children. Three of his sons joined the Marine Corps. Another son served in the submarine service, and his daughter served in the Air Force, according to his son Rick, who is a retired lieutenant colonel in the Marine Corps (email, July 9, 2020).

Richard Inghram died on March 31, 2011, at the age of 85. He is buried in Elmwood Cemetery, Morning Sun, Iowa.

Poem Two

The deck log below, entered on January 1, 1945, by Ensign J.R. Wall, is short and simple, consisting of 16 lines of rhymed couplets. The ship is moored in Ulithi Harbor in the Caroline Islands.

When Ensign Wall stood the midwatch just three months after the atoll was occupied, Ulithi was a bustling Naval operation that included thousands of personnel serving hundreds of ships. Yet the poem has a weary air to it. The war has dragged on for three years, and Wall begins by looking forward to *another* year of war. The ship, powered by boiler number four, is moored in berth 402. The watch is set with guns manned, and the ship is blacked out. It seems to be raining. Wall is three and a half hours into a slow four-hour watch. After apparently being relieved, he expresses a restrained breath of hope in the closing lines: "And so begins one-nine-four-five, / Make my next New Year in a 'Frisco dive."

Here is the poem:

'Tis the downing hour of forty-five,
Another year during which we strive.
Number 4 boiler is still on the line,
In berth 402 where we bide our time.
Ulithi Harbor is the scene this date,
Caroline Islands, this our fate.
The water is deep, twenty fathoms or more,
While riding to port on sixty-four.
Gun three and the twenty, the watch is set,
Ship is darkened, the scene wet.
The watch awake, no whistle did blow,
Almost three-thirty, thirty minutes to go.
Called Old George (CincSacPac) [Commander in Chief Supreme
Allied Command Pacific]
He's on deck, so I'll hit my sack.
And so begins one-nine-four-five,
Make my next New Year in a 'Frisco dive.
J.R. Wall, Ensign (D)L,
U.S.N.R.

Poet Two

Jack Roger Wall was born in Advance, Indiana, on February 4, 1921, to Otis Wall and Nina Waters. According to Jack's son, Jack Jr., Jack Sr. was raised on a 2000-acre farm that his grandfather owned. He attended Purdue University, then transferred to the University of New Mexico to finish his undergraduate degree. While at UNM, he joined the Navy ROTC, which eventually led to his commission as an Ensign and his ticket to *Lansdowne* in 1944. Jack Jr. said that if Jack Sr. was asked about his major at UNM, he would say that he majored in Rodeo because it was his favorite non-academic activity that he was good at and loved to do (email, February 3, 2021).

On March 1, 1944, before shipping out to the Pacific, Jack married Helene J. Higgins in Chicago. In September 1945, Wall was aboard the *Lansdowne* when she ferried Japanese dignitaries to the surrender ceremony in Tokyo Harbor. He can be seen in a photo, kneeling and taking photos as the dignitaries come back aboard the *Lansdowne* after the ceremony.

After the war, Jack joined a partnership with his father, Wall and Son, in Advance, Indiana. Jack and Otis raised thousands of sheep and sold the wool to the U.S. Army up through the Korean War. According to Jack Jr., the development of synthetic clothing in the 1950s led to a reduced demand for wool, leading Jack Sr. to a career in sales of mainframe computers with Sperry-Rand Corporation. In the early

With Jack R. Wall kneeling and taking photos (upper left), Japanese representatives follow their escort officer along the deck of USS *Lansdowne* (DD-486) after the surrender ceremonies. Foreign Minister Mamoru Shigemitsu is leading the delegation, followed by General Yoshijiro Umezu. National Archives Photo SC 329103.

1960s, he moved his family to Washington, D.C., where he became part of a successful sales team selling computers to the Department of Defense (email, February 3, 2021).

Jack R. Wall died on January 13, 1971, at the young age of 49. He is buried in Jamestown Cemetery in Jamestown, Indiana. He had advanced to the rank of lieutenant before he left the Navy.

USS *Dent*

"There's Nothing Like a Dame"

USS *Dent* (DD 116) at anchor, probably in New York Harbor, on December 27, 1918. NH 54693 Courtesy of the Naval History & Heritage Command.

The Ship

USS *Dent* (DD 116/APD 9) was commissioned on September 9, 1918, making her one of the older fighting ladies in World War II. She saw very limited action in World War I. Between September 19 and November 8, she escorted a convoy to Ireland. The Armistice was signed three days later, on November 11. She moved to Guantanamo

Bay for training exercises and in May 1919 she sailed to Newfoundland to support the first aerial crossing of the Atlantic, by a Navy seaplane. In June, she escorted the yacht *Imperator* as it carried the president of Brazil from New York to Newport.

Dent joined the Pacific Fleet in August 1919, and for the next decade and a half she was in and out of the Reserve Fleet. In December 1934, she entered the Rotating Reserve and tested ordnance. She was again commissioned in June 1935, serving on the West Coast and in Hawaii.

When the Japanese attacked Pearl Harbor, *Dent* joined a screen for the aircraft carrier USS *Saratoga*'s (CV 3) high-speed run to Hawaii. Later that month, she was assigned to the Sound School at San Diego, helping to develop sonar techniques. She was sent to Alaska in April 1942 and participated in the Aleutian Campaign until January 1943, when she returned to Seattle for repairs and was converted to a high-speed transport and reclassified as APD 9. Beginning in April, she participated in the Solomon Islands and Bougainville campaigns.

According to the ship's war diary for December 22, she ran aground 3.5 miles off Cape Sudest, New Guinea, during maneuvers. Both of her props were damaged, her keel buckled, and diesel oil leaked into bilges from a ruptured tank (USS *Dent*, 1943). With the damage too extensive for emergency repairs, *Dent* was ordered to Milne Bay at best speed (just seven knots, crawling for a destroyer). She arrived Christmas Day to be checked by the destroyer tender USS *Dobbin* (AD 3). Divers trimmed her propeller blades to decrease vibration. During test runs, she worked out a creative way to maintain a speed of 12 knots, by running the starboard engine at 14 knots, the port engine at 11 knots. According to the diary for December 27, "Backing both engines as much as one third sets up a vibration which in a short time would cause severe structural strains" (USS *Dent*, 1943). The next day, she left for Brisbane, Australia, for repairs. She remained there through January.

After repairs, she transported Marines for landings on Emirau and Aitape, then supported the Mariana and Palau Islands campaigns, taking part in training an underwater demolition team and escorting the Navy ammunition ship USS *Mazama* (AE-9) to Saipan for emergency re-supply of ships bombarding the island. She continued patrol and escort duties in the Mariana and Marshall Islands until returning to San Diego for overhaul in August. She remained with the Amphibious Training Force there until the end of the war. In October 1945, the old girl sailed for Philadelphia, where she was decommissioned in December. She was sold for scrap in June 1946.

Dent received five battle stars for her service in World War II.

Poem One

The deck log for January 1, 1944, was entered by Ensign J.D. Boatman, Jr., USNR. The poem is written in prose paragraphs, though it includes regular rhyme throughout. If it were broken into separate lines, it would be 54 lines long, a bit longer than most of the New Year's deck logs. The rhymes have been marked with slash marks to facilitate reading the deck log as poetry.

Parts of the poem read like notes for the popular songs from the musical *South Pacific,* especially "There Is Nothing Like a Dame." The parallel is not as far-fetched as it might seem, since Rodgers and Hammerstein based their 1949 musical on James Michener's book of stories *Tales of the South Pacific*, published in 1947. Michener, a Navy lieutenant at the time, had been assigned by the Navy in 1944 to write a history of the Navy in the Pacific. He was allowed to travel widely, interviewing many soldiers and sailors. According to Charles Edel, senior fellow at the United States Studies Centre at the University of Sydney, "he attempted to 'report the South Pacific as it actually was,' noting that 'nothing in the manuscript is entirely fictitious.' … For Michener, the Pacific War was a combination of boredom, beauty, 'timeless, repetitive waiting' and spasmodic violence and rapid movement" (Edel, 2020). The stories, like Boatman's poem, reveal the boredom and show the interaction between Navy men, nurses and islanders. Michener won a Pulitzer Prize for the book in 1948.

Boatman writes the poem while *Dent* is moored at West Molle Island off the east coast of Australia on the Great Barrier Reef in Whitsunday Passage in the Coral Sea. The ship is on its way to Brisbane for major repairs after running aground. Since their top speed was 12 knots due to their damaged propellers, they are only a little over halfway to Brisbane on New Year's Day. The ship is darkened. She is alongside the Australian minesweeper and anti-submarine ship HMAS *Bowen* (J285/M285), and Boatman can't resist throwing a little British vulgarity into the middle of the designation: "H. M. bloody A.S. Bowen." The ship is moored to the port side, but Boatman uses the archaic nautical term "larboard" for "port."

Early in the first stanza, he has fun with the rhyming of "bottom" with "gottem" when he gives the anchor bearings. He uses an uncommon descriptor for the left-hand tangent, calling it a "sinister tangent." Contemporary usage of the word "sinister" means some form of evil, but it comes from a Latin word simply meaning "on the left side." The echoes of the musical *South Pacific* become clear when Boatman says that earlier, at dusk, they had decided to take one more sighting for safety's sake, but what they were sighting was a bevy of beautiful ladies. He says the ship "bore but five five degrees / from those lissome, brown, and dimpled knees." Then they all checked a second time to see what the blonde was wearing "above the knees." The first stanza ends with the third repeater signal flag raised to indicate that the skipper is not on board. He has, in fact, gone "ashore to meet her."

In the second stanza, hours later during the midwatch, at 20 minutes after midnight (0020), the coxswain, who would be the crewman in charge of open boats coming and going from the ship, calls lustily to *Dent* before tying up and boarding. The Senior Officer Present Afloat comes aboard, followed by the "liberty lads" from the Higgins boat. Higgins Industries in New Orleans made various surface craft for moving personnel, the best known being the LCVP (Landing Craft, Vehicle,

Personnel) used by the Allies in all the beach landings. But here the Higgins boat is simply the small craft used to transport personnel to and from the ship.

In the opening lines of stanza three, Boatman describes himself, the Officer of the Deck, as "weary and worn." He checks on the engineer to see why the ship's whistle did not sound at midnight to summon the new year. There follows a humorous play on words when he describes himself as returning to the bridge, to the "modified condition" of readiness for the ship, to wait for the Executive Officer to return from shore. He expects that the Exec will also be in a "modified condition" from partying. The closing lines of stanza three bemoan the fact that those who had to remain on duty on the ship had no chance for revelry nor alcohol. How, he asks, can they celebrate "auld lang syne" if "in the proudest fleet upon the sea there is neither whiskey, beer, nor wine?"

Stanza four laments that, though the crew on board has nothing to drink, a drinking contest took place on the beach of the island: "Daydream Island," a name that first appeared in the 1930s when it was a popular resort. The alcohol for the drinking contest had come from the lockers of the HMAS *Bowen*, the Australian ship that was accompanying *Dent* to Brisbane and tied up alongside. Boatman takes another little dig at the Aussies when he calls them "the Wavy Navy." The British and Australian navies differentiated reserve officers from regular Navy officers by using wavy stripes on the reserve officer uniforms. The inherent prejudice toward reserve officers from the regular Navy, which was entrenched in the community of Annapolis grads in the U.S. Navy, bred the derogatory term "Wavy Navy" to describe reservists. Boatman applies the dig to British-Australian sailors but not the Americans. The war had done a lot to change attitudes toward reservists in the U.S. Navy. He judiciously asserts that the contest between the Aussies and the Americans "ended tie score / with both brave allies near the floor."

The fifth stanza offers a melancholy picture of the last of the "liberty lads" paying their respects to the "Christian maidens" and their chaperone, Mrs. Moody, before boarding the Higgins boat to return to the ship. And the short final stanza asserts that this motley crew, including the Executive Officer, "groped and crawled" onto the deck, clearly as he expected in a modified condition. The poem closes with the Exec claiming that he may have to let out some chain—"veer some chain"—if he's going to make it through the night.

Here is the poem:

> Anchored here in this quiet bay, / off the beach of the West Molle, / We with few lights showin,' / lie with H.M. bloody A.S. Bowen. / We swing about in our little nook, / with seven and five to the larboard hook. / Full thirteen fathom lies the bottom. / Here's the anchor bearings as we gottem: / Sinister tangent of North Molle is double zero three, all true, / and at zero thirty one point five, we're looking to / —a cut cut on the left of West Molle, as to the right / of the selfsame island, reads the angle zero double eight. / In gathering dusk we thought for safety's sake, / one more sight we'd better take. / We found we each checked again upon the bearing, / —largely to note what the blonde, above the knees, was wearing. / Shortly up the halyard rose the third repeater / as our skipper went ashore to meet her. /
>
> O'er our heads hours now have passed aplenty / and just as the chronometer reads double zero twenty / the calm is shattered as the lusty lunged coxswain

gives vent, / to the call, grandest and simplest, that of *Dent.* / Saluting and saluted, he, Senior Officer Present Afloat, / is followed by the liberty lads, also in the Higgins boat. /

Weary and drawn, the officer-of-the-deck / upon the engineering makes a check / to find out why the whistle would not roar / as forty-three gave way to forty-four. / (Reason was that boiler four did not count the New Year / as part of the ship's auxiliary gear.) / Then to the modified condition watch he turned to see / and await the Exec., who also would in modified condition be. / Long silent hours passed upon the ship, / for of New Year's revelry there was not a drip. / How take the cup of kindness for auld lang syne / when in the proudest fleet upon the sea there is neither whiskey, beer, nor wine? /

But on the shores of West Molle, / known as Day-Dream, the simple happy natives say, / good cheer in bottles was overflowin' / from out the wardroom lockers of the BOWEN. / In toasting this and drinking that the Wavy Navy with British verve / contended with the pick of the U.S.N. Reserve. / And 'tis but fair to say it ended tie score / with both brave allies near the floor. /

Soon mustered the wearers of the braid to pay their social doody / to the Christian maidens and their chaperone, Mrs. Moody. / Down to the beach and into the boat with its sober crew / marched the gallant remainder, the Last of the Few. /

Back to the ship, up the ladder, and onto the deck, / groped and crawled the Chief, Pills, codes, and the Exec, / —the last named averring that he'd veer some chain / if he in his berth was to bear the night's strain.

J.D. Boatman, Jr.
Ensign, U.S. Naval Reserve

The Poet

James Dulaney Boatman, Jr., was born on August 4, 1916, in Dallas, Texas, to James Dulaney Boatman, Sr., and Kathryn Myrtle Poage. He attended Paris High School and graduated from Paris Junior College as salutatorian (*Paris News*, 1938), then earned his bachelor's degree in business administration at Southern Methodist University. He also earned a law degree from SMU in 1951, graduating second in his class.

Boatman attended midshipmen's school in New York City prior to getting his commission as an ensign in 1942. He spent his early time in the Navy on *Dent* and eventually held positions of first lieutenant and Executive Officer. He left the Naval Reserves at the rank of lieutenant in 1953. He served on *Dent* for a time under T.W. Davison, the former captain of the USS *Finch* who was spirited away from the Philippines by a submarine in early 1942 (see *Finch* chapter for details).

According to a 1966 article in the *Fort Worth Star Telegram*, Boatman worked as an office boy in 1938 for the Atlantic Richfield oil company. He filled the role of senior planning coordinator in 1963 and retired in 1981 as manager of the budget group at the same company.

Boatman died on December 6, 2004, and is buried at Sparkman Hillcrest Memorial Park in Dallas, Texas (James Delaney Boatman Jr.).

Poem Two

The deck log for January 1, 1945, was penned by Ensign J.C. Eschen, USNR. It is a short poem, 12 lines of rhymed couplets. *Dent* had returned to San Diego for overhaul after her stint in the South Pacific campaigns.

As do many other deck log poems, Eschen's mentions the Fleet and District Craft. The *Hoptree* (AN-62), a net-laying ship for harbor defenses, lies to starboard. A personnel transport ship (AP) is positioned "abaft," farther aft, toward the stern. *Dent* lies with her port side to the south side of Pier Two.

Eschen's typical American Navy humor shows up in line six, which originally said that the duty section was "duly" celebrating the holiday. But Eschen marked through "duly" and replaced it with "dryly," a nod to the persistent complaint among American sailors about the lack of alcohol for those on duty. The ship is getting water from the dock, but steam and electricity are provided by boiler number one. Eschen says the Senior Officer Present Afloat (SOPA) is the Commander of the Fleet Air Forces for the West Coast.

Eschen closes the poem with a "glad New Years toast," hailing all those "good fellows who labor and strive / For peace and sweet victory" in the coming year. There will be eight months of bloody jungle fighting from island to island before the surrender of Japan on September 2.

Here's the poem:

> We're at Repair Base, San Diego by name,
> The California locale of great Navy fame,
> All 'round us our fleet and small district craft,
> To starboard there's HOPTREE, an AP abaft.
> To south side pier two, portside to's how we lay,
> Duty section dryly celebrating this cold New Year's Day.
> From the dock we get water, the fire main to sluice
> And from number one boiler our steam and our juice.
> The SOPA we log, ComFairWestCoast [ComFair: Commander Fleet
> Air Forces]
> To close now we give this glad New Years Toast,
> "Hail to those good fellows who labor and strive
> For peace and sweet victory in this year forty-five."
> J.C. Eschen,
> Ensign, U.S.N.R.

The Poet

James C. Eschen was born in Alameda, California, on August 23, 1922, to James N. Eschen and Mae Benedict Silva. His father was a one-time city councilman and mayor of Alameda in the 1930s. His grandfather, Captain James (Jens) Eschen, came to the U.S. from Denmark and was involved in establishing a maritime-based company along with several other prominent families. Initially named Eschen & Minor (Hull, 2007), the company eventually became the California Stevedore & Ballast

Company and operated under that name until the early 1990s (Metro Ports). Captain Eschen personified the salty seafaring skippers of the 19th century in an incident recorded in the March 20, 1901, *San Francisco Examiner.* The crew of the ship *W.H. Macy* found a thief on board and attempted to capture him. The thief used a gang-plank to go from the ship to the dock. Unfortunately for the thief, Captain Eschen was sitting in his buggy nearby and walloped the thief over the head with the handle of his whip. The fugitive continued his escape, but not without continued action by Eschen. According to the newspaper:

> Turning his horse around, the Captain whipped up and was soon upon the man beating him over the head with one stroke and whipping up his steed with the next. The race continued for a few blocks and then the fellow escaped into the lumber yards near the Mall Dock. Captain Eschen had to buy a new whip [*San Francisco Examiner*, 1901].

The Eschen family were well-known within the Bay Area yachting community and had strong ties to the Encinal Yacht Club in Alameda (*Soundings*, 2019).

James C. earned a reputation as an athlete in the Alameda area. He attended the local schools and then enrolled at University of California. When World War II intervened, he entered the Navy in April 1942. During the war, he served on *Dent,* and after hostilities ceased, he commanded USS *Kirwin* (APD 90) for a short time. He eventually finished his time in the Naval Reserve at the rank of lieutenant.

Eschen spent most of his life employed by the company his grandfather founded, eventually becoming its president. After retirement, he remained active in local civic groups and clubs such as the Bohemian Club in San Francisco (James C. Eschen). He died on March 10, 2006.

USS *Bush*

A Brief and Tragic Glory

OFFICIAL PHOTOGRAPH

NAVY YARD MARE ISLAND, CALIF

USS *Bush* (DD 529) off the Mare Island Navy Yard, California, on June 11, 1944. Her camouflage is Measure 32, Design 1d. NH 98928 Courtesy of the Naval History & Heritage Command.

The Ship

USS *Bush* (DD 529) was a Fletcher-class destroyer commissioned on May 10, 1943. After initial training exercises, she began patrols in Alaskan waters and shortly thereafter headed to destinations westward in the Pacific for escort and screening duty. *Bush* maintained a busy schedule until April 6, 1945, when she was hit by three kamikazes in the first wave of ten massive kamikaze attacks against U.S. ships off the coast of Okinawa and sunk. Parts of the Action Report for this event are both gripping and heart-breaking.

At 1515 hours, the first kamikaze hit *Bush*. The plane struck at deck level on the starboard side, detonating an immense explosion in the forward engine room, blasting a six-foot section of blower, weighing 3500 pounds, through the deck and high enough to knock off an antenna and crash onto a wing of the bridge. All the crew in the engine room were killed. Four men escaped from the forward fireroom with severe burns, and eight escaped the after fireroom. While the crew fought the fire and treated the wounded, the captain ordered all crew to go over the side if another kamikaze appeared or if the ship was strafed. Knotted lines were put over the side to facilitate coming back aboard if this happened.

At 1730, another plane crashed into the port side of the main deck, almost cutting the ship in two and igniting another large fire. The bottom and the keel were all that held the ship together. The crew scrambled back onto the ship and began to fight the fire. But 15 minutes later, a third kamikaze dealt the final blow to *Bush*, striking just above the main deck and igniting a third inferno, made worse by the proximity of ammunition.

> Casualties being treated in the wardroom were killed or burned to death. The water stream from the forward handy-billy was shifted from amidships to this fire but the area became untenable as 40mm ammunition and remaining 5" ammunition started to explode [USS *Bush*, 1945].

As the *Bush* practically folded in half, the command was given to abandon her. The captain left the ship last from the aft section. What came next is chronicled in the ship's after-action report. Though the officers and men helped each other and worked to keep morale up, a few men became hysterical and violent.

> Although they were wearing life jackets and in all cases appeared to be physically unhurt they would give up, slip out of their life jackets and go down or swim out into the darkness to meet the same fate. It is hard to believe that such circumstance would arise in a group that had spent any time on or near the water but such was the case. These unfortunates must have believed that rescue ships would never come. Thirty-three men were lost in this period.

As the rescue ships approached, men became excited and swam toward the ships, some losing strength and drowning. Others, when they reached the ships, "were rolled against the hull, knocked out by exhaust, or caught in the screws and lost their lives. About ten were believed lost in this manner."

The ships were blacked out and operated in complete darkness to avoid becoming targets of enemy planes. Twelve men died after being hauled aboard (USS *Bush*, 1945). In all, *Bush* lost seven officers and 80 men killed or missing in action. Before suffering this fate, *Bush* earned seven battle stars for her service.

The crew of USS *Bush* left us two Midwatch poems. They were written on the two New Year's Days the ship was in service. Ironically, both poets transferred off *Bush* just two months before the ship sank with so great a loss of life.

Poem One

The first deck log below was entered January 1, 1944, by Lt. P.A. Lilly, Jr. It consists of 30 lines of rhyming couplets with no stanza breaks. The fact that Lilly packs the poem with all the technical information required in a deck log results in some unevenness in many of the lines. But then, it can be difficult to create rhythm when you are listing ships' identification numbers, as in line ten below.

In addition to all the technical information, the poem is steeped in references to the ongoing action in which the ship is engaged. They are steaming at nine knots "on a mission of war" as part of anti-submarine screen 54, with plenty of steam from their boilers and with guns loaded to "give the Nips hell." All torpedo mounts are stocked, and the crew manning them are ready to "make each fish count." The *Bush* is part of an anti-submarine screen escorting a convoy that is hauling artillery to Port Gloucester on the island of New Britain in the territory of New Guinea. The Battle of Port Gloucester had begun on December 26, and by the end of December the Marines had captured and secured the airports. Lt. Lilly lists five LSTs in the convoy and names three other Fletcher-class destroyers in the screen: USS *Bache* (DD 470), USS *Mullany* (DD 528) and USS *Ammen* (DD 527). Lilly proudly claims they are working for Douglas MacArthur, commander of the Southwest Pacific Force, whom he refers to familiarly as "Doug, ComSouwespac."

The men are under orders from Commander Task Force 76 at battle stations in "condition one easy" and not getting much sleep. Twenty minutes into Lilly's watch, at 0020, all hands are called to General Quarters when a possible enemy contact is made. Twenty-nine minutes later, at 0049, they lose the target and change course for their final approach to the island. The poem closes as the coast of New Britain comes into view, and the poet's final thoughts are: "Bring on the Japs, it's getting mighty late / Our thoughts they be—sail under the gate." The phrase "sail under the gate" may be a personal reference for Lilly. Since he is from Sutter, California, not far from San Francisco, he is likely thinking of the Golden Gate Bridge, which had opened four years earlier. To "sail under the gate" is a phrase used since that time to describe the experience of sailing under the Golden Gate. Lilly is saying, in other words, let's get this thing over with and go home.

Here is the poem:

Steaming as before on true course 054
Checking 061 on a mission of war
Nine knots (88 rpm) is the speed of advance
Patrol thirty degrees, as though in a trance
Got plenty of steam, four boilers in parallel.
Enough stuff at the guns to give the Nips hell
Torpedoes are ready, five at each mount
Personnel stationed to make each fish count
It is degrading business, have amphibs in tow.
LST's 459, 457, 465, 206, 26, all in a row
Anti-submarine screen 54 natural order of ships

BUSH (CDD48), BACHE, MULLANY, AMMEN as in any other trips
Working for Doug, ComSouwespac [Commander Southwest Pacific]
Condition one easy, no time in the sack
Taking artillery to Cape Gloucester-New Britain, not Maine
ComTaskFor [Commander Task Force] 76 orders to blame
—Dated 29 December of year 43
Our operation order 4 dash 43
0020 was disturbed to find,
the radar operator on the line
Range 4.5 miles bearing 316 true [sighting of enemy ship]
The boatswain mate call, all hands to GQ
Target was lost at double 0 four nine
Back to one easy, everything fine
At midnight plus 56 minutes
New course 085(T) our hearts not in it
Checking 091 psc [per standard compass]
New Britain's coast we're beginning to see
Bring on some Japs, it's getting mighty late
Our thoughts they be—sail under the gate.

P.A. Lilly, Jr.,
Lieutenant, USN

The Poet

Midshipman Percy Anthony Lilly, Jr., from the 1941 Naval Academy Yearbook *Annapolis Lucky Bag*.

Percy Anthony Lilly, Jr., was born in Sutter, California, on December 28, 1917. His father and mother were both born in Kentucky and were farmers, according to Percy, Jr.'s, birth certificate. Sometime between Percy, Jr.'s, birth and 1920, the family moved back to Kentucky, and Percy, Sr., became the co-proprietor of the Henrietta Hotel in Princeton.

Lilly attended the Kavanaugh School, a Louisville prep school that was often called "Little Annapolis" because it graduated 150 future Navy officers between 1914 and 1945. Lilly received an appointment to Annapolis in 1937 and graduated in the Class of 1941.

While aboard *Bush*, Lilly was wounded in the shoulder by the tail gunner of a Japanese plane that strafed the ship after dropping a torpedo. In addition to serving on USS *Bush*, he also served on USS *Stack* (DD 406) and USS *Steinaker* (DD 863/DDR 863). Over the course of his naval career, Lilly rose through the ranks, eventually being promoted to captain. Through the 1940s into the 1960s, he commanded five different ships: USS *Newport* (PF 27), USS *Uhlmann* (DD 687), USS *Lindenwald* (LSD 6), USS *Dufilho* (DE 423) and USS *Gridley* (DLG/CG 21). He also served as Executive Officer on the cruiser USS *Boston* (CAG 1/CA 69). Additionally, he commanded Destroyer Squadron 25 and held several high-level Navy administration positions.

By all accounts, Lilly was an affable, competent officer. While aboard the USS *Bush*, he participated in what some called the Great Mustache Contest, during which the officers competed to see who could grow the best mustache (USS *Bush*, no date). While commanding the USS *Lindenwald* in 1955, Lilly and his crew had an interesting encounter with a polar bear. According to a *Baltimore Sun* newspaper article, during a beach unloading operation in the Arctic Fox Basin, the crew adopted a polar bear, which wandered around the camp and was fed by the sailors. When the bear swam out to the ship, anchored a mile offshore, Lilly led two landing craft in a bear-herding operation that ended two hours later with the polar bear, exhausted, climbing onto an ice floe and the crew returning to the ship (*The Baltimore Sun*, 1955).

Lilly also demonstrated a sharp sense of humor. A satirical letter about the height of urinals on ships, attributed to Lilly and often labeled on the Internet as "This correspondence was recently unearthed at Annapolis" and titled "Fire When Ready, Gridley—Navy and Urinals," outlines a request for changing urinal height on ships along with accompanying reasons. Item #3 states:

> A survey of ship's company has revealed that the tallest man in the crew is 6'6" and the shortest is 5'4". In a dry run, these two men have been posed at the urinals, at their present height of 23", and it has been determined that the tallest man has 15 inches clearance and the shortest 4 inches. Although GRIDLEY completely concurs in the desirability of fully documenting its recommendations it is considered that photographs may be, in this instance, omitted due to the delicacy of the subject. At any rate, it may be seen from the above figures that even the shortest man in the crew would still have one inch clearance if the urinals were mounted 3 inches higher. Let there be no thought that there is anything wrong with GRIDLEY's marksmanship. We can hit them, but it must be realized that the longer the drop in flow, the higher the head and consequently the greater the splash. Splash is the nemesis of sanitation.

The letter, which carries his name, has been confirmed as authentic by a member of Lilly's family and by a former *Gridley* crew member, David Brennan, who was, in fact, the one who typed the letter for Lilly (personal communication, October 29, 2020).

The following is taken from the 1958 USS *Boston* Cruise Book about Cmdr. Lilly (Executive Officer): "With an eye for every detail, with a word here, and a steely look there, a smile and a prod, he has contributed immeasurably by interpreting and executing the policies and guidelines laid down by the Commanding Officer" (USS *Boston*, 1958).

He earned many awards during his career, including, among others, the Legion of Merit with one Gold Star, Bronze Star Medal with "V" Device, Purple Heart and several Presidential Citations. After retiring from the Navy in 1970, Lilly became the Harbor Master of Maui County, Hawaii, where he was responsible for harbors on Maui, Molokai and Lanai. He retired from that position in 1980. He died on June 5, 2012, at the age of 94.

Poem Two

A second January 1 deck log appeared one year after Lilly's. Written by Lt. j.g. Newton Perry Foss, the original copy of the deck log is erroneously labeled as January 1, 1944, instead of 1945. Foss transferred off *Bush* 30 days after posting this entry in the deck log and just two months before the ship was sunk.

This poem consists of 54 continuous lines with no stanza breaks. With only a couple of exceptions, it consists of rhymed couplets. The poem opens with a humorous jab at the frequent very short deck logs that appeared on Navy ships, which said simply, "Steaming as before" or "Moored as before." Foss boldly claims his deck log must be the full deal. Writing very late in the war (January 1945), Foss says that they are lucky to be alive. These lines carry a sad irony in that *Bush* will be sunk three months later with heavy loss of life.

Bush is coming from "old Mindoro," in the Philippines, "Where the 'Kamikazis' are plenty thorough." He reveals that the ship is cruising slowly at eight and a half knots leading the submarine screen for the convoy under the command of R.E. Westholm, USN. There are eight "cans" (destroyers) in the screen and 23 LSTs (tank-landing ships), a merchantman and an army ship in the convoy.

In line 21, Foss refers to "31-Knot Burke." Captain Arleigh Burke, commander of Destroyer Squadron 23 (DESRON 23), was given the nickname by Admiral Halsey. Halsey ordered DESRON 23 to intercept a Japanese group "with all due speed." Burke replied to Halsey that the squadron could only go as fast as its slowest destroyer, which was 31 knots (Zimmerman, D., 2013). But Foss declares his ship's loyalty to Captain J.B. McLean, Commander of Destroyer Division 48, which *Bush* is part of. Foss gives McLean his own nickname: "[W]e labor with might and main / For 'Four and a knot Captain McLean.'"

The crew is at condition "one easy," battle stations manned in case of attack. The ship has been in heated action. Line 29 says that the crew had been called to 45 General Quarters in five days. They receive the message "Flash Red, Control Green," requiring them to begin making smoke for cover. Foss adds, "Thirty-nine planes have been the splash" while the guns on *Bush* roared and flashed. When more "bogeys" (enemy planes) are spotted, *Bush* receives the message that there is no CAP (Combat Air Patrol) to help them. Foss says, "The nips from the sun start into their dive," evoking two images: the Japanese symbol of the rising sun on their aircraft and the fact that they attacked from the direction of the sun, strategically making them a tougher target for anti-aircraft fire.

Lines 39 to 46 offer an unusual list of the chain of command from Rear Admiral Struble, who was Commander of Amphibious Group Nine, Seventh Amphibious Force, up to General Douglas MacArthur: "And supreme in command, most resplendent by far / Is 'Dug out the Doug,' the mighty five-star." As opposed to Lt. Lilly's seemingly proud claim in the first *Bush* poem to be working for MacArthur, Lt. Foss uses the derogatory nickname "Dug-out Doug," which MacArthur's own troops gave him in early 1942 before he was ordered off Corregidor by Roosevelt. Though MacArthur was extremely popular with the American media, he was much less popular among his besieged troops in the Philippines. The moniker was "a reference to his practice of remaining holed up in a bunker on Corregidor and never showing himself among them" (Toll, 2012, p. 243). The nickname also casts a perhaps sarcastic shadow over the adjective "mighty."

The final four lines of the poem claim that great progress has been made in the war effort, but that much more remains to be done. In a kind of prophetic closing, the poet says, "The New Year's goal for which we strive / Is Tokyo in nineteen hundred forty five." Eight months later, on September 2, 1945, American ships would indeed be in Tokyo Harbor accepting the surrender of the Japanese Imperial Command. But *Bush* would not be there. Four months before the surrender, she would be a casualty of war, along with seven officers and 80 crew members.

Here is the poem:

"Steaming as before"—that we can't say.
A full log we must write on New Years day.
One January, nineteen hundred forty-five
And, frankly, we're lucky to be alive.
We're steaming back from old Mindoro
Where the "Kamikazis" are plenty thorough.
The mighty BUSH—the fighting five two nine
Using boilers two and three on the line.
That furnished all the power we need
Eight and a half knots—not very much speed.
For we're not alone, we're heading the screen
For that convoy known as Uncle plus fifteen.
Course zero eight five, checking one zero two
The latter magnetic, the former is true.
Commander R.E. WESTHOLM, USN
Skippers us there—and back again.
Eight cans form the screen
For old Uncle plus fifteen.
Twenty three LST's, a merchantman too
And one Army ship completes our screen
Now there are those who sing of "31 knot Burke"
But it is not for him that we do our work.
At one easy we labor with might and main

For "Four and a knot Captain McLean."
ComDesDiv [Commander Destroyer Div] forty eight (sometimes ninety, too)
And also commander of this TU [Task Unit].
Seventy eight dot three dot one five
Has been busy as bees in a hive
Forty five GQ's [General Quarters] in the past five days
Rough on sleep but with the nips it pays.
We can hear him now—"Flash Red, Control Green"
This message comes from Demerit Fifteen.
Thirty-nine planes have been the splash
While the five inch roar and the forty's flash.
The jeep tells us that bogeys are near
The nips from the sun start into their dive
A message comes on the air from Austere
Sorry no CAP [Combat Air Patrol], savannah is five.
Rear Admiral Struble is seventy eight point three
For him we sailed the Sulu Sea.
He got his orders to operate
From Vice Admiral Barbey, CTF [Commander Task Force] 78.
And over him is Com Seventh Fleet
Vice Admiral Kincaid, mighty hard to beat
And supreme in command, most resplendent by far
Is "Dug out the Doug," the mighty five star.
Now we head for San Pedro Bay
And the bogeys over Tacloban way.
Through patrol dog—of Bush reknown
Where we shot those two planes down.
We've come pretty far in forty four
But we've got to go a whole lot more
The new years goal for which we strive
Is Tokyo in nineteen hundred forty five.

N.P. Foss,
Lt.(j.g.), USN

The Second Poet

Newton Perry Foss was born on August 1, 1921, in Portsmouth, New Hampshire. He graduated from the well-known and highly respected Admiral Farragut Prep School in 1940 and entered the Naval Academy. While listed as a member of the Annapolis Class of 1944, he actually graduated from an accelerated program on June 9, 1943. His Academy yearbook entry indicated that he had talent in gymnastics. After undergoing aircraft and ship recognition training at the Naval Air Operational and Training Command School in Jacksonville, Florida, his first duty assignment was on USS *Bush*. He arrived on *Bush* on September 23, 1943, and his time on the ship overlapped with Percy Anthony Lilly, the first poet highlighted above.

On February 25, 1945, Foss married Ada Louise Foster in New Hampshire, and in June 1945 he reported to the Naval Aviation Station (NAS) at Ottumwa, Iowa, to begin flight training. He went on to command Attack Squadron VA-106

Midshipman Newton Perry Foss from the 1944 Naval Academy Yearbook *Annapolis Lucky Bag*.

(the Gladiators) from April 1958 to December 1959 aboard USS *Essex* (CVA 9).

Foss served as Executive Officer on USS *Independence* (CV 62) from August 3, 1963, to December 21, 1964. He commanded two ships during his career. From June 25, 1966, to May 19, 1967, he captained USS *Chara* (AKA 58, later AE 31 upon recommissioning in 1966) that saw service in Vietnam. He took over as captain of USS *Hancock* (CV 19, later CVA-19), an Essex-class aircraft carrier, from February 1969 to June 1970.

Capt. Foss experienced a "first" in 1970 as he brought the *Hancock* back to Alameda, California, after a deployment in the Pacific. According to an article in the *Edwardsville Intelligencer,* U.S. Customs allowed two women inspectors (along with three men) to be helicoptered out to *Hancock* to begin the property declaration process, so that the sailors could leave the ship as soon as it docked. In the past, only men had been given that duty. Capt. Foss said that their visit should be pleasant and that they would be greeted in "true Navy fashion" (*Edwardsville Intelligencer*, 1970). According to *The Argus* (Freemont, California), the crew had a lot to declare. Apparently, Honda motorcycles were very popular in 1970! According to Customs Inspector Doris Mathers, "There were 336 brand new Honda motorcycles onboard—the boys kind of went crazy over Hondas" (Holzmeister and Raimy, 1970).

Foss also held a variety of commands after his service on *Hancock*, including Commander United States Pacific Fleet's Training Command and Chief of Staff for the Pacific Fleet Naval Air Force. He advanced up the ranks, eventually reaching Rear Admiral by July 1972.

Foss' daughter Janice followed in his footsteps by earning a commission as ensign in the Navy on December 22, 1972. Admiral Foss was there to congratulate her after her commissioning (*Newport Mercury*, 1973).

Foss' awards and decorations included the Navy and Marine Corps Commendation Medal (January 14, 1969) and two Legion of Merit Awards (May 20, 1970, and June 28, 1972) along with a host of other World War II– and Vietnam-era medals.

Foss retired from the Navy in 1975 and died on August 20, 1979, in San Diego, California.

USS *Ringgold*

A New Slant on Bunghole

USS *Ringgold* (DD 500) coming alongside USS *Chenango* to fuel on June 16, 1944, while operating as Screen Command for TG53.2. National Archives photo 80-G3-21655.

The Ship

USS *Ringgold* (DD 500), a Fletcher-class destroyer, was commissioned on December 30, 1942. She took her shakedown cruise to Guantanamo Bay and then performed various training maneuvers until July, when she sailed for the Pacific and joined Task Force 50 at Pearl Harbor. After further training, she joined a fast carrier group and participated in strikes against Tarawa and Makin in the Gilbert Islands in mid–September 1943.

After supporting strikes by the fast carrier task force on Wake Island in October, *Ringgold* returned to Tarawa in November, where during a scouting mission she mistakenly fired on the submarine USS *Nautilus*. The ship's first salvo struck the sub's conning tower but did not explode, allowing *Nautilus* to escape. According to the *Ringgold*'s war diary, she also fired two torpedoes at the sub, which did not hit their target but exploded in the vicinity. *Ringgold* had no idea they had fired on an American submarine (USS *Ringgold*, 1943).

On November 20, while performing a close action attack in Betio Lagoon under heavy fire from shore batteries, *Ringgold* took two hits, both of which were duds. One of the shells knocked out the port engine. The conflict with shore batteries was at such close range that the crew could see the batteries they were combatting. According to Robert Dorr, the ship could not depress its guns any lower. They had no charts for the lagoon, and the skipper allowed a New Zealand Royal Navy reserve officer, who claimed to know the lagoon, to navigate the ship. He ran her aground in the lagoon broadside to the beach, and she was forced to spend the next three days battling shore batteries just 700 yards away. Crew members claimed she fired 15,000 rounds in three days, and the guns glowed red hot. The second shell that pierced *Ringgold*, a strike to the hull just below the waterline, punched a hole that threatened serious flooding and produced a memorable act of ingenuity by Chief Engineer Lt. Wayne A. Parker. Parker plugged the hole by sitting in it, stopping the flooding water with his buttocks (Dorr, 2014) and perhaps adding a whole new slant to the old English word "bunghole." Parker received the Navy Cross for his actions, which included, according to the citation, clearing the room of personnel and carrying the live shell topside and throwing it overboard.

After repairs in December 1943, *Ringgold* supported the invasions of Kwajalein and Eniwetok in January and February 1944. She participated in a diversionary bombardment in New Ireland in March and supported the assault on New Hollandia in April and May. In June, she operated in the Marianas, serving as a Landing Craft Control Vessel and providing fire support during the invasion of Guam. After supporting the invasion of Morotai Island, she operated in the Philippines in October before returning to Mare Island, California, for overhaul.

In February 1945, *Ringgold* joined Vice Admiral Mitscher's Task Force 58 for the first air attacks striking deep in the heart of the Japanese mainland. According to the War Diary for March 4, during night battle drills, *Ringgold* and USS *Yarnall* (DD 541) collided, shearing off *Ringgold*'s bow (USS *Ringgold*, 1945). According to *Yarnall*'s War Diary, their own bow was bent to the right and elevated. The following day, while *Yarnall* was being towed stern first, her bow broke loose and sank (USS *Yarnall*, 1945). After repairs, *Ringgold* rejoined the fleet and in June supported the fast carrier task force assault on Okinawa. Through the month of July, she again participated in strikes against the Japanese mainland with Admiral Halsey's Third Fleet fast carrier task force, conducting anti-shipping sweeps and bombardment. Following further coastal operations and escort duty, *Ringgold* underwent further repairs at Guam and then proceeded to the East Coast of the U.S. She was decommissioned on March 23, 1946, remaining in the Reserve Fleet until 1959, when she underwent modernization and outfitting before being handed over to the Federal Republic of

Germany. Redesignated as *Zerstörer 2* (D 171), she served until September 1981, when she was transferred to the Greek Navy. She was broken up for scrap in 1993.

Ringgold received ten battle stars for her service in World War II.

The Poem

The following deck log was entered by Lt. A. John Ruggeri on January 1, 1945. The poem consists of 16 lines divided into four quatrains. There is no reference to the war. Ruggeri offers a straightforward, simple description of the current ship condition. *Ringgold* would have just undergone overhaul at Mare Island and would be waiting orders to rejoin the fleet. She is moored in San Francisco Bay beside USS *Shea* (DM 30) at Pier 54. USS *Sigsbee* (DD 502) is moored to her port side. Ruggeri refers to the "gallant *Sigsbee*, Captain Chung Hoon's pride." Born in Honolulu, Commander Gordon Chung-Hoon was the first Asian-American to graduate from the Naval Academy, where he was a star halfback. He commanded *Sigsbee* from May 1944 until October 1945.

On April 14, 1945, four months after Ruggeri mentions Chung-Hoon in the deck log poem, *Sigsbee* suffered extensive damage when hit by a kamikaze. According to John R. Williams, Signalman Second Class, the explosion knocked out the port engine and disabled steering control. The aft third of the ship was taking on water heavily and the aft main deck was soon a foot under water (Williams, John, 2000). Orders came down for Chung-Hoon to scuttle the ship, but he refused, continuing to deliver fire against the Japanese attack and directing damage control until the ship could make it to port under her own power. Chung-Hoon received the Navy Cross and the Silver Star for his actions aboard *Sigsbee*. He later rose to the rank of admiral, becoming the first Asian-American flag officer in the U.S. Navy (Zimmerman, Alec, 2021).

In the third stanza of the poem, Ruggeri offers the common complaint in deck log poems that, while the on-board watch is set, those who are on liberty are celebrating "wet," enjoying the luxury of alcohol denied to those on duty. All is in order on board, but Ruggeri can't resist taking an indirect jab at the sailors celebrating on liberty when he says, "Not all is at peace with the Shore Patrol." Ruggeri closes by wishing everyone a Happy New Year from the *Ringgold*.

Here's the poem:

As the bells pealed in this joyous day
Ringgold was moored starboard side to the SHEA,
Who in turn was moored as before
To the pier numbered fifty-four.

The gallant SIGSBEE, Captain Chung Hoon's pride,
Was securely moored to our port side.
This was in San Francisco Bay,
And all transpired on New Year's Day.

The in-port watch was properly set,
While the liberty section celebrated it "wet."

The steam for auxiliaries came from Boiler One.
Praise the Engineers for a job well done.

In true Holiday Spirit, these sailors extole.
Not all is at peace with the Shore Patrol.
No unexecuted orders—the slate is clear,
So from RINGGOLD to all, A Happy New Year!
A. John Ruggeri,
Lt (j.g.), U S Naval Reserve

The Poet

Adolph John Ruggeri was born on April 1, 1919, to Giovanni (John) Ruggeri and Paolina (Pauline) Berra in Price, Utah. Giovanni, Paolina and their first-born daughter emigrated to the U.S. from Italy a few years prior to Adolph's birth. Giovanni mostly worked as a farmer, but the 1930 Census also listed him as a coal miner.

Adolph attended grammar school and junior high school at Notre Dame School, which was affiliated with the Notre Dame de Lourdes Church in Price, Utah. He graduated from that school with special recognition in leadership in 1934 (*The Sun-Advocate*, 1934). He went on to Carbon High School in Price, Utah, becoming his class president in 1935 and 1937 and performing in dramatic productions. After high school graduation, Ruggeri attended the University of Utah and graduated with a Bachelor of Law degree.

Nineteen forty-two was a year of change for Ruggeri. On June 20, he married Margaret Lorraine Price of Helper, Utah, and was admitted to the Utah Bar *in absentia* in October because he had been inducted into the U.S. Naval Reserve in September. As with many other enlisted Navy men during this time, Ruggeri likely held an enlisted rating and eventually went to one of the Naval Reserve's Midshipmen Schools. On March 25, 1944, he reported aboard *Ringgold* as an ensign and he served onboard until the end of 1945. His promotion to Lt. Junior Grade came sometime prior to his leaving *Ringgold*.

After the war, Ruggeri maintained a successful law practice and eventually served in city and county judge positions. His final judgeship was as the Seventh District Court Judge, from which he retired in 1988. In 1986, the Utah Bar Association named him Circuit Court Judge of the Year (Johnson, 1988).

Ruggeri died on December 7, 2011, and was buried next to his wife of nearly 60 years, who preceded him in death in 2002. Their graves are in Cliffview Cemetery in Price, Utah.

USS *Mason*

The Grand Experiment

A port broadside view of USS *Mason* (DE 529) underway at Boston on May 26, 1944. National Archives photo 80-G-382866.

The Ship

USS *Mason* (DE 529) was an Evarts-class destroyer escort named for Ensign Newton Henry Mason, a Naval aviator killed during the Battle of the Coral Sea. *Mason*, commissioned on March 20, 1944, held a unique position among World War II Navy vessels. Serving as an experiment for racial integration, *Mason* began her service with a crew that was primarily black, commanded by an all-white complement of officers.

Mason was the only ocean-going vessel in the Navy with this distinction. USS *PC 1264* also maintained a black enlisted-men crew, but she was a coastal patrol vessel while *Mason* made numerous Atlantic Ocean crossings guarding convoys and hunting U-boats. This does not minimize the service of *PC-1264* as she shuttled convoys north and south off the coast of the U.S.

Mason was an experiment testing whether African-Americans could hold positions in the Navy other than stewards and mess men. Some accounts referred to *Mason* as "Eleanor's Folly" because of First Lady Eleanor Roosevelt's opposition to segregation. The history of the *Mason* is nicely outlined in two books, Mary Pat Kelly's *Proudly We Served: The Men of the USS* Mason and Butler, Blackford and Dunn's

Captain W.M. Blackford on the commissioning of the *Mason* (center) with some of the crew standing in ranks behind him. National Archives photo NA 80-G-218856.

Onboard the USS Mason*: The World War II Diary of James A. Dunn*. Both books describe the conditions leading up to the launching of this experiment in integration and the life of the officers and crew as they crossed the Atlantic and visited ports in the U.S. and abroad.

William M. Blackford, the great grandson of an abolitionist, captained *Mason* upon her commission. He often said that he wasn't there to make a statement about race, but to run the best ship in the Navy. The enlisted men referred to Blackford as "Big Bill," but not to his face. He was universally loved by the crew, who often said that they would follow him to Hell and back. Apparently, Blackford demonstrated right from the start that he was not going to put up with crewmen who shirked their duties. The forenoon watch from the March 24, 1944, deck log shows the outcome of a Captain's Mast that meted out punishments for several infractions:

> …1000 Commanding Officer held Mast and awarded the following punishments: CUMMINGS, LeRoy, 812 31 10, S1c, V-6 USNR—Offense: Relieving watch 45 minutes late and standing bow sentry watch inside Compartment A-101-ACL—Punishment—eight (8) hours extra duty. JOHNSON, Eugene Webster, 285 31 11, S1c, V-6 USNR—Offense: Failure to obey orders given by a petty officer—Punishment—five (5) days solitary confinement on bread and water. To be served ashore… [USS Mason, 1944].

Confinement on bread and water was a sanctioned and often-used punishment aboard World War II ships. In fact, this punishment was only officially abolished when a reformed Uniform Code of Military Justice went into effect on January 1, 2019.

The officers, all white, were given the choice of whether to serve on *Mason* or not. According to William Farrell (Engineering Officer), the officers decided that they would discuss whether to serve and that the vote would have to be all "yes" if they were to do it. They were a little concerned about William W. Kitts, the writer of the poem highlighted in this post, because he was from Texas and might object to serving with the black crew members. According to Kitts' 2009 oral history, he had no problems with serving in this experiment due to his positive interactions with blacks in his hometown when he was growing up. Though Kitts was clearly open-minded, and his actions speak to the fact that he had no inclination toward overt racism, the shaping of the following statements reflects the inherent bias of the culture in which he grew up. Regarding African Americans in his hometown, he said:

> We had very, very few problems, because they were all closely associated. They all knew what the ground rules were and everybody behaved properly. So, we didn't have anybody on the street corner shouting, that sort of thing. It was all very, very smooth [Kitts, 2009].

Kitts remembered that his father aided many of the families in the black community financially and helped with food during the depth of the Depression.

> So, people were good to each other, and I remember no unpleasantness from my earlier years until I graduated and left town and everything. I don't really recall anything like that.

Kitts found the decision to serve on *Mason* an easy one. After being told by one of the men who recruited him in Washington that he would "be making a contribution above and beyond," Kitts gave them a quick answer, thinking, "Well, gee, that could be something that could be worthwhile." Kitts, by virtue of his past experiences with African-Americans, became the *de facto* mediator for the black crewmen as ordered by the captain. The captain's request is revealing of the general separation of the races throughout the country at the time. As Kitts put it in his oral history:

> I was also aware of the fact that he expected a lot out of me, because he said, "Hey, you know how to talk to these people. I want you to talk to them." So when we had trouble over here on the beach or some place, I got the finger pointed [at me]: "Go fix it" [Kitts, 2009].

One problem frequently faced by the *Mason* crew was the discrimination they experienced while in ports in the U.S. It was still the Jim Crow Era, and throughout the military and American society, African-Americans had to deal with personal and institutional prejudice. According to Alexis Clark, "Regardless of the region, at all the bases there were separate blood banks, hospitals or wards, medical staff, barracks and recreational facilities for Black soldiers. And white soldiers and local white residents routinely slurred and harassed them" (Clark, 2020). Clearly, "Eleanor's Folly" was far from folly to the men of *Mason*. It was deadly serious business, a chance to prove their value as human beings and warriors.

One of the most poignant accounts of the experience of *Mason*'s crew in port came when they arrived in Northern Ireland in July 1944. *Mason*'s crew found the Irish people to be friendly and welcoming. Lorenzo DuFau gave the following account: "Never in my life had we received such greetings from people, perfect strangers. It's hard to find words to describe the Belfast experience, what we felt to be received the way we were by the people" (Kelly, 2015).

DuFau describes an incident in which a woman apologized for the overcast weather conditions, wishing it was a sunny day so that he could see how beautiful the place was. "We had to travel from our own home country, our own home town, over all this water," he says, "to get to a place where people treated us like human beings" (Kelly, 2015).

One of the *Mason* crew's more harrowing experiences involved their escort of Convoy NY.119 in September-October 1944. *Mason* experienced some of the worst weather the North Atlantic could dish out. High wind and seas led to sinking of some convoy vessels and barges that were being towed. By the time the convoy arrived off the coast of England, it was scattered over a wide area. *Mason*'s crew navigated from buoy to buoy to find their way to port. After delivering the first set of convoy vessels, she returned to gather up stragglers to lead them to port. All of this occurred even though *Mason* had developed a huge crack in her deck and the crew had to take a couple of hours during this shuttle service to weld it shut. *Mason* was to have received a Letter of Commendation for this action, but it did not come. It wasn't until 1995 that President Bill Clinton issued the commendation for the heroic role *Mason* played in the escort of NY.119.

The Poem

The deck log below was entered by Lt. j.g. William W. Kitts on January 1, 1945. It is a joy to read. The poem consists of 21 rhymed couplets, and the tone is light-hearted.

There is some question about whether the poem was written by Kitts, by one of the quartermasters, or perhaps by both. A line late in the poem indicates that the quartermaster may have helped write it. Some of the poems entered in deck logs were actually written by other members of the crew or groups of crewmen, not necessarily the Officer of the Deck of record. The *Mason* had several crewmen with the quartermaster rating, so which quartermaster Kitts refers to may never be revealed.

Couplet 17 seems to say that Kitts is *not* the writer of the poem: "The quartermaster on watch [which would have been one of the black crewmen] is a poet of rare wit." Then the following line asserts, "And here I [the OOD, Lt. Kitts] copy, just as he writ." However, the punctuation of that line, which ends with a colon, could indicate that only the final four couplets of the poem were written by the quartermaster. If this were true, then the first 17 couplets may well have been written by Kitts and the last four by the quartermaster. The last four couplets are the only ones in the poem that

Navigation instruction for quartermasters, during training for *Mason*'s crew at Naval Training Station in Norfolk, Virginia. Instructor is Chief Quartermaster L.J. Russell, USNR. Trainees are (left to right): Quartermaster 2nd Class Charles W. Divers, Quartermaster 2nd Class Royal H. Gooden, Quartermaster 3rd Class Lewis F. Blanton and Quartermaster 2nd Class Calvin Bell. National Archives photo NA 80-G-214543.

include a time signature. But the style of the last four couplets is much like the rest of the poem, and so they may or may not have been written by two different people.

At any rate, if one assumes that the quartermaster wrote the entire poem, it is hard not to sense an underlying irony at points. The second couplet claims they are leaving the state of "Virginny" in the "land of plenty." Virginia was a very Southern state, and the Southern United States was not the same "land of plenty" for African-Americans in 1945 as it was for most white Southerners. But the poet keeps the tone light through the use of double rhyme—a common poetic tool for creating light humor: "Virginny" rhyming with "plenty." The irony in the third couplet is perhaps more revealing. The ship is headed for the French port of Oran in Algeria, "Algiers" in the poem. The French were widely known in the early 20th century for a very progressive, accepting attitude toward blacks. During the Harlem Renaissance in the 1920s, Paris became a haven for African-American artists, perhaps the best-known being Josephine Baker, who worked for the French Resistance during World War II. When the poet says, "Of the Frenchmen there we have not fears," there is a sense that the French may be seen not just as allies in the war but as people potentially sympathetic to the African-American crew. Algeria was, after all, in North Africa, a part of the world where the color of people's skin was closer to that of the crew of *Mason* than to that of her officers.

The poet does an impressive job of including much of the mundane information required in a deck log while maintaining the light tone and occasional personal touch. The final verse offers a last little joke of sorts. "When this watch was over, together we cried, / Tho we didn't par Whitman, My! How we tried." The same self-effacing humor seen throughout the poem shows here in his comparison with the great nineteenth-century American poet Walt Whitman. The writer may not be up to par with Whitman, but he gave it his best shot. The use of "we" in the last line raises again the question of authorship. The poet may be using the royal "we" to refer tongue-in-cheek to only himself. Or he may be referring to the "we" of Lt. Kitts and the quartermaster. It could even refer to several of the crewmen participating in the production. It will remain a mystery.

The poet begins by wishing everyone a Happy New Year. The *Mason* is underway for Algeria as part of "Task Force Sixty-Four." The task force flagship is the destroyer USS *Balch* (DD 363). The task force is made up of Destroyer Division Twenty-Six and Escort Division Eighty. The poet remarks specifically that the Coast Guard Frigate *Gulfport*, which was on her first escort mission, was part of the task force. Their course is zero nine five, speed nine and a half knots. Power is supplied by number two engine on starboard and number four on port. The Commander calls for "Disposition Baker…On Plan Two Able." Section One is standing watch.

Here's the poem:

Here in the beginning while it's so near
I wish you all a Happy New Year!

Underway from Norfolk, the state of Virginny,
In the U.S.A., the land of plenty.

We're bound for a place called Oran, Algiers,
Of the Frenchmen there, we have not fears.

The "Boss" of this "gang," Task Force Sixty-Four,
Is riding the BALCH, and he knows the score.

This "Gang" is made up, if you're interested, matey,
Of DesDiv [Destroyer Division] two-six and CortDiv [Escort Division] Eighty.
Of course the Coast Guard must be along,
They sent the GULFPORT to sing their song.

The "Gang" is escorting merships by the score
It's known as convoy UGS Sixty-Four.

Zero plus nine five is base course, that's true,
As onward we sail o'er the ocean so blue.

The speed we are making keeps us lookin' alive,
Given in knots, it is nine point five.

With fifteen knots as standard speed set,
We're making two-thirds, but we're not there yet.

In order to stay on station right,
Three one five turns we're doing tonight.

Two main engines are runnin'—hear 'em Sport?
Number two on the starboard, number four on the port.

In position three is where we stand,
Thus able to screen on the starboard hand.

"In Disposition Baker" our Command cried,
"On plan Two Able I did decide."

"In case you're interested in who made same"
"You're talking to the one who's to blame."

As the old year has departed, and the New Year has begun,
On the war cruising watch stood section one.

The quartermaster on watch is a poet of rare wit,
And here I copy just as he "writ":

2356–: "Four one five" came to the wheel,
For back into position we must steal

0008–: Now the turns are three twenty, and there they will stay,
Unless Lieutenant KITTS has more to say.

0014–: The Captain called, 'cause he couldn't be near
To wish the O.O.D.'s a "Happy New Year."

0345–: When this watch was over together we cried,
"Tho we didn't par Whitman, My! How we tried"
W.W. Kitts
Lieutenant, USN

Addendum

Lt. Kitts submitted an additional verse for the 1600 to 1800 watch. Perhaps Kitts, if he did not write the earlier poem, could not resist writing his own contribution after seeing how much fun the anonymous quartermaster had writing *his* poem. The rhythm and rhyme scheme are much crisper, more regular here. This would lend some credence to the idea that the midwatch verse was penned by another hand. Regardless, the humor and fun in writing it are the same. A second watch log poem is unprecedented. The evidence of hundreds of deck logs has not shown anyone to violate the "rule" that verse is only appropriate for the January 1, 0000–0400 watch, making the *Mason* a very special vessel once again!

Here is the additional verse.

16–18—Round and round the clock hands go,
The hours pass, but very slow.
I won't say much, tho I could say more,
For this short watch, just—steaming as before.
One other thing I'd better add,
In case it interests some other lad,
At seventeen ten by the wheel house clock,
To three twenty five the turns we did rock.
W.W. Kitts

The Poet

It would be satisfying to write a short biography for the quartermaster who wrote part, if not all, of the midwatch verse. It's ironic, perhaps a kind of poetic irony, that he must remain anonymous. One could wish that he had revealed his name in couplet 17, instead of simply referring to himself, with tongue in cheek, as "a poet of rare wit." But such was life at the time. He was not the Officer of the Deck, and it was the OOD who had to sign off on the poem. We are glad Kitts left an identifiable part of himself in the short later poem.

William Wayne Kitts was born on March 16, 1921, just outside Sulpher Springs, Texas, to William and Dora Kitts. His father Bill was a local political figure and musician who sang with the regionally acclaimed Stamps Quartet in the 1930s. William Wayne also excelled in music. After Kitts broke his nose several times, a physician recommended that he take on fewer contact sports activities and try out for the school band. During his time in the band, Kitts played drums, baritone, baritone saxophone and the clarinet. He was also an accomplished pianist.

He was the valedictorian of his high school class in 1938 before attending the University of Texas. At UT, Kitts had difficulty choosing a major, starting with pre-med, changing to music, and eventually graduating with a physics major. In

Three *Mason* crew members admire their ship while she lies moored at the Boston Navy Yard in Massachusetts on March 20, 1944. The placards indicate that *Mason*'s sister ship *John M. Bermingham* (DE-530) and the tank landing ship *LST-982* are fitting-out nearby. National Archives Photo 80-G-218861.

1942, he enlisted in the Navy and was ordered to the U.S. Naval Reserve Midshipman's School in New York City. During his first day in the Big Apple, Kitts went out to see the sights. He wore a pair of red Nocona cowboy boots that drew considerable attention. According to his oral history, several people approached him and asked if he was in town with a rodeo.

He came aboard *Mason* as an ensign. About a year before the breakout of the Korean War, Kitts became the commander of the Naval Reserve Training Center. Over time, he rose up the ranks in the U.S. Navy Reserve Training Center on the Texas Tech campus. While in that capacity, he was recalled to service in the Korean War. Part of his time during the war, he served as Executive Officer of USS *Hollis* (DE 794). He rose to the rank of captain before retiring from the Naval Reserve.

Over the years, he earned a couple of master's degrees and had a distinguished career in the aerospace industry. Two of his accomplishments were solving the problem of Vought F7U-3 Corsair's arresting hook not catching cables on carrier landing due to bouncing. He also led the team that designed the Lockheed/LTV S3-A aircraft. He was a 32nd degree Mason. Kitts was also active in his local Southern Baptist congregation. He died at the age of 96 on January 31, 2018.

Kitts' cooperation with the "experiment" to integrate the U.S. Navy cannot be minimized. At a time when blacks were treated so poorly by many in the U.S. population, Kitts seemed to accept them as equals to the task of defeating the enemies of the U.S.

USS *PC 1264*

An Inglorious Fate

USS *PC 1264* crew man the rails in dress whites circa 1944. Collection of Jack Sutherland. Donated by Laura Sutherland. NH 106733 Courtesy of Naval History & Heritage Command.

The Ship

USS *PC 1264*, a PC 461 class submarine chaser, was commissioned on April 25, 1944. Like USS *Mason* (DE 529), *PC 1264* was part of "The Grand Experiment" in which the ship was crewed primarily by African-American enlisted personnel and led by white officers. Petty officers were also white with the remainder of the crew being black. In theory, as black crew members became petty officers, the white crew would be rotated off the ship with the goal of having an entirely black enlisted crew. Unlike *Mason*, *PC 1264* accomplished the goal of an all-black enlisted crew before being decommissioned in 1946. Both *Mason* and *PC 1264* allowed black sailors for the first time to obtain occupational specialties other than stewards and messmen.

Sub chasers filled an important role during the war. Instead of protecting convoys against enemy subs while crossing an ocean, these vessels, smaller and slower than destroyers, protected convoys shuttling up and down the coast of the U.S. Like hundreds of other smaller vessels designated by a number rather than a name, *PC 1264* was crewed by Navy Reservists and often commanded by lieutenants or lieutenants junior grade, and even ensigns for smaller vessels. They often referred to themselves as "The Donald Duck Navy" after Disney's sailor-suit–wearing cartoon character Donald Duck.

Just like the USS *Mason* crew, the *PC 1264* crew suffered indignities dealt to them by white residents any time they sailed into a port, particularly in the Southern U.S. Even fellow Navy crewmen made disparaging remarks. Once while pulling into port, a chief petty officer on a passing PC beckoned his crew to the deck by saying, "Hurry up, you guys! Here comes a ship full of cooks!" (Purdon, 1972).

Over time, the *PC 1264* crew transformed the ship into one of the most efficient PCs in the Atlantic fleet. The upper echelon of the Navy brass and fellow patrol craft crew members began to recognize the level of competence of the crew. Eric Purdon, *PC 1264*'s first captain, described two instances of that recognition in his book *Black Company: The Story of Subchaser* PC 1264. The first account involved civilian guards at a Miami shipyard where *PC 1264* was moored for repairs. The guards frequently hassled the black crewmen with overly enthusiastic scrutiny of liberty passes and identification papers. The crew had come to expect it. However, shortly before the crew took back their repaired ship, the hassles stopped. It was not known until later that the guards had good reason to back off: Apparently, the crew of another PC, all white men, overheard several of the guards in a local drinking establishment plotting to go down to the docks and "shoot up the nigger ship" (Purdon, 1972). They went back to their own ship, roused their shipmates and, without informing any officers, broke into the arms lockers and took possession of several rifles and pistols. The impromptu commando squad then deployed to the entrance to the docks and thwarted the white guards' alcohol-fueled siege. While not all white sailors were as magnanimous as this PC crew, the gesture demonstrated that at least some within the Navy felt that the *PC 1264* crewmen were worthy of respect and defense (Purdon, 1972).

A second example of the regard given *1264* occurred in late April 1945, just before the end of the war in Europe. The ship received the following notice:

> PROCEED IMMEDIATELY CHARLESTON NAVAL SHIPYARD X REPORT PORT DIRECTOR FOR INSTRUCTIONS AND ROUTING OF CHARLESTON SECTION CONVOY KN-382 X ASSUME COMMAND ESCORT GROUP THIS SECTION.

Finally, *1264* was given the lead position for protection of a convoy that was to rendezvous with ships sailing north from Key West to New York. *PC 1264* had the enviable position of shepherding several dozen merchant ships. So, on April 27, she moved out of Charleston Harbor and began her first, and only, mission in command of a convoy escort. The next day, *1264* rendezvoused with ships from Key West and handed command over to one of their escorts, becoming once again just another ship escorting the nearly four dozen merchant ships. But the *1264* crew felt pride in their brief time in charge. Clearly, someone up the line of command had confidence in them.

Two other notable events occurred aboard the ship. One involved the arrival of Ensign Samuel L. Gravely, USNR, on May 2, 1945, at 1820 hours. Gravely was *1264*'s first black officer and the first black Naval officer assigned to a fighting ship. Gravely became a trailblazer for future African-Americans in the Navy. He went on to be the U.S. Navy's first African-American commander, captain, rear admiral and vice admiral. He was the first African-American to command a warship, a warship in battle, and a Navy fleet.

The second event occurred in *1264*'s wardroom. In his book, Captain Purdon described an encounter he had with Ensign Stanley Rhodes. Rhodes inquired about the captain's knowledge of how to publish a song. The captain expressed his lack of knowledge about such a procedure and asked if the ensign wanted to sing it. So Rhodes sang the song he had written, much to the surprise of a passing crewman, who simply heard one of the ship's officers singing a love song to his captain. Purdon's review of Rhodes' singing was less than stellar. What he heard, however, was probably the premiere of a song that Rhodes eventually published (with collaborators) entitled "A Sunday Kind of Love," which was recorded by luminaries such as Etta James, Reba McEntire, Frankie Laine, Ella Fitzgerald, the Four Seasons, Jan and Dean, and Jerry Lee Lewis, to name a few. Rhodes went on to publish more than 80 songs.

After the war in Europe, *PC 1264* received orders to escort one more convoy from New York to Key West. However, before reaching their destination on May 15, the convoy was ordered dispersed due to the lack of any additional threat from U-boats. *PC 1264* steamed independently toward Key West, arriving there on the 16th. For a time, the fate of *1264* and other similar vessels remained unknown, but finally the ship's captain received orders that would lead to refitting and training and eventual transfer to the Pacific Fleet. They were not out of the war yet.

In Miami, while awaiting this assignment, another notable incident occurred that reflected the racism that still gripped the U.S. Navy. Ensign Gravely and several of his black sailors gathered in a restaurant that was known to serve blacks. At some point, a scuffle erupted, and someone called the Shore Patrol. All was calm again by the time the patrol arrived. Two of the three members of the patrol came into the establishment; one was an Army MP, the other a sailor. A Chief Petty Officer remained outside. Seeing Gravely in an officer's uniform, the constabulary told him that the Chief wanted to see him outside. Thinking they were referring to a Chief from *1264*, Gravely informed them that the Chief could come inside to see *him*, consistent with protocol.

Suspecting that Gravely was not really an officer, likely due to his skin color, the MP pulled him out of his seat and informed him that he was going outside to see the Chief. This led to an immediate reaction by the *1264* crew. They were not going to let their ensign go quietly. Gravely tried to settle down the crew by telling them that it was all a misunderstanding, but by that time, additional gendarmerie arrived and many of the crew, including Gravely, were carted off to Shore Patrol Headquarters. Eventually, word got back to Capt. Purdon, who rushed to headquarters and took custody of his men. He intended to hold a Captains Mast to deal with the charges that included "Drunk," "Interference with Shore Patrol" and the like. All would likely have ended with the Mast, except the base duty officer informed Capt. Purdon that "the Admiral" wanted him to bring court martial proceedings against Gravely for fraternizing with enlisted men and conduct unbecoming an officer. Purdon informed the base duty officer

> that the commanding officer of a commissioned ship was The Captain, regardless of rank; that a junior grade lieutenant in command of an SC had the same responsibilities, the same powers under Navy Regulations as the four-striper captain of a battleship. "Sir, I am the commanding officer of USS PC 1264. The Commandant of a Naval District cannot order me to bring charges against any officer under my command.... And, I won't do it" [Purdon, 1972].

Purdon took no action against Gravely. But Captain's Mast and Deck Court were held for the enlisted men for certain legitimate charges. According to deck logs, punishments varied: ten hours extra duty for I.T. Alkins, Motor Machinist's Mate 3rd Class, for "dirty white uniform," confinement to ship for 20 days for D.C. Brown, Fireman 1st Class, and ditto for A. Simon, Seaman 1st Class, for "drunkenness." C.S. Harvey, Chief Motor Machinist's Mate, was hit with a hefty fine of $21 per month for four months for "drunkenness" (USS *PC 1264*, 1945).

After the end of hostilities in the Pacific, one final honor awaited *PC 1264*. She was selected as one of the dozens of ships to be reviewed by President Truman on Navy Day, October 27, 1945. The ship was readied, and *1264* took her place at the end of the line of ships. USS *Missouri,* over five times the length of *1264,* headed that line with her huge presence. According to the *St. Louis Star and Times*, "[A]t the northern end of the line, the doughty little PC 1264, too small to be given a name, [was] a proud ship this day." When the president passed *1264* aboard USS *Renshaw*, the crew saluted, and a 21-gun salute went off without a hitch (*St. Louis Star and Times*, 1945).

Eventually, *PC 1264* met the fate of thousands of vessels that helped win the war. On February 7, 1946, a decommissioning ceremony was held and *1264* was sold for scrap. Unlike so many other World War II–era warships, which were cut up and repurposed, she was towed to a scrapyard only about ten miles away from her former home base, where she has remained for 80 years. The photo below shows *PC 1264* and *PC 1217* languishing, rusting away, in the former Witte Brothers Marine Scrapyard, now DonJon Recycling. An inglorious fate for such a "doughty" ship, no matter how small.

Final resting place for PC 1264 and PC 1217 in a Staten Island ship graveyard. (Google Maps, January 20, 2022.)

The Poem

The following New Year's deck log for *PC 1264* was entered on January 1, 1945, by Lt. W.F. Otto, USNR. The poem is short, 12 lines divided into two stanzas. The lines too are short—two and three beats with a simple rhyme scheme. The structure imitates the A.A. Milne poem "Disobedience," which was probably familiar to Lt. Otto: "James James / Morrison Morrison / Weatherby George DuPree, / Took great / Care of his mother / Though he was only three." Milne's poem appeared in the anthology *When We Were Very Young* in 1924. His famous character Winnie the Pooh was introduced in one of the poems.

When the deck log is written, *PC 1264* is moored port side to the quay on the north side of Pier Seven on the "outboard" side of her sister ship *PC 1265*. They are at the U.S. Navy Frontier Base in Staten Island, New York. *PC 1264* had returned to Staten Island just the day before from the Navy Yard Annex in Bayonne, New Jersey, which was just a short distance away. She had spent three weeks in Bayonne for repairs to her main engine. Evidently the engine had a catastrophic failure, because *1264* was towed to Bayonne from Staten Island by a Naval tugboat.

Nothing of the ship's engine troubles and repairs appears in the New Year's deck log. Other than the information on her mooring, Lt. Otto reveals no details of the ship's condition or operations. He makes no reference to the war or to any ship activities related to the war. The notable events involving the ship's crew mentioned above—commanding a convoy escort group, the arrival of the first black officer to serve on a fighting ship, President Truman's review—were still months in the future, as was the end of the war later that year.

Here's the poem:

Moored fast are we
Port side to quay
Outboard the 1265
PC is she
And so are we
With a crew that looks alive.

This side of heaven
North side pier seven
United States Naval Frontier Base
The Island of Staten
Close to Manhattan
In the state of New York is our place
W.F. Otto, Lt.,
USNR

The Poet

Wilbur Frank Otto was born on August 19, 1918, in Modesto, California, to Frank Ferdinand Otto and Lillian Agnes Holmann. Wilbur spent much of his childhood in Downey, California, where his father worked as a public-school teacher, principal and district superintendent. This likely set the stage for Wilbur's choice of profession later in life.

Wilbur, or Will as he was often called, attended University of California School of Agriculture, but like many other men of his generation got the call to military service. He received his commission as ensign in the U.S. Navy on April 20, 1942. Before attending Submarine Chaser Training Center, he received gunnery training in San Francisco and commanded a merchantman armed guard (Purdon, 1972). Prior to arriving on the USS *PC 1264* for her commissioning, he was promoted to lieutenant junior grade. Captain Purdon described Otto as

> a young man with an insatiable appetite for adventure, new experiences; the possibility of serving aboard such a distinctive ship whetted his already instinctive enthusiasms. "Boy, oh boy!" he kept repeating during his interview in a deserted classroom on Pier 2, his face breaking into a series of ingenuous grins. "Sounds great!" He was nominated to be Gunnery Officer [Purdon, 1972].

Otto served on *1264* until May 1945, when as a newly minted lieutenant he shipped out to the Pacific Theater to command USS *YF 1042*, a wooden-hulled supply ship that carried a variety of goods between the islands that made up the Marshalls. He continued in this for six months after the war (Purdon, 1972).

Otto had a distinguished career in numerous educational positions in the Covina, California, school system, including vocational agriculture teacher, boys' counselor and principal.

Otto died in April 2014 just five months after his wife. Both were cremated and their ashes spread at sea off the coast of British Columbia.

USS *Pennsylvania*

"Old Falling Apart"

USS *Pennsylvania* (BB 38) underway off New York City during the Naval Review before President Franklin D. Roosevelt on May 31, 1934. *Pennsylvania* was then serving as flagship of the Commander in Chief, U.S. Fleet, Admiral David F. Sellers, USN. NH 67583 Courtesy of Naval History & Heritage Command.

The Ship

USS *Pennsylvania* (BB 38) was commissioned on June 12, 1916, at the Newport News Shipbuilding Yard in Virginia. She did not see service in Europe during World War I due to her oil-burning propulsion system. Oil was not nearly available enough in Europe to meet her needs. She served as the flagship of the Atlantic Fleet in the

1920s and 1930s before moving to the Pacific, where she operated mostly off the coast of California. In early 1941, she sailed to Pearl Harbor, where she was dry docked on December 7 during the Japanese attack. *Pennsylvania* shared the dry dock with destroyers *Cassin* (DD 372) and *Downes* (DD 375). While she was most likely the target of the attacking planes, it was the destroyers that were most devastated by the attack. She took some damage from a single bomb hit and from flying debris from *Cassin* and *Downes*. Twenty-eight men died in the attack (two officers and 26 crew). *Pennsylvania* moved out of dry dock and headed back to the mainland on December 20.

By August 1942, *Pennsylvania* was sailing back to Pearl Harbor sporting new technology and armament. According to her ship record, this new version bristled with nine 14-inch guns, 16 five-inch guns, 40 40mm guns, 50 20mm guns and eight 50-caliber machine guns. So furious was her ability to lay down fire with her huge arsenal that a reporter wrote, "The boys call the *Pennsy* 'Old Falling Apart' because she turns such a volume of gun fire that you'd think she was falling to pieces" (USS *Pennsylvania*, 1942). Serving often as a flagship, she boasted 24 radio transmitters and 41 receivers that were manned by 127 radiomen.

Most of her time from 1942 through 1945 involved bombarding shore and island fortifications during the eight campaigns for which she earned battle stars. Being a relatively slow vessel of World War I vintage, *Pennsylvania* could not keep up with the fleet carriers. Instead of accompanying carriers to support air actions, she essentially became a formidable floating gun platform. Her actions at places like the Aleutians, the Gilbert Islands, the Mariana Islands and the Philippines earned her the Navy Unit Commendation.

While moored in Buckner Bay, Okinawa, on August 12, 1945, just three days before the Japanese surrender was announced by Emperor Hirohito, *Pennsylvania* took a hit from a Japanese torpedo dropped by a plane to her aft starboard side. The torpedo blew a 30-foot diameter hole in her hull, killing 20 of her crew. Excellent damage control saved the ship, but *Pennsylvania*'s war was over. One sailor remarked, "We didn't get the Jap plane, but we sure busted hell out of her torpedo." She began the trip back to the U.S. for repairs.

However, before she returned home, she embarked a young ensign who would later become a legend as a late-night talk-show host: Johnny Carson. Carson was commissioned in 1945 and assigned to *Pennsylvania* just at the war's end. There is some disparity among various biographical sources about the date of his embarkation, some claiming that Ensign Carson reported aboard the "*Pensy*" sometime in early August while others indicate he arrived in early September. Even the official *Pennsylvania* records offer conflicting reports. The dates August 6 and September 6 both appear as dates of embarkation. The records are clear, however, on the date of his detachment: November 19, 1945.

An unauthorized biography quotes Carson as saying he embarked the day after the Japanese torpedo hit, and as a young ensign had to supervise the recovery of bodies from the attack (Corkery, 1987, p. 54). (According to the ship's war reports, the remaining bodies of missing crewmen entombed in the bowels of the ship were recovered in September while she was in floating dry dock securing repairs for the torpedo damage.) Carson was definitely on board at the time, assigned to damage control. He is also said to have served in communications, decoding encrypted messages. but this would probably have been when he was sent to Guam after *Pennsylvania* returned home. An amateur boxer in the Navy, Carson racked up a 10–0 record, supposedly most fights occurring while on *Pennsylvania*. But he was hardly on the ship long enough—two or three months—to have had so many matches there. He apparently entertained the crew as a ventriloquist with his dummy, and it seems to have been his success at entertaining Secretary of the Navy James Forrestal, not known for his sense of humor, with a card trick that convinced Carson he had to be an entertainer (Stilwell, no date; Cockery, p. 55).

A 1982 article in the *Santa Cruz Sentinel* describes one of the more interesting sagas aboard the ship while Carson was there. It was a "contest between the enlisted men who wanted to steal the ship's beer, and the officers ... who didn't want the whitehats to have the beer." After the enlisted men's first caper, the officers locked all the beer in the brig. But the determined whitehats crawled in through the fresh air vents and stole several more cases. The episode reflects the high value placed on alcohol by the sailors, a fact reflected in so many deck log poems.

In 1946, *Pennsylvania* was tapped to be a target ship in the Operation Crossroads nuclear tests in Bikini Atoll. She survived the bomb explosions and became the object of radiological studies until 1948, when she was stricken from the Navy's rolls and scuttled off Kwajalein.

Pennsylvania earned eight battle stars and a Navy Unit Citation for her service in World War II. Her bell is now on the campus of Penn State University near the Wagner Building that houses the university's ROTC programs.

The Poem

The midwatch deck log for January 1, 1945, was entered by Lt. R.E. Hayes, USNR. For readers familiar with Rudyard Kipling's 1890 poem "Gunga Din," Hayes evokes an undercurrent of pathos in his imitation of Kipling's distinctive style. Kipling's character Gunga Din is an Indian water carrier, much mistreated by the British soldiers during the Indian Mutiny of 1857. He is killed while saving the life of the narrator. The poem is mostly remembered for its final line, "You're a better man than I am, Gunga Din." And so, almost a century later, Lt. Hayes, an American sailor, attempted to put his World War II experience onto paper borrowing the rhythms of "Gunga Din."

Pennsylvania is anchored at Kossol Road in the Palau Islands, which from September through November 1944 was the site of some of the most vicious and costly fighting of the Pacific War. *Pennsylvania* had participated in the bombardment of the island of Peleliu, where the most intense fighting took place. After the ten-week siege of Palau, Kossol Anchorage became a major re-supply and repair base for the Pacific Fleet.

As Hayes begins his deck log, *Pennsylvania* is moored in 18 fathoms of water on 75 fathoms of line in Berth 26. Power is being supplied by boiler number two, and readiness is at Condition III. The Material Condition of the ship is set at Yoke, and the ship is blacked out. A variety of American ships are anchored with *Pennsylvania*, along with ships of the Australian Navy. At 0200, the ship adjusts her clocks to align with Greenwich Mean Time ("zone minus nine"). Then at 0140, an engineer lights boiler number one and later is heard to mutter profanities when he brings the boiler online at 0309. A little less than 30 minutes later, at 0333, he lights boilers three, four, five and six.

Hayes' poem describes a typical midwatch during wartime: details of anchorage, conditions of readiness, blackout, sources of steam. But his nearly perfect imitation of the steady rhythm and complex rhyme scheme of "Gunga Din" makes the poem a technical triumph and a joy to read. The American war machine, after three years of fighting, is grinding toward Japan. The slow march to victory will persist for eight months more. The final lines of Hayes' poem express the typical American optimism and hope for the future as he prays for warm and clear weather for the "*Pennsy*" and her crew throughout the year.

Here is the poem:

It's the *PENNSYLVANIA*'s privilege to be in KOSSOL ANCHORAGE,
On the 1st of January 1945.
Yes, in the Islands called PALAU our port anchor dangles now,
And its' length in fathoms measure 75.
Oh a look beneath our keel will at a glance reveal,
The water there is 18 fathoms deep.
And the Navigator's fix says we're in Berth 26,
A position that he really wants to keep.......
In engine rooms below, every man is sure to know,
That boiler number two is on the line.
And as New Year's Bells do toll, far above in Sky Control
Condition III is thought to be quite fine.
Down in Central Station our Material Condition,
Is certainly not treated as a joke.
They would likely be quite sad, and maybe even mad,
If I failed to mention here that it is Yoke.
Now the First Lieutenant's Crew has so many things to do,
That to their lessons they have always hearkened.
And so I'm glad to say on this new-born New Year's Day,
That our ship is very safely darkened.
All about on every side on the Kossol waves to ride,
Other vessels large and small of Uncle Sam.
And full many an "Aussie Crew" is here beside us too,
To aid us in destruction of Japan.
Now to continue this rhyme, we changed the time,
At two o'clock to zone minus nine.
Though the clocks went back we still kept track,

Of the boilers on the line.
An engineer was sighted just as he coyly lighted
The fires 'neath number one at oh-one-forty.
And he put it on the line at zero-three-oh-nine,
As he muttered words that were a little naughty.
We hoped that this might be the last activity,
Among our busy boilers for the night.
But there was even more, three, five, six and four,
At oh-three-thirty-three were set alight.
I am happy though to say that on this the New Year's Day,
The weather, it is warm and very clear.
And as I close I pray that 'twill always stay that way,
For the "*Pennsy*" and her crew throughout the year.
R.E. HAYES, Lieutenant (j.g.),
U.S. Naval Reserve

The Poet

Raymond Eric Hayes was born on September 11, 1917, in Detroit, Michigan, to Herbert Hayes and Dorothy Ada Pope. He graduated from Denby High School in 1935 and enrolled at Wayne State University. According to Hayes' papers, he majored in speech-forensics and showed considerable aptitude for public communication. After graduation in 1939, he joined General Motors' "Parade of Progress," a traveling exhibition that highlighted futuristic cars and technologies. The Parade moved from town to town, easily identifiable by a convoy of Fisher Body–built Futurliner vans.

In a 1977 interview, Hayes reminisced about his involvement in the program.

> The three guys I broke in with were from Harvard, Columbia, and Brown—all Eastern guys. We were all hired as lecturers, but there was an apprenticeship period. While you were

General Motors Futurliners during a 1936 GM Parade of Progress. Photo from GM Heritage Center.

> apprenticing, they put you on the utility crew—we called it the futility crew—and that meant you didn't lecture until you learned every other job and also until one of the regular lecturers dropped out. What you did—you reported from the hotel to the show at about six o'clock in the morning in coveralls, and you waxed floors, took a stick with a nail on the end of it, picked up papers—that sort of thing [Williams, B., 1998].

On April 5, 1941, Hayes married Alice Kingsley Donald in Detroit. In mid-1941, he was contacted by his local draft board regarding future military service. General Motors requested a three-month deferment from being drafted so they could hire and train Hayes' replacement. The Selective Service board approved the deferment (Hayes, 1941). As the draft neared, Hayes decided to enlist in the Navy just six days prior to the Pearl Harbor attack. Two days later, Hayes arrived at the recruiting office to take the Navy's intelligence test. According to newspaper accounts, he turned in his exam in 19 minutes, much faster than expected of new recruits. The recruiting office staff expected a dismal score only to be astounded by Hayes' score of 100 percent. The average score was 60, and 85 was considered very good. Lt. Cmdr. Carson R. Miller, commander of the recruiting station, exclaimed that this had never happened before (100 Per Center).

Hayes joined the Navy as a Yeoman 2nd Class and shipped out to the Great Lakes Training Base for his initial training, then came back to the Navy Recruiting Station in Detroit. Two years later, he, like many other young men, was sent to Naval Reserve Midshipmen's School at Notre Dame University. After his commissioning on May 27, 1943, he went off to sea on USS *Pennsylvania*. He served on *Pennsylvania* for seven of her eight credited campaigns. Having been awarded honors in navigation during Midshipmen's school, Hayes was her Assistant Navigator. He also served as "N" Division Officer and, for a time, Assistant Censor.

Raymond Eric Hayes as an enlisted sailor, probably in 1942. Courtesy of Robert W. Hayes.

On August 12, 1945, according to Hayes' daughter-in-law, he visited some of his "N" Division crew and left them just before their quarters were devastated by the Japanese torpedo. Hayes' immediate actions after the explosion are unknown, but his separation papers indicate that he was recommended for an

Funeral services for four of Raymond Hayes' "N" Division crew members killed by a Japanese torpedo on August 12, 1945. Hayes is standing between a Marine and a chief in the upper right. (Courtesy of Robert Hayes.)

individual commendation on that date. Funeral services for four of his "N" Division men are memorialized in photographs from Hayes' papers.

After the war, Hayes went back to General Motors and worked until his retirement in 1980, when he held the position of director of communication and marketing. He was highly respected in forensics and for his service to that discipline. In 1970, he received the Distinguished Alumni Award from Wayne State University and in 1976 received a similar award from the National Honorary Forensic Society (Delta Sigma Rho-Tau Kappa Alpha). To this day, Wayne State University grants the Raymond and Alice Hayes Endowed Scholarship Award Fund for Forensics Students.

Raymond Eric Hayes died on November 24, 1991, in Palm Beach, Florida, and is buried at White Chapel Memorial Cemetery in Troy, Michigan.

USS *South Dakota*

Battleship X

USS *South Dakota* (BB 57) off the Norfolk Navy Yard, Virginia, on August 20, 1943. NH 97264 Courtesy of Naval History & Heritage Command.

The Ship

USS *South Dakota* (BB 57), the lead vessel of the four South Dakota–class fast battleships, was commissioned on March 20, 1942. On her shakedown cruise in July, while zigzagging she joined the "whale-bangers club," hitting a large whale. She passed through the Panama Canal and into the Pacific on August 21 and with

Lansdowne (DD 486), *Lardner* (DD 487) and *Meade* (DD 602) headed for Tonga. She reached the Tonga Islands on September 4.

On September 6, *South Dakota* struck an uncharted shoal, causing extensive underwater damage to her hull. After temporary repairs by USS *Vestal* (AR 4), she sailed to Pearl Harbor Navy Yard, where she received a permanent patch to her hull. As was being done to all the battleships in the fleet as part of a necessary change in battle philosophy since Pearl Harbor, she also got additional anti-aircraft armament (Toll, 2012, p. 57). She then returned to Tonga, joining Task Force 16.

In the Battle of the Santa Cruz Islands in October, *South Dakota* provided anti-aircraft support to USS *Enterprise* and suffered repeated aerial attacks, with planes dropping out of clouds as low as 500 feet and sometimes flying just above the water between ships to avoid anti-aircraft fire. According to the ship's action report for October 26, several of her Filipino and African American mess attendants manned anti-aircraft guns at their own request: "Every member of these crews courageously and fearlessly served their guns." Eight of the 11 mess attendants were wounded. On the fourth wave of attacks, a bomb struck the ship's forward main battery but did not penetrate the shell. The explosion killed two men and wounded over 50, including Captain Thomas Gatch, who was on the bridge wing spotting bombers. The withering anti-aircraft fire of *South Dakota* and the other screening ships saved *Enterprise*, but the carrier *Hornet* was sunk. Because of his wounds, Gatch had to hand over his command to the XO. He received the Navy Cross and a Purple Heart. After the battle, Gatch praised his crew: "[N]o one of the *South Dakota* flinched from his post or showed the least sign of disaffection. As long as we raise such men we are safe" (USS *South Dakota*, 1942).

In the heat of battle, *South Dakota* gunners nearly shot down some U.S. aircraft returning to *Enterprise*. According to one Navy veteran, *South Dakota* had a reputation for shooting first and asking questions later. According to him, Navy fliers had a simple rule for *South Dakota*: "Don't fly anywhere near that big so-and-so; she'll shoot you down" (Miller, 1993, p. 151).

While returning to Noumea from the battle, *South Dakota* attempted to avoid a submarine contact and collided with USS *Mahan* (DD 364), causing significant damage to both ships. Though no one was seriously injured, *Mahan* left an anchor in *South Dakota*'s wardroom.

In the Second Naval Battle of Guadalcanal in November 1942, the ship took a heavy beating when, in a rare occurrence, U.S. and Japanese battleships engaged in direct surface action. The Japanese focused all their attention on *South Dakota*, and she received a total of 42 hits, though most were to her superstructure and did not compromise her buoyancy. During the battle, she experienced multiple electrical power failures, some from enemy hits and some caused by the shock of her own guns. She also endured radar failure, communications failure, fires, loss of power to gun mounts and fire control, and ruptured oil compartments. In addition to extensive damage to her systems, she suffered heavy personnel losses: 40 killed and 180 wounded. She left the battle at full speed. Her rapid disappearance caused the Japanese to believe she had been sunk. To encourage this belief, Naval Intelligence began referring to her as Battleship X in their dispatches. The press later referred to her as "Old Nameless" (Miller, 152). She received the Navy Unit Citation for her actions. Halsey said of the ship, "My pride in you is beyond comparison. No honor for you could be too great. Magnificently done!" (Evans, 2015).

One of those wounded aboard *South Dakota* at Guadalcanal was 12-year-old Calvin Graham, the youngest person to serve the U.S. in World War II (he lied about his age to enter the Navy). For his actions in helping others after being wounded himself by shrapnel, Graham received the Bronze Star and Purple Heart. The medals were revoked, however, and he was sent home and served time in the brig after his mother, seeing promotional photos, called the Navy. The Bronze Star was reinstated later in his life, the Purple Heart posthumously (King, 2012).

In December 1942, *South Dakota* returned to the Navy Yard in New York for repairs. By May 1943, she was operating with British ships in the North Atlantic and escorting convoys to the Soviet Union. In June, she joined an effort to lure the German battleship *Tirpitz* into a trap, sailing with USS *Alabama* in Norwegian waters. The effort was fruitless, and in November 1943, she moved back to the Pacific Theater and participated in campaigns in the Gilbert and Marshall Islands. In February 1944, she participated in campaigns at Truk and the Marianas, and in March the campaign in the Carolines, screening for the carrier fleet. In April, she supported the campaign in Western New Guinea. Operation Forager, the invasion of the Marianas and Palau in June, saw *South Dakota* escorting the fast carrier force and repelling numerous air attacks. The *Kingfishers* launched from *South Dakota* flew rescue duty for downed airmen.

On the morning of June 19, 1944, the first wave of Japanese strike aircraft broke through U.S. air cover and attacked the U.S. fleet in the Battle of the Philippine Sea. A dive bomber hit *South Dakota* with a 500-pound bomb, blasting an eight-by-ten-foot hole in the deck, killing 24 men and wounding 27. She continued in action, and in the following days supported air invasions of nearby islands. On June 27, she headed for Puget Sound, Washington, for repairs, stopping at Pearl Harbor on July 2 to embark 248 wounded, 279 sailors and 90 Marines for transfer to the mainland.

After repairs at dry dock in July, *South Dakota* participated in sea trials, maneuvers and further repairs through August and September 1944. She returned to the fleet at the end of September and participated in the raids at Okinawa and Taiwan. Then on October 24, she supported the Fast Carrier Force's engagement of Admiral Kurita's Center Force at the Battle of the Sibuyan Sea. The following day, she headed north with Task Force 34, screening the Fast Carrier Task Force in Admiral Halsey's pursuit of the decoy Japanese Northern Force. When the Japanese Center Force attacked the small U.S. force left behind to guard Leyte, Halsey was forced to send Task Force 34 back. They arrived too late to support Taffy Three in the heroic Battle off Samar.

In January 1945, *South Dakota* supported various raids against the mainland. From February to May 1945, she engaged in battles at Iwo Jima and Okinawa and supported further raids on Tokyo and other areas in Japan. During ammunition replenishment on May 6, a tank of high-capacity powder for the 16-inch guns exploded, causing four more tanks to detonate and igniting a serious fire. Eleven men died and 24 others were injured. According to her War Diary for that day, only superb damage control and firefighting averted a major disaster (USS *South Dakota*, 1945). *South Dakota* continued in the assault on Japan through July and early August. She entered Tokyo Bay on August 29 and embarked Admirals Halsey and Nimitz, becoming Nimitz's flagship and delivering the admirals to USS *Missouri* for the signing of the Japanese surrender four days later. After the surrender, she served as Halsey's flagship during the early occupation of Japan. She returned to San Francisco in late October.

In February 1946, *South Dakota* became the flagship of the Fourth Fleet reserve unit. She was decommissioned in January 1947 and stricken from the Naval Register in June 1962. She was sold for scrap in October of that year, though parts of the ship were retained for a memorial in Sioux Falls, South Dakota.

South Dakota received 13 battle stars for her service in World War II.

The Poem

The deck log below was entered on January 1, 1945, by Lt. J.C. Hill II. This is one of the longer poems at 54 lines. Interestingly, the first six lines of the poem imitate the rhythm of Rudyard Kipling's famous poem "Gunga Din" (see USS *Pennsylvania* chapter for a more extensive example), but the rest of the poem (48 lines) consists of quatrains of the old ballad stanza, with a varied rhyme scheme.

The ship is steaming at 24 knots with Task Force 38.1, minus USS *Massachusetts* (BB 59), which has departed for repairs accompanied by USS *Taussig* (DD 746) and USS *Maddox* (DD 731). Having endured Typhoon Cobra 12 days earlier, the task force is now cruising to a position off Taiwan, where the attack will begin on January 3. The carrier *Yorktown* (CV 5) hosts the Officer-in-Tactical Command (OTC), who is Rear Admiral Arthur W. Radford, and the radar search is set for "Able" (aircraft). Hill shows his sense of humor when he calls the idea of writing a deck log in verse a "fable."

He claims that the "heavy ships," meaning the battleships and cruisers, are the axis of the formation. It's not clear initially what he means when he says, "The planes are in an awful state," which is "[i]ndictive of the crew." "Indictive" would mean "proclaimed or declared," and Hill may have intended to say "indicative." He clarifies why the planes and men are in an awful state in the following lines (23–30) when he says that New Year is a traditional time for celebration, but in fact both the aircraft and the crew are "as dry as dry can be." The planes are "de-gassed," and the crew is without alcohol, as so many of the deck logs complain.

The ship is darkened and in Material Condition Yoke. The gun batteries are in readiness Condition Three. She changes course a half-hour after midnight. The engineers blow her tubes at 0140 hours. At 0210, orders come over the TBS (Talk Between Ships), the radio frequency used for tactical maneuvering, to change course and speed. Then comes Admiral Halsey on the air, and in his typically audacious way, he wishes them Happy New Year by saying, "The best of everything to come, / And keep the bastards dying!"

Hill closes the poem with the hope that the war will end in 1945. And though *South Dakota* will still see action at Iwo Jima and Okinawa and experience tragedy when her powder tanks explode, she will pull alongside USS *Missouri* to deliver Admirals Nimitz and Halsey for the signing of the surrender on September 2 of that year.

Here's the poem:

0000–0300
For the progress of the war
We are steaming twenty-four,
In company with thirty-eight point one;
And the *Massachusetts,* screened
By the *Taussig-Maddox* team,
Has departed 'till all repairs are done.
The *Yorktown* has the O.T.C. [Officer in Tactical Command],
The radar search is "Able";
All boilers on the line for we,
While logs in verse are fable.
The heavy ships on seven-oh
As axis do remain,
While one-two-oh the carriers
Consider as their claim.
The base course now is two-nine-five,
And so we set our helm;
Though *Yorktown* as the guide,
Can meander in her realm.
With radio and radar
Set in Condition Two,
The planes are in an awful state
Indictive of the crew.
For on this great eventful day
When New Year's feels its birth,
And celebration's been the way
For years and years on Earth,
The aircraft are, and so the crew,
As dry as dry can be,
For planes are in Condition Nine,
As de-gassed as are we!
New "Yoke" is set, and batteries
Are in Condition Three;
The ship is darkened fore and aft,
To keep us fighting free.
In disposition Roger (five)

We steam into the night,
And changed to new course three-oh-five
At thirty past midnight.
At forty after one o'clock
The engineers made known
Their need to start the New Year clean,
And so our tubes were blown!
At ten past two the T B S [Talk Between Ships radio]
Came forth with something new,
And changed our course to three-one-oh,
And speed to twenty-two.
Came Admiral Halsey on the air—
His words, they rung out, crying
"The best of everything to come,
And keep the bastards dying!"
As with this watch the year came in—
We helped it to arrive!
So hope we the war will end
In 1945!

J. C. Hill II
Lieut., USN

The Poet

John "Jack" Clayton Hill II was born on August 30, 1919, in Newport, Rhode Island, to Harry Wilbur Hill and Margaret Harwood Hall. Hill was one of two boys born to the family that day. His brother, Harry Wilbur Hill, Jr., died on September 2, 1919, and is buried with the rest of his family at the U.S. Naval Academy Cemetery.

John followed his father's lead and attended the Naval Academy, graduating in the Class of 1942. His father, Harry, graduated from Annapolis in 1911 and served on a variety of ships during World War I and throughout the 1920s. Harry also received appointments to the Office of the Chief of Naval Operations. When World War II broke out, the elder Hill commanded a battleship division. Ultimately promoted to the rank of vice admiral, he served as Commander Fifth Amphibious Force at Okinawa. He received three Distinguished Service Medals for his service. In 1979, the destroyer USS *Harry W. Hill* (DD 986) was commissioned. John Clayton Hill II had big shoes to fill.

After graduating from Annapolis, Ensign Hill boarded USS *South Dakota* and served in the gunnery and fire control divisions. On January 8, 1943, he married Mary Helen Rodman at St. Peters Episcopal Church in Raleigh, North Carolina. She was the daughter of William Blount Rodman, Jr., who served as North Carolina attorney general and on the North Carolina Supreme Court. During *South Dakota*'s time in the Atlantic, Hill earned the Bronze Star Medal with "V" device for his actions in the gunnery division. He also served on USS *Roanoke* (CL 145) as navigator and USS *Borie* (DD 704) as executive officer and navigator (Hill, John).

Midshipman John "Jack" Clayton Hill II from the 1942 Naval Academy Yearbook *Annapolis Lucky Bag*.

During his time in the Navy, Hill commanded three ships. From September 1945 through November 1945, he captained USS *Sturtevant* (DE 239), from August 1952 through January 1954, USS *Parle* (DE 708), and from July 1959 through July 1961, USS *Mullinix* (DD 944). He retired in April 1969 at the rank of captain.

In the 1950s and 1960s, Hill joined the editors and authors of *Dutton's Navigation and Piloting*, one of the most widely used textbooks on navigation (first published in 1926 and was continuously published in a number of forms through the early 2000s). Hill contributed to several editions, a testament to his proficiency in navigation. The early 1970s found Hill employed as Director of Planning Services at COMSAT, an organization founded in the early 1960s to develop commercial and international satellite communications. The company continues to operate in 2021.

John Clayton Hill II died on January 19, 2003, in Washington, D.C., and is buried at the U.S. Naval Academy Cemetery in Annapolis, Maryland.

USS *Ticonderoga*

The Indestructible Captain Dixie

USS *Ticonderoga* (CV 14) at Ulithi Fleet Anchorage on December 8, 1944. National Archives Photo 80-G-K-2589.

The Ship

USS *Ticonderoga* (CV 14), the fourth ship of that name, was an Essex-class aircraft carrier commissioned at Norfolk Navy Yard on May 8, 1944. After embarking Air Group 80, she headed for the West Indies on June 26. There she spent several weeks in training operations before returning to Norfolk for post-shakedown repairs. On September 4, she transited the Panama Canal and steamed to San Diego, where she refueled, stocked and sailed for Hawaii.

Ticonderoga spent a month at Pearl Harbor running tests and conducting air operations. She then joined Task Force 38 at Ulithi Atoll in late October 1944. On November 2, she joined the ranks of ships supporting the Leyte invasion, and over the next few days her planes pummeled enemy shipping, bombed and strafed airfields, and aided in the sinking of Japanese heavy cruiser *Nachi.* On November 5, she survived unscathed an attack of kamikazes that damaged the carrier *Lexington* (CV 16). Through the middle of November, Task Force 38 continued highly effective attacks on Japanese ships and positions in the Philippines. The Task Force then retired to Ulithi for replenishing, refueling and rearming.

The last week of November, *Ticonderoga* returned to battle in the Philippines with TF 38 and again attacked Japanese airfields and ships, including the heavy cruiser *Kumano.* While their planes wreaked havoc on the enemy, TF 38 again suffered aerial attacks, including kamikazes that exploded into the carrier *Essex* (CV 9), inflicting severe damage. Retiring once more to Ulithi, a refreshed *Ticonderoga* returned to the battle on December 11, attacking airfields on Luzon and elsewhere. When, on December 16, she and the rest of TF 38 withdrew for refueling, they were caught in Typhoon Cobra. Unlike the smaller ships of Halsey's force, which were heavily damaged, the carriers rode out the storm with minimal effect. *Ticonderoga* returned to Ulithi on Christmas Eve.

It is difficult to appreciate the history of *Ticonderoga* without being aware of the life of the dynamic captain, Dixie Kiefer. According to David Poyer, Kiefer was quite a prankster during his time at the Naval Academy. Later, during his service, he often broke the mold of a commanding officer, and he was loved by all those who served under him. On Armistice Day, November 11, 1924, he made the first night takeoff from a battleship in San Diego Harbor. He rose through the ranks during the 1930s, and in 1942 he became the Executive Officer of USS *Yorktown* (CV 5). For his leadership in the Battle of the Coral Sea in May of that year, he was awarded the Navy Distinguished Service Medal (Poyer, 2019).

A month later, while fighting at the Battle of Midway, *Yorktown* was hit by three bombs, one of which wounded Kiefer in the shoulder and leg. Despite his wounds, he was the first to grab a hose and begin fighting a dangerous fire in the photo lab (Poyer, 2019). Two days later, after further hits to the ship from torpedo planes, Kiefer was again injured when his hands were burned lowering a wounded man from the ship. He then fell as he attempted to lower himself and suffered compound fractures of his foot and ankle. He still pushed the life raft toward the rescue ship until he had to be pulled aboard (Ferro, 2015).

In June 1944, Kiefer was put in command of the newly minted *Ticonderoga.* Though he guided her brilliantly and safely through the early months of combat in the Pacific, January 1945 would be the turning point in her service. The first week of that month, the ship joined attacks on Luzon and Formosa. The middle of the month saw TF 38 off the coast of Indochina, where on the 12th their 850 planes, performing anti-shipping sweeps, sank a total of 44 enemy ships. After continuing attacks on Japanese airfields on the China coast, the task force headed back to rejoin the attack on Formosa on January 20.

On the morning of January 21, *Ticonderoga*'s luck at escaping the "Divine Wind" ran out when a kamikaze crashed through her flight deck and its bomb exploded just above her hangar deck. During this attack and the one that followed, Kiefer and the damage control work of the crew saved the carrier from a watery grave. According to the after-action report, an intense fire from the explosion ignited on the hangar deck among thickly parked planes. Its progress was slowed by sprinklers and water screens and "the heroic efforts of the fire fighters … [and] plane handlers who removed smouldering [*sic*] and burning planes and shoved them over the side" (USS *Ticonderoga*, 1945). Captain Kiefer changed course to take the wind out of the fire, then ordered magazines and other compartments on the port side flooded to avoid further explosions and to correct a ten-degree list to starboard. He then continued flooding port side compartments to create a ten-degree list to that side, which dumped much of the fire (burning fuel) overboard.

But other kamikazes smelled blood and swarmed to *Ticonderoga*. A desperate screen of anti-aircraft fire downed three enemy planes, but 38 minutes after the first hit, a fourth plane struck the starboard side near the island. According to the after-action report, the enemy plane "passed completely through sky forward and the sky lookout platform." The 550-pound bomb exploded, "spraying fragments which made a sieve of the forward side of the stack and surrounding superstructure.… [The] No. 1 5-inch AA director was nearly severed from its base, and barely hanging by a few plates.…" Burning debris set fires throughout the superstructure, even igniting many life jackets on killed and wounded men. The explosion also ignited another fire among the flight deck planes, but quick firefighting action limited the damage (USS *Ticonderoga*, 1945). Casualties were heavy: 143 killed, 202 wounded, including Captain Kiefer. With the flames under control, the ship was able to retire from the battle without further hits. Arriving at Ulithi on January 24, she transferred her wounded to the hospital ship *Samaritan* and transferred her air group to USS *Hancock* (CV 19). Captain Kiefer had been severely wounded, riddled by 65 pieces of shrapnel, his arm shattered, but had remained on the bridge for 12 hours directing the ship before allowing corpsmen to remove him on a stretcher. He received the Silver Star for his actions. The ship returned to Puget Sound for repairs, docking there on February 15 (Naval History and Heritage Command, 2015).

Secretary of the Navy, James V. Forrestal, called Kiefer "the indestructible man." But in a heartbreaking irony, he was killed in November of that year, less than three months after the end of the war, in the crash of a Navy plane on a short flight returning from the Army–Notre Dame football game, his arm still in a cast from the battle aboard *Ticonderoga* (Ferro, 2015).

With her repairs completed April 20, 1945, *Ticonderoga* sailed for Hawaii without her indestructible captain, arriving at Pearl Harbor on May 1. She embarked Air Group 87 and spent a week training before returning to battle. She then steamed for the Western Pacific, rejoining the Fast Carrier Task Force on May 22. For the final weeks of the war, *Ticonderoga* operated in Japanese home waters, striking airfields on Kyushu, riding out a second typhoon in six months, and joining aerial bombardment of areas in Okinawa. Her planes struck ships in the Inland Sea and airfields at several cities on Mainland Japan. In late July and the first two weeks of August, she helped destroy the remaining Japanese navy and joined the bombardment of major cities, including Tokyo. On August 15, she launched an attack on Tokyo before receiving word of Japan's surrender.

Ticonderoga entered Tokyo Harbor on September 6, four days after the formal signing of surrender. She participated in Operation Magic Carpet, delivering thousands of veterans to the West Coast. On January 9, 1947, she was decommissioned and put in the Reserve Fleet. She received five battle stars for her service in World War II.

In September 1954, *Ticonderoga* was recommissioned after extensive modernization and performed routine operations over the next few years. She was very active during the Vietnam conflict and for her performance there received three Navy Unit Commendations, one Meritorious Unit Commendation, and 12 battle stars. In April 1972, she participated in the recovery of the Apollo 16 moon mission capsule and astronauts near American Samoa. She was decommissioned in September 1973 and sold for scrap in November.

The Poem

The following deck log was entered on January 1, 1945, by Lt. R.F. Harbison, USNR. The poem differs from most in that it consists of 26 rhymed couplets, prefaced by an energetic "Happy New Year!!" and followed by a short prose statement giving course, speed, propeller rpms and steam pressure. *Ticonderoga* has just returned to the Philippine Sea after a brief rest over Christmas at Ulithi Atoll. Just two weeks earlier, she had survived Typhoon Cobra.

The first four lines of the poem reflect the common theme that the focus aboard Navy ships on New Year's Day is performance of duty, not celebration: "No wine, no women, no nightclubs, no song." They are cruising with "T.G. 38.3" (Task Group 38.3, part of Task Force 38) in "Cruising disposition … 5 Roger." Cruising disposition is a smaller segment of the larger ship formation, having its own internal organization similar to the larger group. The Officer in Tactical Command is aboard the carrier *Essex* (CV 9), which is the "guide." Standard speed is 18 knots. Harbison says that the "Formation axis" is "one zero zero True." Using the polar coordinate method of stationing ships, this would put the axis of the formation along a line from the formation center pointing 100 degrees from true north (Naval Operations, 1967).

Like so many other deck log poets, Harbison cannot help thinking of home. If they were in the States, they would be "raising a rumpus" instead of cruising a course "per standard compass." When the ship's speed is bumped up to 25 knots, "[t]hey cut in superheat." Power plants on World War II carriers and several other classes had divided boilers, one set controlling steam pressure and the other controlling steam temperature (superheat). The second set could not be lit until the ship was up to a steady speed of at least 10 or 12 knots to prevent the superheater tubes from overheating. When used, they allowed steam pressure to go from the normal 600 psi to as much as 850 psi (Stewart, 2013).

Material condition Baker and Condition of Readiness II are maintained, and "degaussing is secured." Degaussing was a system of neutralizing a ship's magnetic signature by means of charged cables and coils running the length of the ship's hull or other methods in order to avoid exploding magnetic mines. The ship is darkened so that "the sons of Heaven"—a phrase used by Chinese and Japanese royalty to describe themselves but used by Harbison here to mean the Japanese in general—will not see them.

The final two lines of the poem offer an odd contrast to the typical desires of the writers. It seems likely that the lines are a bit of tongue-in-cheek satire. Harbison says they are "happy as a lark" and would rather be there "than in New York." Another example of the enduring sense of humor found in the deck log poems? Very likely.

Here's the poem:

Happy New Year!!
With little hilarity and practically no jive,
We here on the bridge ushered in '45.
No wine, no women, no nightclubs, no song,
Nothing but water as we go along.
Steaming in the Philippine Sea,
In company with T.G. [Task Group] 38.3.
Cruising disposition is 5 Roger,
Which means for us, very little bother.
ESSEX is guide and OTC [Officer in Tactical Command],
Steaming along in the Philippine Sea.
Standard speed at 18 knots,
Keeps the engine room happy and helps us lots.
Formation axis one zero zero true,
As we steam along on the ocean blue.
Were we in the States, we'd be raising a rumpus,
And not on course 295 true and per standard compass.
25 knots, 191 turns,
Keeps us sailing, but oh! the fuel that it burns.
Engine room gives us power on boilers three through eight,
They cut in superheat so we won't be late.
Material condition Baker assured,
Condition II maintained, degaussing secured.
Ship completely darkened, steaming as we be,
So the sons of Heaven, us, they no see.

So here we be, happy as a lark,
We'd rather be here, than in New York.
0020 Changed course right to 305 (T) pgc and psc. Slowed
to 22 knots, 166 rpm. Average rpm 169.4. Average steam 600 psi.
R.F. Harbison
Lieut., USNR

The Poet

Robert Fulton Harbison was born on January 16, 1921, in Imperial, California, to Ira Fulton Harbison and Gladys Annabel Gray. During Robert's early years, the family lived in National City where father Ira was a beloved public servant. In the early 1930s, with only an eighth-grade education, Ira became judge of the Police Court and eventually city judge in National City. The city's esteem for Harbison led to the eventual naming of a street and a school after him. The school's current incarnation is Ira Harbison Elementary School in the National School District.

Robert graduated from Sweetwater High School in 1938 and enrolled at San Diego State College. After two years at SDSC, he joined the U.S. Navy and spent his early training as an apprentice seaman on the USS *Wichita* (CA 45). After earning his commission as an ensign in early 1941, he boarded USS *Enterprise* (CV-6) where he would remain for over two years. Posted in fire control, Robert served during ten of *Enterprise*'s early campaigns, earning a Bronze Star, Navy Commendation Ribbon and a Presidential Unit Citation (*National City Star-News*, 1947). He rose to the rank of lieutenant while he was just 21 years old, a feat that few managed to accomplish. In a 1943 interview, Harbison claimed to have seen a Japanese aircraft only once during his time on *Enterprise* due to his damage control duties being below decks (*National City Star-News*, 1943). He served on USS *Ticonderoga* for over a year and was aboard for two of her World War II campaigns.

In the fall of 1946, Robert married Laurrine Mildred Berger of Froid, Montana. At the time, Robert was stationed in the Chief of Naval Operations Office in Washington, D.C. Laurrine was employed by the War Department (*Great Falls Tribune*, 1946). Robert eventually rose to the rank of commander and from May 16, 1957, to August 20, 1958, captained USS *Cone* (DD 866). He retired from the Naval Reserve in 1961. After retirement, he served as a teacher and school administrator in the La Mesa Spring Valley School District in California.

Harbison died on January 12, 2016, in Escondido, California, and is buried in the Fort Rosecrans National Cemetery, San Diego, California.

USS *Idaho*

Perdition to Our Axis Foes

USS *Idaho* (BB 42) in 1934, following modernization. NH60632 Courtesy of Naval History & Heritage Command.

The Ship

USS *Idaho* (BB 42) was a New Mexico–class dreadnaught battleship commissioned March 24, 1919. After a shakedown cruise in April of that year, she transported the president of Argentina from New York to Buenos Aires in July. The ensuing years saw a series of maneuvers, training exercises and ceremonies, including Fleet Reviews by President Wilson in 1919 and President Harding in 1923. While returning from exercises in the western Pacific in late 1925, *Idaho* carried the famous Naval airman Commander John Rodgers back to San Francisco from Hawaii after his failed attempt in a PN-9 flying boat to fly non-stop from California to Hawaii.

From September 1931 until October 1934, *Idaho* underwent an extensive overhaul and modernization at Norfolk Navy Yard; new turbines and boilers increased her speed to 22 knots. Her main battery turrets were modified. She was given increased firepower, improved armor and submarine protection, and a new bridge, including a flag bridge for the admiral and his staff.

With World War II approaching, *Idaho* participated in fleet tactics and gunnery exercises before arriving at Pearl Harbor on July 1, 1940. In June 1941, as the Battle of the Atlantic raged between Germany and the European allies, she was sent to Hampton Roads in Virginia to begin patrolling the East Coast in support of the Atlantic Neutrality Patrol.

In September, *Idaho* was sent to Iceland to protect forward bases and was still there on December 7 when the Japanese attacked Pearl Harbor. She then joined the Pacific Fleet and performed battle exercises between the West Coast and Pearl Harbor for most of 1942. From October to December of that year, she was regunned at Puget Sound Navy Yard, adding new anti-aircraft guns and other armament.

From 1943 through the remainder of the war, *Idaho* was active in the Pacific campaigns. She began in the Aleutians, where from April to August 1943, she participated as flagship of the force attacking Attu, giving artillery support to the invasion. In November, she joined the assault fleet headed for the Gilbert Islands, where she provided artillery and anti-aircraft support for the invasion of Makin Atoll. She remained in the Gilberts until December 5, then returned to Pearl Harbor.

Idaho remained busy throughout 1944, participating in campaigns in the Marshall Islands, Saipan in the Mariana Islands, Peleliu, Guam and the Philippines. Sandwiched between the Marshall Islands and Saipan, she was sent to New Ireland in Papua New Guinea for a diversionary bombardment. She returned to Bremerton, Washington, in October 1944 for repairs.

In January 1945, *Idaho* joined a battle group at Pearl Harbor, and from February 19 to March 7, she provided artillery support for the invasion of Iwo Jima. Two weeks later, as part of Rear Admiral Deyo's Gunfire and Covering Group, she served as flagship of Bombardment Unit 4 in the invasion of Okinawa. When the land assault began on April 1, Japanese air forces began furious suicide attacks. According to battle reports, the first attack on *Idaho* came at 0610 by a Japanese dive bomber, followed by another dive bomber attack at 0620. *Idaho* destroyed both planes. Over the next 11 days, she continued fighting off attacks and downing planes. On April 12, she performed heroically, downing five Japanese planes before receiving damage herself. The battle report for 1448 hours that day describes the action as follows: "While TF 54 was under attack by 'suicide' planes, USS *Idaho* (BB42) splashed two (2) 'Vals' and three (3) 'Kates.' All planes approached low over the water and pressed the attack" (USS *Idaho*, 1945). "Vals" was the nickname U.S. forces gave the Japanese Achai D3A dive bomber, and "Kate" referred to the Nakajima B5N torpedo bomber. At 1450, the battle report says that a "Kate" landed a bomb close enough to the ship to blow an 18-inch hole at the waterline, flooding several compartments and requiring counter-flooding to offset the list. The shock caused a steam leak in one of the engines, and shrapnel rendered one radar inoperative and limited the rotation of another. In addition to other minor damage, ten crewmen were superficially wounded.

Idaho returned to Guam for repairs in late April, then steamed back to Okinawa in late May. There she offered fire support until June 20, when she sailed for Leyte Gulf in the Philippines. Hostilities with Japan ceased on August 15, before *Idaho* saw further action. She arrived in Tokyo Bay on August 27, carrying occupation troops, and was present for the signing of the surrender on USS *Missouri* on September 2. She arrived back in Norfolk in October and was decommissioned eight months later, on July 3, 1946. She remained in the Reserve Fleet until being sold for scrap on November 24, 1947.

She received seven battle stars for her service in World War II.

Poem One

The deck log for January 1, 1942, was entered by Ensign E.B. Childs, USN. The Pearl Harbor attack had happened just three weeks earlier, and *Idaho* would be joining the Pacific Fleet later that month. She had just come from Iceland and was spending a brief time in dry dock at Portsmouth Naval Shipyard in Virginia. For the most part, Childs' short poem, only 12 lines of rhymed couplets, describes the activity in the shipyard.

An underlying sense of impatience pervades the first two lines as *Idaho* rests on keel blocks in the Yard, but Childs says, "the nation is at war." The ship is receiving all its services from shore. She is surrounded by ships of the Atlantic Fleet. The Senior Officer Present Afloat, the Commander of Battleship Division five, is ensconced on the battleship *New York* (BB 34). Like so many other midwatch poets, Childs praises the "Yard and district craft"—tugs, cranes, barges and rafts—as "the unsung workers of the Navy." The support craft were clearly appreciated by the combat crews.

The poem's final two lines exhibit the common optimism and confidence of many January 1942 deck log poems. We have allies. We will fight. We have nothing to fear. He closes with typical American brashness: "Perdition to our Axis foes, to all friends a Happy New Year."

Here is the poem:

Resting on the keel blocks in Dry Dock Number Four,
In Portsmouth Yard, Virginia, and the nation is at war.
Receiving all our services, water, phone, and steam,
From the people of the Navy Yard, whose kindness we esteem.
Present in the yard with us, they look so very neat,
Are units large and various of our Atlantic Fleet.
Commander Battleship Division Five, the S.O.P. Afloat,
Is located in U.S.S. New York, a rugged battle boat,
Also here to do the work, tug, crane, barge, and raft,

The unsung workers of the Navy, "Yard and district craft."
With friendly aid we'll fight the war, there is nothing we shall fear,
Perdition to our Axis foes, to all friends a Happy New Year.
E.B. Childs,
Ensign, U.S. Navy

The Poet

Earle Boucher Childs was born on March 30, 1918, in Brooklyn, New York. His mother, Gertrude Boucher Childs, was already a widow. His father, Earle Wayne Freed Childs, a U.S. Navy submariner, perished when the British sub on which he was an observer was rammed by a merchant ship on March 2, 1918. The ship misidentified the sub as a German U-boat. *The Courier News* referred to the newborn as "a posthumous child" (1918). The U.S. Navy awarded his father the Navy Cross "for exceptionally meritorious and distinguished service engaged in the important, exacting and hazardous submarine duty in the war zone" (Childs, Earl W. F.).

In 1920, Gertrude Childs sponsored the launch of a destroyer named after her late husband (USS *Childs*—DD 241). According to her obituary, she met naval officer Arthur Tenney Emerson at that ceremony (Gertrude Emerson). They were married aboard USS *Utah* in Naples, Italy, in December 1921 (*New York Times*, 1921). Emerson went on to be a short-term governor of American Samoa. Gertrude and Arthur had a son who also pursued a career in the U.S. Navy.

Midshipman Earle Boucher Childs from the 1940 Naval Academy Yearbook *Annapolis Lucky Bag*.

Following in his father's footsteps, Earle attended the U.S. Naval Academy. He graduated in 1940. His *Lucky Bag* entry described him as being most knowledgeable about all things naval. On April 11, 1942, he married Catherine Rita Henry, and they eventually had four daughters. After he served on USS *Idaho,* he became division commander of a group of five PT boats. His Navy career was cut short when a 500-pound Japanese bomb directly hit his unit, leading to the loss of his right leg. After retiring from the Navy, he became a real estate broker and a planner for National Steel and Shipbuilding Company. Active in his community, Childs held a Coronado, California, councilman position and was president of the Coronado Lions Club (Childs, Earl B., 2010).

Childs earned a reputation as an excellent builder of boats that measured in the 25-to-36-foot range. He built and sold several to Coronado residents. He served as Commodore of the Coronado Yacht Club. His grandson followed in his footsteps by attending the Naval Academy from 1988 to 1992 (Childs, Earl B., 2010).

Earle Childs died on August 2, 1966, in San Diego and was buried at the Fort Rosecrans National Cemetery.

Poem Two

The deck log poem from *Idaho* for January 1, 1946, entered by Lt. P.V. Kortkamp, USNR, consists of 32 lines of rhymed couplets, broken into eight four-line stanzas. His poem creates a bookend for the 1942 deck log poem. Ensign Childs in the earlier poem, three weeks after Pearl Harbor, seems anxious to get to the action. Kortkamp, four months after the surrender of Japan, calls the end of the war "a blissful state." Ensign Childs wrote the earlier poem while *Idaho* lay in Dry Dock Number Four at the Portsmouth Navy Yard in Virginia. Kortkamp writes his poem while *Idaho* again lies in Portsmouth Navy Yard, in berths seven and eight, with 12 lines holding the ship starboard side to the dock.

The war is over. No threat to the ship. No danger of attack. No imminent bad weather. No more Material Condition Yoke or Zebra, with battle stations manned and the watches on alert. *Idaho* is set to condition X-Ray, used in peacetime in port. The ship is secured, with power coming from the shore station, just as it was four years earlier when Ensign Childs wrote his poem. Senior Officer Present Afloat is located on USS *Midway*. When Kortkamp refers to the Atlantic Fleet, he adds a note, as Childs did in the earlier poem, about the Yard and District Craft.

Kortkamp calls the Iwo Jima campaign the previous year "dreary," but calls Okinawa, where the fleet experienced massive Japanese air attacks, including kamikaze, "frightening." And he complains that *Idaho* was credited with downing only nine planes, while he is sure they destroyed many more.

The last four stanzas of the poem list the mundane events of a midwatch shift. The ship is being dehumidified in preparation for going into the Inactive Fleet. At 0005, R.E. Snyder and D.L. Ritter come aboard absent over leave and are put on report, each becoming a prisoner at large on the ship. At 0030, Lt. Mountjoy, a "real good boy," leaves the ship for demobilization in San Francisco and civilian life. At 0300, Machinist's Mate 2nd Class Jones reports aboard from Shore Patrol after a "rugged" night. The two closing lines are a bit of "That's All Folks" and a Happy New Year wish.

Here is the poem:

The war is over, what a blissful state.
So the "Big I" occupies berths seven and eight,
In Norfolk Naval Shipyard, Portsmouth, Virginia,
Starboard side to dock, 12 lines hold her fast.

Wartime cruising conditions are o'er,
So modified condition "X-RAY" is in store.
Our boilers are secured, engineers on vacation,
Steam, power, water, and phones supplied by a shore station.

SOPA now rests with the U.S.S. MIDWAY,
She has seniority over quite an array
Of various units of the Atlantic Fleet,
District, harbor, and patrol craft quite neat.

1945 saw "Ida's" war burden lightening,
Only Iwo dreary, and Okinawa frightening.
On Jap planes were credited with only 9 hits,
But we feel sure we knocked many more to bits.

Now all our days of combat are done
And we're being de-humidified, what fun.
Soon we'll retire to the Inactive Fleet,
And leave the job for others to complete.

At 0005 two men reported aboard AOL [Absent Over Leave],
Both were placed on report, each is now a PAL [Prisoner at Large].
SNYDER, R.E. and RITTER, D. L., B Division both,
Are all engineers as slow as a sloth?

Demobilization has snatched a real good boy,
For at 0030 we detached Lieut. MOUNTJOY.
His points are up, to ComFive [Commander 5th Naval District] he goes,
For transportation to Frisco, and then civilian woes.

At 0300 Jones, MM2e, reported aboard with his shore patrol.
And although their duty had been rugged, reported "All is under control."
Nothing more to report in this first log of 46,
Except that the wish of "Happy New Year" always clicks.

P.V. KORTKAMP
Lieutenant, U.S.N.R.

The Poet

Paul VanArsdale Kortkamp was born in Alton, Illinois, on July 16, 1910, to Alfred Warren Kortkamp and Eva M. Otwell. His father was a Pentecostal minister in Moline, Illinois. Paul graduated from Alton High School, then attended Shurtleff College for two years. He graduated from University of Illinois with a degree in transportation. He married Georgia Martha Glisman on June 30, 1934, in Moline at the Moline Pentecostal Temple. His father officiated the service.

In the 1930s and into the early 1940s, Kortkamp worked for Dohrn Transfer Company, based in Rock Island, Illinois (the company still operates today), and Rock Island Motor Transit. In 1942, he took a position as district manager of the Office of Defense Transportation in Davenport, Iowa. His position involved the coordination of all truck lines in the area with a focus on gasoline, oil, tires and equipment during the war (*The Daily Times*, 1942).

By 1944, the war called for Kortkamp to have a more direct role in fighting the enemy. On February 8, 1944, he received a commission as a lieutenant j.g. in the Navy and went aboard USS *Idaho* to serve as a division and radar officer. After discharge from active duty in 1946, he was appointed to a position in the Moline–East Moline Naval Reserve Unit. In 1947, Kortkamp received an appointment as representative of the 9th Naval District for the Naval Reserve (*Rock Island Argus*, 1947). At the outset of the Korean War, he was recalled to active duty and spent time on the carrier USS *Midway* (CV 41) serving in the position of first lieutenant (*Rock Island Argus*, 1951). The first lieutenant on a ship is not a rank, but a position: He heads the Deck Department and is responsible for the ship's appearance, mooring and anchoring, underway replenishment and the like. On a carrier, it is a position of high responsibility.

Promoted to lieutenant commander in November 1952, he became commander of the Naval Reserve Training Center in McAlister, Oklahoma, and remained in that position until early 1955. He then was ordered aboard USS *General A.E. Anderson* (AP 111) to assume the position of first lieutenant (*The Daily Oklahoman*, 1955). After going back to civilian life, Kortkamp worked at Central Freight Line in Texas.

Paul V. Kortkamp died on January 1, 1986, 40 years to the day after he penned his midwatch poem on *Idaho*. He was buried at Fort Bliss National Cemetery in El Paso, Texas, with full military honors.

USS *Alabama*

Very Well Done

USS *Alabama* (BB 60) anchored in Casco Bay, Maine, circa December 1942. NH 57209 Courtesy of Naval History & Heritage Command.

The Ship

USS *Alabama* (BB 60) was a South Dakota–class battleship commissioned on August 16, 1942. After a shakedown cruise and operational training, she spent the first four months of her duty in a temporary assignment, alongside her sister ship *South Dakota* (BB 57), with the British Navy covering northern convoy routes supporting the invasion of Sicily. Detached from the British Home Fleet on August 1, 1943, she sailed for Norfolk for overhaul and repairs before being assigned to the U.S. Pacific Fleet. She arrived in the New Hebrides on September 14.

Over the next two years, *Alabama* participated in a laundry list of Pacific campaigns, spending most of her time screening fast carriers and providing bombardment support for landings. She was active in the assaults on the Gilbert Islands and the Marshall Islands. At Nauru in December 1943, she was part of the first Pacific gunfire strike carried out by that type of warship. In February 1944, she joined *Bunker Hill* (CV 17) in attacking Truk Island, the main Japanese naval base in the South Pacific.

Then on February 21, while repelling air attacks, the ship met with tragedy. According to the Action Report, Gun Mount Number 9 fired two five-inch rounds into Gun Mount Number 5, killing five men and wounding 11. The mounts were set on automatic fire mode, and because of the low elevation of the aircraft off the starboard beam and the ship turning right, the gun mounts went into the "stops," which cut off the firing mechanisms, though the mounts continued to follow the target. However, the crewman serving as gun-striker in Mount No. 9 bypassed the safety feature and released the clutch lever by hand on the mechanism, allowing the guns to fire. One shell pierced the rear plate of Mount No. 5 and exploded inside. A second shell nicked the shield and exploded outside the mount. The gun striker, a crewman with nine months experience at the job, told investigators he thought the guns were clear of the other mounts (USS *Alabama*, 1944).

In the Caroline Islands in March, *Alabama* was credited with downing one attacking enemy aircraft and assisting in downing another. In April, she screened *Enterprise* (CV 6) in campaigns in New Guinea and in June supported operations in the Marianas and participated in the Battle of the Philippine Sea. In that battle, she provided the first warning of a massive incoming air strike, allowing the carriers to scramble their aircraft and engage the enemy at a greater distance than otherwise would have occurred. In what became known as the Great Marianas Turkey Shoot, Vice Admiral Willis A. Lee recognized the key role the ship played, announcing to the fleet: "In the matter of reporting initial bogies, to *Iowa* well done, to *Alabama*, very well done."

In an October operation at Luzon, *Alabama* claimed three enemy aircraft downed and a fourth damaged. She supported operations against the Japanese Southern Force at Surigao Strait, then against Admiral Kurita's Center Force approaching San Bernardino Strait. Then, in the incident involving Task Force 34, she screened the fast carrier task force as it pursued the decoy Japanese Northern Fleet to Cape Engano. When news of the Center Force's surprise arrival off the island of Samar came, *Alabama* reversed course and steamed to aid the far outnumbered American force, Taffy 3, that confronted Kurita. The Japanese retreated before she arrived. In December, she was caught with the rest of Admiral Halsey's force in Typhoon Cobra, where she experienced rolls of 30 degrees. Both her Kingfisher planes were destroyed. She also received minor structural damage.

In May 1945, *Alabama* supported the landings at Okinawa, where she downed two enemy aircraft and assisted in downing two more. Throughout July, she participated in strikes on the Japanese homeland and in the first night bombardment of six major industrial plants near Tokyo. During that action, she embarked a special guest, Rear Admiral Richard E. Byrd, the famous polar explorer, as an observer. After the capitulation of Japan, she served in the occupation force and screened carriers conducting reconnaissance flights to locate prisoner of war camps. She then helped return servicemen and servicewomen to the U.S. in Operation Magic Carpet.

Alabama was decommissioned on January 9, 1947, in Seattle and struck from the Naval Vessel Register on June 1, 1962. She was given to the state of Alabama in 1964 and towed to her permanent berth in Mobile.

She received nine battle stars for her service in World War II.

Poem One

The crew of *Alabama* left three deck log poems during her war service. The log below was entered on January 1, 1944, by Lt. Daniel B. Elmore, USNR. The poem consists of 26 lines of rhymed couplets, and it is one of the most accomplished poems technically in all the deck log entries. Elmore maintains an almost perfect waltz-like rhythm (in poetry studies known as *anapestic* rhythm), which is a difficult rhythm to manage. He handles the rhythm and rhyme beautifully, including several variations worthy of a professional poet.

The ship is moored in Havana Harbor on the island of Efate in the New Hebrides, where a seaplane base had been built by Seabees in 1942. She has been escorting carriers and will head to Pearl Harbor for repairs in a few days. Lt. Elmore provides much of the expected deck log detail, giving the depth, length of chain, bearings by beacon, material condition of readiness Yoke, boilers in use, generators, location of SOPA and names of ships surrounding *Alabama*.

Elmore weaves into the second half of the poem a bit of the droll American humor that appears throughout the deck logs. He says that the oil eaten up by the auxiliary boiler that's steaming "keeps the taxpayers screaming." He refers to USS *South Dakota*, which is her sister ship, as "the too famous Battleship 'X.'" He closes the poem with a tongue-in-cheek observation: "There are other small craft which are many and various, / Not to list them is handy and really not serious."

Here's the poem:

At Havana, our harbor this hour so late,
  At anchor we're sitting in berth number eight.
Near the Isle of Efate in New Hebrides,
  A bottom of sand our port anchor doth seize.
The water is deep, forty fathoms at best,
  And of chain ninety fathoms has kept us at rest.
Of beacons for fixes we have only three;
  (The bearings are true to the nearest degree).

It's one twenty-nine to the beacon marked "E,"
While the beacon marked "Z" cuts at zero one three.
At zero eight one is light "F" at this hour,
While at one eighty-six stands the old signal tower.
The book says we're darkened (that's really a joke!)
But for hatches and doors we have modified "Yoke."
For auxiliary use boiler one we are steaming,
And the oil that it eats keeps the taxpayers screaming.
For the juice that we use in our many small stators,
We've pulled from the hat "one" and "two" generators.
The ships here at anchor are many and fine,
And our S.O.P.A. now is ComBatDiv Nine [Commander Battleship Div];
He's embarked in the too famous Battleship "X,"
(U.S.S. South Dakota whose rhyme is complex).
INDIANA, MEDUSA, and old KANKAKEE,
MASSACHUSETTS, ALDEBARAN, STACK we can see.
There are other small craft which are many and various,
Not to list them is handy and really not serious.

Daniel B. Elmore
Lieut. USNR

Poet One

Daniel Bruce Elmore was born on July 9, 1916, to Wilbur Bruce Elmore and Annette Maud Wright in King, Washington. His father, a prominent surgeon in the Northwest, served in the U.S. Navy Medical Corps. Daniel graduated from the prestigious Brentwood Preparatory School in Canada and the University of Washington. When President Roosevelt announced the U.S. Navy's V7 Program to train junior officers, Daniel was one of the first to volunteer in 1940. His training prior to being commissioned an ensign occurred aboard USS *Wyoming* (BB 32) and USS *Illinois* (BB 7, AKA USS *Prairie State*).

In 1941, Elmore received orders to board USS *Nevada*. He was aboard *Nevada* during the Japanese raid on Pearl Harbor. His family received notice shortly thereafter that he was among those killed in action during the attack (*The Spokesman-Review*, 1941). On December 12, requiem high mass was sung for Daniel at St. Joseph's but less than a week later, the family was notified that the death notice was in error. Elmore's mother exclaimed, "That's the greatest thing in the world for me. I just can't express myself" (*Times Colonist*, 1941). This was not the first time Elmore raised concern for the family due to maritime events. In 1935, he and a friend sailed on a yacht that failed to arrive at its destination on time. For a while, no one knew what had happened to the yacht. But the pair showed up after being delayed by a course change (*Nanaimo Daily News*, 1935).

Elmore remained on *Nevada* until 1942 when he transferred to *Alabama* and eventually to USS *Indiana* (BB 38). In 1946, he was deployed to a new cruiser for commissioning: USS *Oregon City* (CA 122). By the late 1940s, Elmore began many years of service at the Department of the Navy in a variety of administrative roles.

On November 18, 2011, Daniel Bruce Elmore died in McLean, Virginia. His obituary published in *The Washington Post* states, "His wish to return to the sea will be fulfilled on a US Navy Ship, accompanied by men and women of our armed forces deployed to defend our country" (*Washington Post,* 2011).

Poem Two

The deck log below was entered on January 1, 1945, by Lt. E.R. Blair, Jr., USN. The ship is nearing Pearl Harbor on her way to Puget Sound for overhaul. She has just come from the attack on Luzon, after which she survived Typhoon Cobra, though with some damage. The poem consists of 20 lines of rhymed couplets without stanza breaks. The first line of the poem claims a holiday mood on board, but in fact the mood of the poem is solemn, with no humor and only a couple of supplementary comments to the business at hand. Most of the poem simply presents the required information—ship formation, course, zigzag, speed, boilers, material condition, condition of readiness and the names of other ships.

Lines three and four provide one of the side comments when Lt. Blair plays with the traditional idea of the full moon being associated with love. (Their formation is three-love.) Line six reflects the reality that the constant change of speed and direction in a zigzag pattern could be a thorn in the OOD's flesh. The closest Blair gets to humor occurs in lines 15 and 16, where he uses the phrase "from Natchez to Memphis," taken from popular songs (possibly by blues singer Robert Johnson in the 1930s) to refer to the ships "NEW ORLEANS and MOBILE abaft our beams."

The poem closes with what seems to be a satirical comment on the lucky bluejackets working at a desk, who will ultimately read the deck log: "Happy New Year gentle reader at your desk in the bureau, / From your colleagues who've fought in Nauru and Majuro."

Here's the poem:

In a holiday mood on this tropic sea
We're steaming for Pearl in thirty-point-three.
The ships are disposed in formation three-love,
Appropriate surely, a full moon's above.
Both axis [center line of formation] and course are nought seven seven
The zigzag's two five, not a watchstander's heaven.
Though standard speed's fifteen, we're doing three more,
With eight boilers available, we're using but four.
Two, four, five and seven are the boilers on the line,
ALABAMA is guide, and she's keeping station fine.
Her skipper embarked is the OTC [Officer in Tactical Command]
And of thirty-point-three he is CTG [Commander Task Group].
Yoke's the condition in doors and hatches,
And III the gun watch, dozing only in snatches.
Though "from Natchez to Memphis" is for song and dance teams,
We've NEW ORLEANS and MOBILE abaft our beams.
Our protection, we hope, from a Nip submarine

Lies in OAKLAND, BROWN, and COWELL in a forward, bent screen.
Happy New Year gentle reader at your desk in the bureau,
From your colleagues who've fought in Nauru and Majuro.
E.R. Blair, Jr.
Lieut., USN

Poet Two

Edward Russell Blair, Jr., was born on April 6, 1916, to Edward Russell Blair, Sr., and Sam Berry in Arkansas. He attended Central High School in Memphis, graduating in 1935. He received an appointment to the Naval Academy at Annapolis in 1937. While there, Blair, who was dubbed "Flash," was a sports encyclopedia. His *Lucky Bag* entry stated, "He can tell you the name and laundry number of past or present great athletes." He played on the basketball team but mainly excelled in tennis. He captained the Academy tennis team in his final year.

Upon his graduation from the Academy in 1941, Blair received orders to board USS *California* (BB 44). Just a few months later, he was aboard that ship when the Japanese attacked Pearl Harbor. When general quarters was called on December 7, Blair was still undressed in the forward bunk room. He left the room just as the first torpedo hit *California*. He climbed up to one of the gun directors to assist targeting of the attacking planes, but it was inoperable. Noticing that the .50 caliber machine gunners below him were running out of their "ready" ammunition, he decided to take a group of ten men below to retrieve ammo to fend off the planes. Blair divided up the munitions and sent the men to specific machine gun locations. Eventually, he assisted other sailors in loading gun belts while on deck. He abandoned ship when that order came and swam to shore (Pearl Harbor Survivor Accounts).

After serving on *California*, Blair transferred to USS *Alabama*. On January 24, 1943, he married Mary Helen Rowe of Tutwiler, Mississippi. After serving on *Alabama*, Blair occupied a variety of positions including captain of USS *Waller* (DD 466) from 1952 to 1954. He retired from the Navy in 1961 at the rank of commander. After retirement, he maintained a law practice in Tupelo, Mississippi, until his death on June 4, 1992. He is buried in Oxford Memorial Cemetery in Oxford, Mississippi.

Poem Three

The log below was entered on January 1, 1946, by Lt. j.g. A.W. Kelly, USNR. The poem consists of 44 lines of rhymed couplets without stanza breaks. *Alabama* is moored at San Pedro Bay, California, where she has been for two months after Magic Carpet duty and where she will remain for two months more before moving to Puget Sound for decommissioning and overhaul. Surrender of the Japanese empire occurred four months earlier, and most of the combatants have returned.

Lt. Kelly dutifully offers the necessary content of a deck log—water depth, length of chain, ship's bearings on various points, material condition, boilers and generators in use, and a long list of other ships present. There are only four deviations from the standard. Lines 25 and 26 contribute a creative and humorous rhyme—"if I hadda" with "the NEVADA." Line 28 expresses the only real reference to peace in the hope that the carriers (flat tops) will never be needed again. In line 41, Kelly can't resist a bit of bragging on his ship when he says that all the others dote on *Alabama*. The poem closes by wishing everyone luck in the coming New Year.

Midshipman Edward Russell Blair, Jr., from the 1941 Naval Academy Yearbook *Annapolis Lucky Bag*.

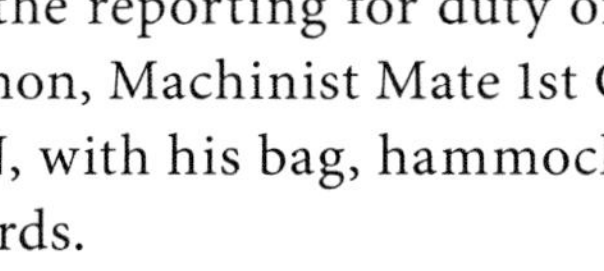

Following the poem, Kelly adds a brief paragraph registering the reporting for duty of B.E. Sigmon, Machinist Mate 1st Class, USN, with his bag, hammock and records.

Here's the poem:

Anchored at last in San Pedro Bay,
In berth 21, so the Navigator does say,
7–1/2 fathoms of water neath our bow is the flood,
On 45 fathoms chain rests the port anchor in mud.
The following bearings mark our anchorage berth,
Of excellent landmarks there's surely no dearth,
In the East toward the sun is East Breakwater Light,
Bearing 090.2°T and it fits the fix light.
To Southwest is a bright light just two miles away,
Bearing 238°T, it's the Harbor Light of L.A.
Down to the South on the breakwater's back,
Bearing 167°T is a ramshackled shack.
And off to the North lettle more than a hole,
Bearing 340.2°T is the number two mole.
In our doors and our hatches our condition is modified Yoke
For the setting in port, flooding's no joke
Of the eight boilers we have, only number four is in use,
And generators three and four take lots of abuse.
That about finishes the dope on this boat.
Now let's look at the others who are here in the moat.
The battleships anchored in the harbor are six,

Enough guns to make the foe look sick.
There's IOWA, WISCONSIN, SOUTH DAKOTA,
TEXAS and WEST VIRGINIA,
And the sixth is one I wouldn't rhyme if I hadda;
So pardon the grammar and let's name the NEVADA.
Our carrier force is impressive indeed,
Let's hope for our flat tops, we'll never have need.
There's INTREPID, POINT CRUZ, CAPE GLOUCESTER, and BENNINGTON,
SHAMROCK BAY, KODASHAM BAY, and LEXINGTON.
The other two flat tops anchored a distance away,
Are the MANILA and COMMENCEMENT both suffixed by Bay.
The last to be named is a long list of cruisers,
Both heavy and light, all powerful bruisers:
CAMBERRA, CHICAGO, MINNEAPOLIS, DULUTH,
And seven more I'll tell you the truth:
VICKSBURG, MIAMI, TOPEKA, ASTORIA,
AMSTERDAM, DAYTON, and last the ATLANTA.
And with us we have all our small friends of the sea,
Various destroyers, small craft, and ships of auxiliary.
And in ALABAMA, on whom all others dote,
Is ComBatDiv [Commander Battle Div] Three, Senior Officer Present Afloat.
And this ends our poem on a mote of good cheer,
We wish you all luck in the coming New Year.

0030 pursuant to orders of Commanding Officer, U.S. Receiving Center, Terminal Island, San Pedro, California, dated 31 December 1945, authority Pers 6303-VIJ-1 P16–3/MM of 27 June 1945 Sigmon, B.E., MM1c, USN, 552 52 86 reported aboard for duty with bag, hammock, and records.

A.W. Kelley
Lt (j.g.), USNR

Poet Three

Arthur Wilson Kelley was born on November 21, 1922, to George Washington Kelley and Fannie Obenour in Moon Run, Pennsylvania. He graduated from Westminster College in 1943 with a bachelor's degree in chemistry. Shortly thereafter, he earned his commission as an ensign in the U.S. Naval Reserve and was posted to USS *Alabama*.

On November 29, 1945, while home on leave, Kelley married M. Lois Keiser at her parents' home in Point Marion, Pennsylvania. He returned to *Alabama* to complete his service the following year.

In 1950, Kelley graduated from the University of Pittsburgh School of Medicine. He opened a practice near Point Marion in 1951. After several years of practice, he moved to Morgantown, West Virginia. He practiced medicine at Mileground Medical Center until his retirement in 1989.

Arthur Wilson Kelley died on June 1, 2010, in Morgantown, West Virginia, and is buried in the Pleasant Hill Cemetery.

USS *Enterprise*

The Big E

USS *Enterprise* (CV 6) en route to Pearl Harbor on October 8, 1939. Photographed from USS *Minneapolis* (CA-36). National Archives photo #80-G-13554.

The Ship

USS *Enterprise* (CV 6), the seventh U.S. Navy vessel of that name, was a Yorktown-class carrier commissioned on May 12, 1938. After her shakedown cruise and brief service in the Atlantic and Caribbean, she was assigned to the Pacific Fleet in 1939. In the early days, not everyone saw the grandeur of the ship. A USS *California* (BB 44) radioman on board said she rolled arthritically, adding

> the flattop reminded me of a huge but decrepit old man with an entourage of bodyguards. If some seer had told me then that the *Enterprise* would steam to glory on one of the most brilliant combat records of any ship in the history of the navy, I would have given him the pitying smile one reserves for fools. From where I stood, it looked like she might have trouble reaching the West Coast [Evans, 2017].

Enterprise spent most of the next two years operating between the West Coast and Hawaii in exercises and maneuvers. In the summer of 1940, she took part in the filming of the Warner Brothers movie *Dive Bomber*, starring Errol Flynn. The excitement of the crew for the two-day filming is wryly noted in a deck log for July 17: "Making movies, no absentees" (Naval History and Heritage Command, 1940).

The ship narrowly missed being in Pearl Harbor when the Japanese attacked on December 7, 1941. In the last days of November, Admiral Halsey detached a small convoy, including *Enterprise*, from Pearl Harbor to carry a dozen Wildcat aircraft to Wake Island. On December 5, the planes departed the carrier for Wake, and she turned back for Pearl. Heavy weather for the next two days slowed her return, and though they had been due back Sunday morning, a mishap between a destroyer in the group and the cruiser *Northampton* on Saturday delayed them. The group arrived off Oahu early on December 7. Halsey received word of the attack on Pearl a little after 0800 and launched Wildcats to fly Combat Air Patrol. Though he ordered the ship's bombers prepared for an attack on Japanese ships, it was not until 1700 that a reported sighting occurred south of the islands. *Enterprise* pursued, launching Devastators, Dauntlesses and Wildcats, but the enemy could not be found, Admiral Nagumo's carriers having fled north. According to Ian Toll, had Halsey been able to engage Nagumo, the ship would likely have been lost to the Japanese superiority in numbers and experience. *Enterprise* accomplished the first U.S. Naval night recovery of the war, turning on her searchlights to aid the returning planes (Toll, 2012, p. 40).

With the water covered in oil and fires still burning, *Enterprise*, low on fuel, entered Pearl Harbor on December 8. She hastily refueled and brought provisions and ammunition aboard, then left the harbor the next day, fearful of another attack.

On February 1, 1942, she participated in attacks on the Gilbert and Marshall Islands. Commander Thomas P. Jeter, *Enterprise*'s executive officer, wrote the following verse on the ship's plan of the day: "An eye for an eye, / A tooth for a tooth, / This Sunday it's our turn to shoot. / —Remember Pearl Harbor." During a Japanese counterattack on the ship, a Japanese Mitsubishi crashed on the flight deck, causing some surface damage and damaging a nearby Dauntless. For the crew of the "Big E," it was full steam ahead from this point forward: The ship participated in more major actions of the war than any other United States ship and became the most decorated U.S. ship of the war.

On April 18, 1942, she was part of the daring Doolittle Raid, the U.S. attack on Tokyo and other major Japanese cities, led by Lt. Col. James H. Doolittle, who led a squadron of 16 B-25 bombers that lifted off from the carrier *Yorktown*. All of

Yorktown's fighters were stowed below decks to make room for the bombers topside, so fighters from *Enterprise* provided protection and reconnaissance. As soon as the B-25s were clear of the task force, the ships headed east at flank speed and made a clean getaway.

From June 4 to 7, *Enterprise* participated in the decisive Battle of Midway, in which the carrier *Yorktown* was sunk. Though *Enterprise* suffered losses to her air group, her planes sank the Japanese carrier *Kaga*, and *Enterprise* was not damaged. In August, she supported the Guadalcanal Campaign and the Battle of the Eastern Solomons. On August 24, she suffered significant damage when 30 planes attacked and she was hit by three bombs; a fourth detonated 12 feet off the port quarter. According to the war damage report, the first hit was from a 1000-pound bomb that detonated between the second and third decks, blowing 24-foot craters in both decks. The second deck bulged up across the entire width of the ship, and both decks were badly distorted. Adjacent areas were destroyed, including the brig, and the starboard section was flooded. Damaged fire lines made it difficult to fight the multiple fires. A second bomb, 500 pounds, penetrated the flight deck and detonated, exploding 5" 38-caliber ammunition, causing fierce fires in the gun mounts and killing 38 men. The third bomb, also 500 pounds, blew a ten-foot hole in the flight deck. The near-miss on the port side lifted the after section of the ship two to three feet, but the hull was not punctured. Steering problems resulted, and when her rudder jammed in a full right position, it nearly led to a catastrophic collision. The attacks resulted in 74 killed and 95 wounded. In September, she headed to Pearl Harbor for repairs and re-gunning.

On October 26, at the Battle of the Santa Cruz Islands, the carrier *Hornet* was severely damaged, but *Enterprise* escaped into a rain squall. When she emerged, a swarm of Japanese aircraft attacked her. American Wildcats and devastating anti-aircraft fire from the battleship *South Dakota* attempted to protect her, but she was struck and severely damaged by two bombs which killed 44 and wounded 75 crewmen. Japanese aircraft continued to attack *Enterprise*, and she avoided an estimated nine torpedoes by making desperate turns. After the battle, during which *Hornet* was sunk, *Enterprise* was withdrawn to Noumea for repairs. She was the only U.S. carrier left in the South Pacific Fleet.

After repairs and further training, she participated in the Battle of Rennell Island, after which she operated for three months in the Solomon Islands. While she was moored in Pearl Harbor Navy Yard for repairs in May, Admiral Nimitz presented her the Presidential Unit Citation. From July to September, she received a much-needed overhaul at Puget Sound Navy Yard. In November, she participated in the occupation of the Gilbert Islands, followed by the Marshall Islands Campaign in January 1944. From there, she supported the attack on Truk Lagoon and other islands in the Carolines. She spent most of April supporting the New Guinea Campaign and then in June moved to support Operation Forager, the invasion of the Marianas. During the invasion of Saipan on June 15, accidental hits from friendly fire killed one crewman and wounded 26.

During the Marianas Campaign, Cmdr. William R. Kane, also known as "Killer" Kane, who commanded Fighting Squadron 10 (the "Grim Reapers") on *Enterprise*, was shot down, possibly by friendly anti-aircraft fire. Kane was rescued and returned to *Enterprise* by USS *Patterson* (DD 392). According to *Patterson*'s deck logs, at 1425 on June 16, 1944, the ship "Transferred Commander W.R. Kane to *Enterprise* via breeches buoy" (USS *Patterson* 1944). Legend has it that before the transfer, the OOD on *Patterson* asked, "How much ice cream is Killer Kane worth?" Since carriers had ice cream makers and destroyers typically did not, it was common for carriers to transfer ice cream to destroyers that repatriated downed flyers.

On June 19, *Enterprise* was one of four U.S. carriers participating in the Battle of the Philippine Sea, the "Great Marianas Turkey Shoot," where U.S. fighters and bombers sank three Japanese carriers and decimated Japanese air power. She continued to support the Saipan invasion into July; beginning in late August, she supported various Pacific Island campaigns, including Palau, Luzon and the Battle of Peleliu. She then participated in raids on Okinawa and the Ryukyus before heading for Leyte on October 7. Over the next couple of weeks, she supported raids on Okinawa, Formosa and Luzon.

After supporting the U.S. Army landings on Leyte on October 20, *Enterprise* participated in the Battle of Leyte Gulf. She first supported the Battle of the Sibuyan

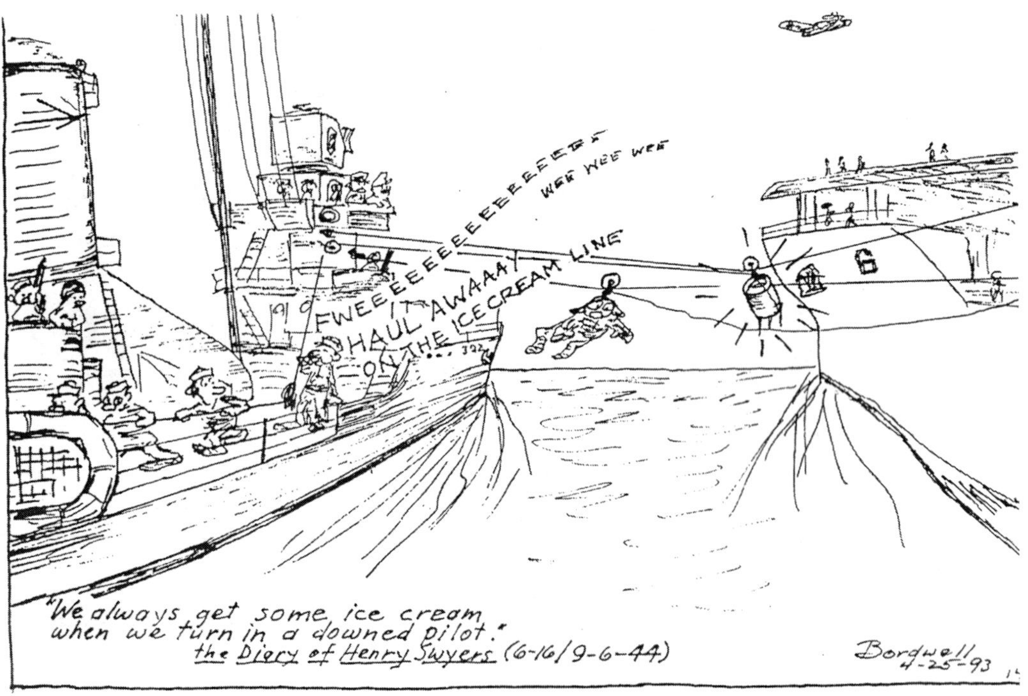

Artist Andy Bordwell's cartoon depicting transfer of William R. Kane (Killer Kane) from USS *Patterson* (DD 392) to USS *Enterprise* (CV 6). From *The USS Patterson DD 392: Shipmates and Memories* (1994).

Sea against the Japanese Center Force as well as sending aircraft against the Japanese Southern Force. The following day, she sailed with Task Force 34 as part of Halsey's Third Fleet, pursuing the decoy Japanese Northern Fleet, and participated in the Battle off Cape Engano. In December, she had her propellers replaced at Pearl Harbor, then returned to the Philippines on Christmas Eve.

Enterprise was active in the landing on Iwo Jima in late February and early March 1945 and then took part in Operation Iceberg, the invasion of Okinawa. At Okinawa on March 18, a 550-pound bomb dropped midship bounced and ricocheted, ending up on the deck. It was a dud, but it had killed one man and wounded two more. Two days later, three near-misses exploded off the starboard side, port side and stern, knocking out the starboard steering. As other ships opened fire on the Japanese planes, two five-inch rounds exploded over *Enterprise*, killing two men and starting a small fire in the ammunition of Gun Mount 6. Fragments from the first shell ruptured fuel tanks on two Hellcats. The burning fuel spread across the deck, igniting two more aircraft and setting off 40mm and 50-caliber ammunition stacked on the deck. Primary flight control, the main communication office, radio central and CIC all had to be evacuated because of thick smoke until the ship could be turned so that wind cleared smoke and heat from those areas. Fire control and repair parties worked amid exploding ammunition and continued attacks, and the fires were controlled within 35 minutes. On March 22, she retired to Ulithi for repairs.

Enterprise returned to Okinawa the second week of April, just in time for a series of ten massive Japanese kamikaze attacks. On April 11, a Zeke struck the port side, damaging two-gun mounts and sliding off the deck into the sea. But the Zeke's engine careened off the ship's side at the waterline, opening a two-foot hole. The Zeke's bomb detonated beneath the ship, causing significant structural damage and rapid flooding of inboard tanks. A little more than an hour later, another Japanese plane crashed into the water 50 feet off the starboard bow. Its bomb exploded, throwing one of the plane's wings onto the flight deck. After the battle, the crew hung the wing on the quarterdeck as a trophy. That night, an Avenger returning from a mission crash-landed on the deck, destroying four Hellcats and starting another fire, which was quickly extinguished.

Early on the morning of May 14, *Enterprise* again took a direct hit by a kamikaze Zeke. Though it was the last wound of the war for *Enterprise*, it was nearly mortal. The Zeke punched a 12- by 20-foot hole in the flight deck, and the bomb penetrated the second deck before exploding, causing extensive damage and igniting a large fire. The explosion hurled the forward elevator into the air and catapulted three quarters of the decking 400 feet above the ship and into the sea. The blast killed 13 and wounded 68, but *Enterprise* remained in formation and continued to fight off enemy aircraft. After the battle, she steamed for Puget Sound, stopping at Ulithi and Pearl. She finally moored at Port Townsend and then went to dry dock for repairs and overhaul. She was still there in August when the news came of Japan's surrender.

After the war, *Enterprise* participated in Operation Magic Carpet, transporting over 10,000 veterans back to the U.S. in her final service to the country. On November 1, President Truman approved a letter recommending that *Enterprise* be preserved as a historic ship in the U.S. Navy. She was decommissioned on February 17, 1947, and in October 1952 was reclassified to an attack aircraft carrier (CVA 6). The following year, she was again reclassified to an anti-submarine support aircraft carrier (CVS 6). Fourteen hundred of those who had served on *Enterprise* formed the Enterprise Association, attempting to save the ship from being scrapped. Admiral Halsey led the organization for a while, and in 1957 the 85th Congress passed a law authorizing her establishment as a national memorial. Despite these ongoing efforts, in the end significant difficulties with the project and inadequate funding caused her to be stricken from the Naval List of Vessels in 1956 and sold for scrap in 1958.

The Naval Aviation Museum in Pensacola has had a permanent *Enterprise* exhibit since 1984, housing artifacts, photos and other items. The stern nameplate of the ship is displayed at a little league park in River Vale, New Jersey. The ship's bell resides at the U.S. Naval Academy and is rung after victories over West Point.

Enterprise was awarded the Presidential Unit Citation and received the Navy Unit Commendation and 20 battle stars for her service in World War II.

The Poem

The following deck log was entered on January 1, 1946, by Ensign E.J. Adams, USN, four months after the signing of the surrender by Japan. The poem consists of 48 lines of rhymed couplets broken into stanzas of varying lengths, from two to six lines. It seems appropriate that the first four lines reflect on the harrowing year the ship has just endured. She is beat up and patched and barely survived. The ship is moored in New York Harbor preparing to leave for the Azores to bring back another load of war-weary veterans. It will be her final voyage of Operation Magic Carpet, and she will bring back 3,557 personnel, including 212 WACs, arriving again in New York on January 17. The next day, January 18, she will enter the Naval Shipyard for deactivation.

As Ensign Adams writes the log, *Enterprise* is refueling, laying in stores, and bringing all the crew back aboard from shore leave by 0400 so the ship can depart by 1400 hours. Adams says the ship is securely moored by spring lines (restraining from two directions) and breast lines (from only one direction) of strong manila rope and wire. The number one boiler is providing steam, and water is being supplied from the dock.

The Senior Officer Present Afloat is aboard the battleship USS *Missouri* (BB 63), "the old Missou," who had entered the war in January 1945, and was honored as the site of the Japanese signing of surrender. Adams hints at the rapid decommissioning process of ships and men when he says that ships are "anchored all over the place," more ships than slips to hold them, and that the men who came on them "have now flown the coop." At 0154 the fueling is complete, "the fuel's all below / Some twenty five thousand barrels or so," and the weather is clear and cold. In the closing lines, though the men standing watch pound their feet and their ears to stay warm, they look forward to a Happy New Year—the first New Year celebrated in peacetime since January 1941.

Here's the poem:

The Big E in the year forty five
Fought the war and just barely survived,
A bit beat up and patched up too,
She somehow managed to struggle on thru

To find herself on New Year's Eve
In New York Harbor preparing to leave

For Azorean waters and GI Joes
Who wait for passage in awful throes

Of longing and some little despair
Since during the holidays they were put there.

We're topping off fueling and laying in stores
And bringing the crew back from all out doors,
By zero four hundred this New Years day
So by fourteen hundred we can head out the bay
In compliance with CNO's [Chief of Naval Operations]
message this date,
Comply says CINCLANT [Commander in Chief Atlantic Fleet]
and comply we do make.
The ship is made fast by springs and four breasts
Eight manilas two wires hold us very close to, lest
A foul wind or tide carry us so
Before the Captain gives the word to "let go"

The number one boiler is cooking with steam
Supplying the power to cook up the beans
The fresh water's no problem along side this lock
We're taking our share right from the dock.

The old Missou is S-O-P-A
And probably will be for many a day
With the Cruisers and BatShips she's in for a spell
To enjoy the leave we've been promised so well.

The harbor is filled with a lot of new ships
Who've anchored all over the place, with no slips
To take them, they lay in a loop
And the crew that brought them has now flown the coop.

The Captain's aboard and the full duty crew
As well as the officers of old Section Two
The Navigator's back from a very short leave,
And the rest of the ship will be ready to heave

In on the lines by fourteen hundred today,
At least that's what it says in our plan of the day.

At one fifty four the fuel's all below,
Some twenty five thousand barrels or so.
The draft's twenty nine feet three by the stern,
We acquired a two foot drag, so we learn.

The weather is clear and somewhat cold
The front has passed, clear weather's foretold

And so this starts out the year Forty Six,
While the crew finds out what makes Gotham tick,
The watch aboard pounds their feet or their ear
And looks forward to a Happy New Year.
E.J. Adams
Ensign, U.S.N.

The Poet

Emil "E.J." John Adams was born on August 11, 1923, in Northampton, Massachusetts, to John Adams, Sr. (aka John Adamec) and Kristina Duga. The Adamses emigrated to the U.S. from Eastern Europe, settled in Massachusetts, and began farming.

Three of the Adams boys served in the Navy during World War II. Edward was an Aviation Machinist's Mate. Samuel attended the U.S. Naval Academy at Annapolis and became a Naval aviator. Samuel distinguished himself in air action near New Guinea and at the Battle of the Coral Sea. During the Battle of Midway, he was lost and presumed dead in 1942. For his service, he received three Navy Crosses and an Air Medal. Emil also attended the Naval Academy and graduated in the Class of 1946. Eventually becoming a Naval aviator, he served in Fighting Squadron 144 while aboard USS *Boxer* (CVS 21) in the 1950s. During his career, he served during several cruises aboard aircraft carriers in the Far East and the Mediterranean. He flew the following aircraft: F6F Hellcat, F8F Bearcat, F4U Corsair, F2H Banshee and F9F Panther. During his career, he amassed over 3,500 flight hours and over 200 arrested carrier landings (Adams, no date).

Midshipman Emil John "E.J." Adams from the 1946 Naval Academy Yearbook *Annapolis Lucky Bag*.

Adams retired from the Navy at the rank of commander in August 1967 with 25 years of service. He then took a position at Pratt & Whitney Aircraft Corporation as a consultant on jet engine design. In the 1970s, he became a branch manager for the American Savings Bank in Glastonbury, Connecticut, from which he retired in 1976.

Emil John Adams died on March 20, 2017, in Glastonbury at the age of 93 (Emil J. Adams, Obituary).

Addendum

After reading the deck log poem written by Ensign Adams, his daughter Kris, a singer and songwriter, wrote a delightful poetic supplement to her father's biography, using internal rhyme in most of the lines. As with all the other family members of midwatch verse writers, Kris knew nothing of the poem her father had written and was delighted to read it. Connecting with family member of the sailor poets in *Midwatch in Verse* was for the authors the most fulfilling part of the project, and the responses to the poems by fathers, grandfathers and uncles was very rewarding.

Here is Kris' poetic tribute to her father:

Ode to E.J. Adams

He was born on a farm near Northampton's tobacco barns
The last in a crew of a Slovakian brew
For his father came west to make their lives best.

Working the land, they all gave a hand
Tending the soil that they all had to toil
In this their new country, they did not go hungry.

The war was upon them, it caused a great mayhem
And his brother named Sam defended the land.

One day in June, flying over the Midway
He spotted the last ship and radioed her way
She suffered much damage out there on the sea
And for this heroic flight, Sam was awarded for his bravery.

This was the story that brought the family much glory
And so, as a lad, this dream E.J. had,
To follow his brother, if he had his druthers.

He studied hard in school for he was no fool
He came second in line when it was time
To enter the academy and for this he was happy.

Having graduated school early, he started his service
Not flying yet, and boy, he was nervous
An ensign was he and in January
Set sail for the Azores for what they would carry
To bring back the soldiers, heavy weight on their shoulders.

And thus, it began, his post in the Navy
And a long, fruitful life, its bounty had he.
—Kris Adams

USS *Huse*

The Hunter Killer

USS *Huse* (DD 145) in harbor, circa the 1950s. NH 82337-KN Courtesy of Naval History & Heritage Command.

The Ship

USS *Huse* (DE 145) was commissioned in August 1943, and during the rest of 1943 and early 1944, she escorted convoys to Europe and Africa. In March 1944, she teamed up with several other destroyer escorts, destroyers and the escort carrier USS *Croatan* (CVE 25) to locate and attack German U-boats. Escort carriers were smaller, slower, and carried fewer planes than their larger cousins, but they were very effective in this capacity. This hunter-killer mission began to take a toll on the German Kriegsmarine due to the ability of carrier planes to sight subs and direct attacks on them. Improved sonar and radar also helped the Allies more easily locate subs underwater and on the surface.

On April 7, 1944, the German U-boat U-856 came under attack by USS *Boyle* (DD 600), USS *Champlin* (DD 601) and *Huse*. After several depth charge runs, the sub surfaced and began to engage the ships with deck gun fire. The ships returned fire, with *Huse* getting many hits on the enemy according to *Champlin*'s official report. At one point in the battle, *Champlin*'s captain was killed by a 20mm shell after the ship had collided with U-856. *Huse* then prepared to depth charge the sub's survivors in the water but was warned off this action by *Champlin*. *Champlin*'s log states, "Depth charging survivors in water considered advisable against Japanese who refuse to surrender but not against Germans who were very anxious to be picked up." U-856 sank and exploded. Twenty-eight survivors were retrieved from the water (USS *Champlin*, 1944).

Nineteen days later, USS *Frost* (DE 144), USS *Inch* (DE 146) and *Huse* led a series of depth charge attacks on a suspected submarine contact. The attack resulted in the sinking of U-488 with all hands aboard. *Huse* found herself in a cat-and-mouse game with another submarine on June 11, 1944. After expending many depth charges, *Huse* was joined by *Frost* and *Inch* in the search for the sub. Shortly after midnight, the sub was spotted on the surface and engaged by *Frost* and *Inch* with deck guns. U-490, a re-supply submarine with little armament, gave little resistance and sank under the ships' fire. All its crewmen survived.

For the remainder of 1944 and into 1945, *Huse* continued hunter-killer operations with the escort carrier *Croatan*. On at least three occasions, *Huse* picked up downed pilots from the carrier after they ditched in the sea.

On April 12, 1945, in the early morning hours, *Frost*, USS *Stanton* (DE 247) and *Huse* investigated a reported sub contact. Depth charge attacks by *Frost* and *Stanton* resulted in a huge underwater explosion. Later, an oil slick appeared on the water's surface. U-880 had sunk with all hands aboard.

In July 1945, *Huse* began her journey to the Pacific to assist in operations to defeat the Japanese Empire. While she sailed from the mainland U.S. to Hawaii, the Japanese surrendered. *Huse* engaged in exercises in Hawaii until she returned to Norfolk, Virginia, for her decommissioning and placement into the reserve fleet in March 1946.

The Navy recalled *Huse* to duty in 1951 for service during the Korean War. She served mostly as a training vessel, although years later she saw duty off the coast of Florida supporting the embargo associated with the Cuban Missile Crisis. She was again decommissioned in 1965. The Navy struck her from the Naval Vessel Register in 1973. *Huse* was sold for scrap in 1974.

She earned five battle stars for her actions in World War II.

The Poem

The deck log below was entered on January 1, 1946, by Ensign F.W. McCabe, USNR. As with many of the other amateur poets in uniform, McCabe handles his material with skill. The poem consists of five stanzas of six lines each, with three rhymed couplets in each stanza. McCabe deftly creates a lilting waltz-like rhythm. These rhythmic echoes of the dance seem perfectly appropriate for the ship's first New Year's deck log of peacetime.

The war had ended four months earlier. Men were being released from the Navy and ships decommissioned at astonishing rates. On December 7, 1941, the U.S. Navy had an active ship force of 790. By the time the atomic bombs were dropped on Japan in August 1945, American industrial production had pushed that number to 6,768 ships. By the end of June 1946, only ten months later, the number had shrunk again to 1,248. Some ships (including *Huse*) were put in reserve and used during the Korean War; others were sold to other countries. Most were sold for scrap.

McCabe's deck log is notable because of its focus on peace, hard-earned after almost four years of war, and his look to the future. He speaks well of the millions of "citizen sailors" who served in the Naval Reserve. Over three-fourths of those serving in the Navy during World War II were reservists. Note that the ship was being prepared for the reserve force. Consequently, the watches tended to be longer than during battle conditions. This entry is for midnight through noon on January 1.

The poem begins with the celebratory whistles, bells and voices of cheer ringing through the night. But McCabe quickly offers a thought-provoking challenge: Though the fighting is over, he warns, "peace must be won." The post-war world offered no guarantee of peace. It would take work. The last lines of the first stanza and the first lines of the second stanza offer a snapshot of the massive decommissioning process that was ongoing. *Huse* was docked in Jacksonville, Florida, "on the St. Johns." She would have been at Lee Naval Air Station in Green Cove Springs at the mouth of the St. John's River. The base operated until 1962 and was the site for the mothballing of hundreds of ships after the war.

McCabe describes the process—a crew, which is fast being demobilized and dispersed, chipping, painting, preserving the ship. The old paint was being scraped off, the hull coated with oil, scraped again, and then coated with red oxide paint to prevent rust. *Huse* is tied up alongside "Mother *Melville*, old AD2." *Melville* was a destroyer tender—a depot ship that ran with destroyers and other small warships. The tenders carried some ammunition and depth charges but focused mostly on repairs. *Melville* was built in 1913 (thus "old mother"). She served in both World Wars I and II in both the Atlantic and Pacific theaters. She was stationed at Lee Naval Air Base to aid in decommissioning destroyers, and then was decommissioned herself in August at Norfolk. On the starboard side of *Huse*, the destroyer escort USS *Scott* (DE 769) is moored.

McCabe's three stanzas wax philosophical, and it is here, in these closing stanzas, that he looks to the future with the hope that must have been shared by all the war-weary veterans. At 9:15, they muster the crew with all hands on deck. It is mid-morning on January 1, and all those with liberty are leaving the ship early. Though New Year's Day in 1946 was on Tuesday, there would have been many special religious services that day, and McCabe says that the men on liberty "all went to church to earnestly pray" for peace. An exaggeration perhaps, reflecting McCabe's own strong religious grounding (see his bio below), but surely an accurate indication of how intensely they all felt the need for peace so soon after the long years of war. He adds that they prayed that "all would be right / For the 'civilian in uniform' who was called out to fight." The prayer seems to foreshadow the struggle many men who were not professional soldiers and sailors would have when they returned to civilian life after the horrific experience of war.

The last two stanzas manage a fine balance between tongue-in-cheek humor and serious observation. The sailors of the regular Navy, who will remain in the service, McCabe says, "will do well to remember" that all the sailors from the reserves and all those who volunteered "don't 'hate' the Navy, but this sea-going stuff / Is not to our liking and we've had enough." He closes the stanza with a brief political note: Congress will start cutting money to get votes as they always have, which McCabe calls "the usual rut."

Then the final stanza offers a heartfelt plea, in which McCabe addresses members of the regular Navy directly, telling them things are different now. The United States, he says, has the greatest Navy in the world, which will be a powerful diplomatic tool, and it will be left in the charge of "you," the regular Navy. And he closes the poem with a powerful call to action, that by the grace of God, "we hold to our principles and never give in." But he softens it with a note of self-deprecating humor in the last line, "So that we soft civies won't be back in."

Here's the poem:

0000–1200
Whistles and bells with voices of cheer
Ring through the night to bring in the year;
A new year of peace, the fighting is done,
Yet all is not over for peace must be won.
In Jacksonville, Florida, on the St. Johns,
Preservation of ships is being carried on.

Alongside "Mother Melville," old AD2
We're chipping and painting with a fast leaving crew.
To starboard, the Scott, DE 769
Is also preserving and doing quite fine;
Both DE's receiving steam and fresh water,
But we also get power and flushing water.

At nine-fifteen, we mustered the crew,
All hands were present and none overdue
The men that had liberty left early today
And all went to church to earnestly pray
That peace would be kept and that all would be right.
For the "Civilian in uniform" who was called out to fight.

With these ships laid up, fender to fender,
Those USN left will do well to remember
We don't "hate" the navy, but this seagoing stuff
Is not to our liking and we've had enough,
The vote-seeking congress appropriations will cut
As in history past—the usual rut.

Yet this time its different, you have all these ships
And diplomatically, Uncle Sam has a whip.
The world's greatest Navy is in your charge;
So let us all pray by the grace of God
That we hold to our principles and never give in
So that we soft civies won't be back in.

F.W. McCabe,
Ensign, USNR

The Poet

Farrell Wilbur McCabe was born on February 26, 1924, to Michael Christopher McCabe and Eva Mary Corbin in Fall River, Massachusetts. One of Mr. McCabe's sons, David, reported that his father left seminary after the Pearl Harbor attack and enlisted in the Navy (email, January 14, 2020). During his early days in the Navy, McCabe served as an Aviation Machinist's Mate 3rd class at the Naval Aviation Facility at Argentina, New Foundland. On April 28, 1943, McCabe boarded USS *Barnegat* (AVP 10), bound for Midshipman training at the University of Notre Dame. He eventually boarded *Huse* and served as her Assistant Gunnery Officer until she was decommissioned in 1946.

Ensign Farrell Wilbur "Truck" McCabe, circa 1946. Courtesy of David McCabe.

While at Notre Dame, McCabe met Dorothy Edna Saunders, a Navy WAVE. According to McCabe's son, the two met while on watch on Thanksgiving Day. They returned to Notre Dame three years later, after the war, and were married in the Notre Dame Log Chapel on July 6, 1946 (email, January 14, 2020).

The Navy released McCabe from active duty in 1946, after which he returned to college and earned a BA in Economics from Tufts College (now Tufts University). He held several sales and managerial jobs until the U.S. needed him to go to war once again. During the Korean War, he served on USS *Willard Keith* (DD 775), USS *Bisbee* (PF 46) and USS *Horace A. Bass* (APD 144). *Horace A. Bass* played a major role in landing commandos on reconnaissance missions and raids to disrupt the North Koreans' supply lines.

After the war, McCabe served as the commander of Navy and Marine Corps Reserve Training Center in Tucson, Arizona. In 1955, he traveled to Turkey as an Engineering Advisor to the Turkish Navy. After release from active duty in 1958, he worked for Navy contract companies in Charleston. His retirement from the Naval Reserve as a lieutenant commander occurred in August 1969. McCabe eventually took a position with Charleston County Planning, Development and Zoning where he continued to work until his retirement in the early 1990s.

He was ordained to the Permanent Diaconate in the Roman Catholic Church in 1979.

McCabe's children were unaware of the deck log poem their father posted. After reading it, one of his sons said that it sounded a lot like his father. McCabe died on February 23, 1997, and is buried in the Holy Cross Cemetery in James Island, South Carolina. In an online obituary for McCabe, a nickname "Truck" appears. According to his son David, McCabe was a talented lineman on his school's football team. One day, he left a dent in the coach's truck after an attempt at "tackling" it. The nickname Truck was born and stuck with him throughout his life (email, January 18, 2021).

Conclusion

In the study of ships and the men who sailed them in wartime, certain truths become apparent. The men—in this case American men—are courageous, resilient, creative, and carry within them a seemingly inexhaustible capacity for loyalty, sacrifice, compassion and humor. Though combat itself is pitiless, dehumanizing and inhumane, the men of the U.S. Navy who found themselves caught up in World War II and who believed they were fighting for a greater good cause, could exhibit the most human and humane character in their thoughts and actions. This book is ultimately a tribute to humanity, that mixture of good and evil, of compassion and violence, love and hate that under the worst of conditions often lives up to its best potential.

The ships, masses of metal configured to accomplish a particular purpose, become almost human themselves in the minds and hearts of the sailors who live and work on them. The human pronouns used to refer to a ship—"she" and "her"—reinforce that tendency. It rings somewhat ironic when, time after time, a ship that performed through tragedy and triumph ends up being sold for scrap, out of practical necessity. A poignant example is USS *Enterprise*, the most decorated of ships, whose sailors (and many others) worked so hard to save her. She was scrapped because the cost was too high.

The poetry in these pages is good poetry. Perhaps it's not great literature, but it does a great job of shining a light on the very human nature of the young men who wrote it. Appendix D below offers a humorous sampling of the very human responses many of them had to that poetic call.

The authors hope that this book inspires the current generation of sailor poets to carry on the tradition.

Appendix A

Material Conditions in Navy Ships

Use of the word "condition" in relation to Navy ships can be confusing to land lubbers. There are two common ways of identifying the readiness of a ship for engagement. One is stated as the Material Condition of Readiness, which deals with the airtight compartmentalization of the ship, creating varying levels of protection, and includes three basic conditions—XRAY, YOKE, and ZEBRA—and some modifications of these. The second way of identifying ship's condition is usually stated simply as Condition of Readiness, which includes five levels of readiness for action for personnel and gun stations.

The following description of Material Condition of Readiness is taken from *Basic Military Requirements* NAVEDTRA 14325, page 341.

Material Conditions of Readiness

XRAY. Provides the least watertight integrity and the greatest ease of access throughout the ship. It is set when the threat to the ship is minimal. Condition XRAY is set during working hours when the ship is in port, when there is no danger of attack, and when there is no threat from bad weather. All fittings marked with a black X and circle X are closed when condition XRAY is set.

YOKE. Provides a greater degree of watertight integrity than condition XRAY but to a lesser degree than the maximum condition. YOKE is normally set at sea and in port during wartime. All fittings marked with Xs and Ys, Circle X, and Circle Y are closed when condition YOKE is set.

ZEBRA. Provides the greatest degree of subdivision and watertight integrity to the ship. It is the maximum state of readiness for the ship's survivability system. Condition ZEBRA is set when the following situations occur:

1. Immediately when GQ is sounded
2. When entering or leaving port in wartime
3. To localize damage and control fire and flooding when the crew is not at GQ
4. At any time the CO deems the maximum condition of survivability should be set.

All fittings marked with X or Y, Circle X, Circle Y, Z, Circle Z, and DOG Zs are closed when condition ZEBRA is set.

The terms "A" (Affirm or Able), "B" (Baker), and "C" (Cast) were also used for material conditions. "Affirm" represented the maximum watertight integrity of the ship when General Quarters was called and action was imminent. "Baker" was required at sea and in port during war when there was a likelihood of action but freedom of movement below decks was maintained. "Cast" represented normal peacetime cruising conditions.

The following description of Conditions of Readiness is taken from the Federation of American Scientists, Military Analysis Network, Navy Documents.

Conditions of Readiness

Condition I—General Quarters, all hands at battle stations
Condition II—Modified General Quarters, used in large ships to permit some relaxation among personnel
Condition III—Wartime Cruising, generally one third of the crew is on watch, and strategic stations are manned or partly manned.
Condition IV—Optimum Peacetime Cruising, provides adequate watch manning, provides personnel economy. It is normal peacetime cruising condition.
Condition V—Not normally a condition, IN-PORT ROUTINE.

Appendix B

How Ships Get Their Names

To the casual observer, U.S. Navy ships have a bewildering set of names and hull designations. For example, what is the difference between BB 24 (USS *Idaho*) and DD 392 (USS *Patterson*)? Each ship has a name, a type designation (BB and DD), and a hull number. In this case, *Idaho* is obviously named after a state, but *Patterson* is named after Daniel Todd Patterson, a U.S. Naval officer of the early 19th century. *Idaho* was a battleship that was the 24th of its designation and *Patterson* was a destroyer that was the 392nd ship built within its designation. To a large extent, lower hull numbers equate to older ships. We know this because of the relatively standardized way that the Navy chooses names and designations.

March 3, 1819, ushered in the requirement that all U.S. Navy ships be named by the Secretary of the Navy. An act passed by Congress stated that

> all of the ships, of the Navy of the United States, now building, or hereafter to be built, shall be named by the Secretary of the Navy, under the direction of the President of the United States, according to the following rule, to wit: those of the first class shall be called after the States of this Union; those of the second class after the rivers; and those of the third class after the principal cities and towns; taking care that no two vessels of the navy shall bear the same name [Naval History and Heritage Command, 2019].

As new types of ships entered service and old types became obsolete, this three-class system failed to capture the diversity of the fleet. So, by about 1920, a more complex system developed that with some alterations over the years remained in effect for the next 40 to 50 years. The Secretary of the Navy still maintains the responsibility for naming ships, but new classifications emerged, and some old ones faded away.

There are too many different types of ships in the Navy inventory to outline here. Below are some of the most common.

Battleships

BB: This designates a battleship. Battleships tended to be large floating gun platforms with an armor belt to protect against torpedo attack. They were considered the capital ships of the Navy from World War I until World War II, meaning they were considered the most important asset possessed by the Navy. Battleships primarily took the names of U.S. states.

Aircraft Carriers

CV, CVE, CVL: As World War II unfolded, it became clear that battleships no longer provided the comprehensive utility needed for modern warfare. They were too restricted by speed and range. The U.S. Navy realized that the aircraft carrier allowed commanders to broaden their reach well beyond the range of the battleship's big guns. Aircraft carriers could send planes in any direction to find and then attack the enemy. Carriers received several designations depending mostly on their size and number of aircraft they deployed. CV designated fleet carriers such as *Enterprise* and *Lexington*. CVE designated escort carriers that were much smaller and slower than their fleet counterparts. CVL designated light carriers that were like the CVEs but were built to be faster. Naming was not as restricted for carriers as it was for battleships. Carriers tended to be named after important old ships or past battles (e.g., USS *Enterprise* and USS *Guadalcanal*).

Cruisers

CA, CL: Cruisers fell into two categories: Heavy (CA) and Light (CL). They were smaller and faster than battleships but had smaller caliber guns and less armor. Cruisers mostly took on names of cities in the U.S., although there were exceptions. For example, USS *Canberra* (CA 70) was named after the Australian cruiser HMAS *Canberra* that was sunk at the Battle of Savo Island off Guadalcanal in 1942. A U.S. cruiser, USS *Quincy* (CA 39), was also sunk in that battle and another *Quincy* (CA 71) was commissioned. It was not unusual for a second ship within a designation to have the name of an older ship that was no longer in commission.

Destroyers and Destroyer Escorts

DD, DE: Destroyers and Destroyer Escorts were the smaller ships that accompanied the carriers and cruisers of the fleet. World War II destroyers were fast, being able to make 32–37 knots. They contained virtually no armor and they performed a wide variety of duties. They screened the larger ships from submarine and surface ship attack. Torpedoes and depth charges provided destroyers these capabilities. They also possessed small guns such as 5"/38 caliber, 40mm and 20mm for offensive action against surface vessels and aircraft. In addition to their protection of the capital ships, destroyers delivered mail, picked up persons in the water, and transferred personnel from one ship to another. Destroyer escorts tended to be slightly smaller and slower than destroyers. They performed essentially the same duties but were better equipped to escort slower ships such as convoys and escort carriers. By mid–World War II, the naming convention for DDs and DEs had evolved to the use of "Deceased American Naval, Marine Corps and Coast Guard Officers and enlisted personnel who have rendered distinguished service to their country above and beyond the call of duty; former Secretaries and Assistant Secretaries of the Navy; members of Congress who have been closely identified with Naval affairs; and inventors" (Martin, 2020).

Auxiliary Ships

This category of ships contains a wide range of types. They have in common a specific role to play in the conduct of war. They also generally have ship designators that begin with "A." AK stands for cargo ship. Naming was not consistent over time, but many received the name of heavenly bodies or constellations. AO stands for oiler. These ships fueled up the other ships in the fleet. Many of the oilers in World War II were named after Native American tribes.

Thousands of World War II ships were given hull designations and numbers but carried out their duties without names. Landing craft, PT boats and small submarine chasers fell into this category.

The Navy evolves over time, so some of these naming conventions from the 1940s no longer hold. Battleships are a thing of the past so state names now get attached to submarines. The modern Navy needed warships that could operate closer to land and in places of shallower water. So ships with the designation Littoral Combat Ships (LCS) emerged in the early 2000s. Many of these new ships were given names of U.S. cities.

Appendix C

U.S. Navy Hull Designations in This Book

AD: Destroyer Tender
AE: Ammunition Ship
AGS: Survey Ship
AH: Hospital Ship
AKA: Attack Cargo Ship
AM: Minesweeper
AMc: Coastal Minesweeper
AO: Fleet Oiler
AP: Transport
APA: Attack Transport
APD: High Speed Transport
AS: Submarine Tender
AV: Seaplane Tender
AVP: Seaplane Tender, light
BB: Battleship
CA: Heavy Cruiser
CAG: Heavy Cruiser, Guided Missile
CG: Guided Missile Cruiser
CL: Light Cruiser
CV: Aircraft Carrier
CVA: Attack Aircraft Carrier
CVE: Escort Aircraft Carrier
CVL: Light Aircraft Carrier
CVS: Anti-Submarine Aircraft Carrier
DD: Destroyer
DDR: Radar Picket Destroyer
DE: Destroyer Escort
DLG: Guided Missile Frigate
DM: Destroyer Minelayer
LSD: Landing Ship, Dock
LST: Landing Ship, Tank
PC: Patrol Craft
PCS: Patrol Craft, Submarine Chaser
PF: Frigate
PY: Seagoing Gunship
PYc: Coastal Gun Ship
SS: Attack Submarine
COAST GUARD:
WAVP: Casco-Class Cutter
WHEC: High Endurance Cutter (designated in 1965) WMEC Medium Endurance Cutter is a historical designation

Appendix D

Candid Comments by Poets in the Poems

Standing the watch at midnight was not a popular duty under the best of circumstances. But standing the watch from midnight to 4:00 a.m. on New Year's Day was perhaps the most unpopular duty. The young officer and enlisted men on the bridge toiled for four long hours, painfully aware that their crewmates were celebrating the New Year. It's no wonder they so often lamented the absence of alcohol and female companionship in their deck log poems. Many of them went a step further and complained not just about having to stand the watch but also about having to write the log in verse. The complaints have stood the test of time. Here are some selected lines from poems dated 1927 to 1970.

USS *Idaho* (BB 42), 1927

To cook our chow and give us heat
Steams boiler number nine.
From ten days leave came Ensign Clark
To finish this damned rime.
F.N. Kivette
Ensign, U.S. Navy

USS *Helena* (PG 9), 1928

That's all for this watch, naught else has transpired,
I'll turn me in now for I'm pretty damn' tired,
But the wish of this pitch-pounding, worn-out O.O.D.,
Is to all ye who read this,—Happy New Year to thee.
E.C. Rook, Lieut. (j.g.) U.S.N.

USS *Daly* (DD 519), 1952

My log has been writ, the saying's been said
To hell with mid-watches, I'm headed for bed.
W.E. Norton
Lt., USNR

USS *Beale* (DDE 471), 1952

This little rhyme is poor I know;
But on this night of parties gay with most the crew away
I end this cold, lonesome, and thankless watch with nothing more to say.
Paul T. Quinton,
ENS., USN

USS *Atka* (AGB 3), 1953

No use griping but still a hell of a way
To welcome in the year, wet as a fish & cold as the day.

But into every life some rain must fall
Nothing else to report, so that's all.
R.E. Deamer, Lt. USN

USS *Cutlass* (SS 478), 1953

For the first log of the year,
To follow tradition I fear,
....
Now my log has come to an end,
Of many rhymes its been a blend,
As a final small touch,
You'd all say as much,
Happy New Year to all we extend.
H.J. Estelman
Lt. USN

USS *Newport News* (CA 148), 1956

So this log I will close and relinquish my place
As I enviously watch those who have spliced the mainbrace.
["Splice the mainbrace" is an old Navy term for doling out alcohol.]
R.B. Lawson, LTJG, USNR

USS *Point Cruz* (CVE 119), 1956

The watch 'though unique must come to a close
But harken ye, Matey, 'tis not one I chose,
For many and fierce are the hazards here
When returneth the celebrant loaded with cheer.
N.L. Bausch
Lt., USN

USS *Alstede* (AF 48), 1958

And thus on this New Year's, with phrases so "cherce"
in fine old tradition, the log's writ in verse.
W.A. Wenker
Lt. USN

USS *Ford County* (LST 772), 1958

A poet I never claimed to be,
After this, I'm sure you'll agree,
But because its tradition
My duty I could not shun.
16 Bells, on time, were struck
To bring us all the best of luck.
The watch is over, it was a lark
So now to this, I'll affix my mark.
F. Gordon
QM1, USN

USS *Radford* (DDE 446), 1959

New Year's Eve duty, and to make the matter worse—
The mid-watch entry to be written in verse.
And so says tradition, as we enter 59.
"Call forth your talents for rhythm and rhyme."
R.D. Murphy, LTJG, USN

USS *Steinaker* (DDR 863), 1964

Well, I've rambled along and the rhyme's not to hot.
And, I must confess, my mind's about shot.
But, this log has been written—Perhaps ashore I shall go.
After the XO sees this, He'll probably say "No"!
F.R. Whalen
Ens. USN

USS *Midway* (CVA 41), 1965

Tis hard enough these words to weave
On every duty night.
But when we come to New Year's Eve
This curse in verse we write.
We're bound by duty, per navy regs,
To give our hard earned time.
Yet this question for an answer begs
Why must this __________thing rhyme?
J.N. Lorton, JOOW NNR.W. Lewis
LTjg, USNR Ensign, USN

USS *Ability* (MSO 519), 1966

Listen, old log, and none of your tricks,
As this day dawns on nineteen sixty-six;
I'm a fellow whose troublesome job was again,
To enter the record in metric refrain
F.G. Clark, Jr
LTJG USNR

USS *Dupont* (DD 941), 1966

I'm standing my watch, the normal routine;
It's the usual kick, but the New Years scene.
And tradition demands a little bit more
Than the standard old phrase "Moored as before."
We're charged with the duty (I and my pen)
So I'll log it in verse, and here I begin:
E.C. Holloway
LTJG, SC, USN
[Sidenote: The New Year's log for 1967
on *Dupont* uses Holloway's log almost word for word.
What's a little plagiarism among friends?]

USS *Current* (ARS 22), 1966

I'm certainly glad this poetry's o're,
Now I'll get back to "Moored as before."
Larry B. Hachtel
LTJG USNR

USS *Graffias* (AF 29), 1968

Tis New Years Eve and here I stand,
Writing the deck log with a frozen hand.
As Navy legend goes, so the log must rhyme,
So might as well sit and take my time.
R.G. Sanders RD2 USN

USS *Davidson* (DE 1045), 1969

Again New Year's Eve! I've the duty again!
While I'm freezing I'll break out my government pen
And describe for posterity, sort of in rhyme,
Where Davidson's at, whom we're with, and the time.
....
Meantime I have only one wish: Let me say
I had this watch last year and I've had it today!
So if anyone cares, as I put up my pen,
Could you see that next year I don't get it again?
T. J. Nicarico, LT. USN

USS *Agile* (MSO 421), 1969

Before ending this wonderful rhyme
And taking my place with great poets of time
I shall wish everyone the happiest of New Year's
And a year of peace with the world and few tears.
Ralph M. Mitchell, Jr.
LTJG, USN

USS *Rupertus* (DD 851), 1970

With screaming and shouting
And rushing about
We praised sixty-nine
And ushered her out.
With seventy here,
We think of the past;
This damned log is written,
This line is the last.
B.C. Adams
Ens., USN

USS *Shelton* (DD 790), 1970

T'is a week after Christmas, The duty is mine.
As tradition prevails, this log entry must rhyme.
J.M. Chevrier, Ens, USN

Appendix E

Non-World War II Poems

Below is a selection of non-World War II era poems from January 1 logs. The first is from 1929, followed by poems from the 1950s and 1960s. Times change, but the midwatch poems remain similar. Note that the poem from the USS *Serrano* is in free verse, a rarity in midwatch poems.

USS *Helena* (PG 9), January 1, 1929 (log incorrectly states 1928)
[With a nod, perhaps, to "The Rime of the Ancient Mariner"]

Again we ride in Yangtze's tide, (the same as a year ago)
The yellow stream reflects the beam of a moon serene and low
Two anchors hold our vessel bold, one up the stream, one down,
With five and forty fathoms each, off ancient Hankow Town.

Beneath our keel 'tis good to feel six feet of water clear;
From nor nor east the cold wind breathes a note of New Year's cheer
While crew asleep in hammocks deep, dream on of peace or fights
And boiler two provides the steam to give us heat and lights.

So small in size, the PANAY lies two hundred yards or less
And twinkles back a New Year's wish for joy and happiness.
Not far away, Republique Francais has a ship—without a mar
A lovely sloop, so trim and neat, the BELLATRIX—a star.

HINAKI, SAGA, TONE, KASHI, Nippon's ships are these;
Stalwart and strong, they hold the fort, against the new Chinese
And lying there, serene and fair, are Britains iron walls—
COCKCHAFER, BEE, CASTOR, PETREL—will hold e're Britain falls.

But whats that gleam, far up the stream, that shows so clear and bright—
The CHING KIANG and KIANG SIEN—to show New China's might.
The vigil ends; the cold moon sends its farewell rays to cheer—
And soon the sun will wish us all a happy, bright New Year.

K.R. Belch, Lieutenant, U.S.N.

USS *Bayonne* (PF 21), January 1, 1952
[With a nod, perhaps, to "Gunga Din"]

00–04 We are steaming on two boilers, In vicinity of Oilers, for, you see, we had replenished yesterday. Oh the radar it is searching as the ship is gently lurching and the sonar gear is busy at its play.

Now the sky is overcast (tho' we know it won't last) and the temperature is under thirty-nine. The watch is at its place, as must always be the case, and generator two is on the line.

For Operational Control who has the role but Commander Niner Five Point Two and Two,

and he told us to remain, through the wind, the snow, and rain at our post whatever else that we might do.
Our nightly set of orders has us staying in the waters, in vicinity the Island of Yang Do. Our mission is blockading to insure against the raiding of these out-posts we have wrested from the foe.

We have set condition three for readiness at sea and condition Baker's set throughout the ship. Eight Point Five knots is our speed, Seven Five turns does the deed, to move us through the water on our trip.

True and Gyro Course is set Two Three Five Degrees will get us on the track desired, we make good. The Standard Compass Check—Two Four Four Degrees—By Heck! Is found down where the helmsman's watch is stood.

The Oh Two Oh Eight prediction, of our job of interdiction, is that targets that we fire on tonight had better be prepared to have their foxholes aired, because, by God, they'll know they've had a fight.

In the star shell's eerie glow, above the hills of snow, we see our target clearly now and shout, Fire One and Two and Three, as we press on through the sea, maneuvering to turn the ship about.

Now we'll keep on at our task, as long as it may last, and do the job we know that we must do, and hope the dawning year, will bring us that great cheer of going home some time in Fifty-Two.

G.C. Krauleidis, LTJG, U.S. Naval Reserve

USS *Philip* (DDE 498), January 1, 1962
[With an obvious nod to "'Twas the Night Before Christmas"]

'Twas New Years Eve and all through the ship,
Not a sailor was stirring, all was silent in the slip.
The new watch cap covers were hung on each stack,
They looked shiny now, but would soon be black.
The watch was set in its usual way,
OOD in the wardroom drinking café.
The Captain, Exec, and all others were ashore,
All was quiet like a tomb in the morning at four.
The six standard mooring lines were first taught, then slack,
As the wakes from harbor boats, rocked us in, then back.
The cables and hoses from the services on the pier,
Were visible, though silent, if you looked there and here.
There were not many ships present, diversified was our might,
A few fleet, yard and district types moored silently in the night.
Admiral Sides who was SOPA was partying high on the hill,
Though it's certain, as CINCPACFLT, he extended his good will.
At Pearl Harbor Shipyard in berth B-17 were we,
The quarterdeck on the starboard side so the OOD could see,
Down the pier with his ever vigilant eye,
Thinking to himself "perhaps tonight I'll catch me a spy."
When all of a sudden out of the dark does appear,
Eight stumbling, drunken sailors with a cold case of beer.
They try to hide it, but try too late,
For the OOD is alert and says to them, "wait."
"You can't bring that on board, it's against regulations,

I'll put you all on report with no hesitations."
They stop for a moment, when one says, "I think,
He might let us on if we offer him a drink."
"What ho there mate, how about a wee cup of ale,
I have one right here, and it's not even stale."
The OOD's tongue twitches, the temptation is strong,
But he says, "no thanks, you men run along."
They turned on their heels and toddled into the night,
To walk, it looked like it took all their might.
Well, that was one problem solved, how many more to go,
This is something that no one would know.
The OOD lets his thoughts drift away,
He pictures a party, where folks swing and sway.
At this party he sees all his shipmates together,
Some of them heading towards strong, stormy weather.
He reflects for a while on the past of his friends,
Of some he laughs so hard he nearly gets the bends,
There's the skipper, "Ol' Honest Ted," as he's known to some
Always with a smile and a hearty welcome,
A ship handler supreme, twenty knots toward the pier,
"All back full," he roars, "we'll stop her here."
Then there's the old X.O. "Uncle Gordo" by name,
Who due to his antics won dubious fame.
When he flew to the bridge to see what was the matter,
All that could be heard when he landed was "scatter"!
He was soon replaced by "Easy John Bond,"
Who seems to always know just what's going on.
So be aware there sailor, better not skylark,
For the XO's bite can be worse than his bark.
And of course, we have to have a Chief Snipe,
He's atypical, unusual, the only one of his type.
There's only one thing that saves him from impending disgrace,
About fifty pounds of "Devcon" smeared all over the place.
All of a sudden the OOD comes back to reality,
What in the world can all that racket be?
Whistles are blowing, a bell is ringing near,
Oh, it's just the PHILIP wishing the world a HAPPY NEW YEAR!

David T. Halverson
LTJG, USNR

USS *Serrano* (AGS 24), January 1, 1967
[Hand-printed, all upper case, free verse]

NOW BRINGS THE GENTLE MUSE, POOR GODDESS
UNFAMILIAR IN THESE BOUNDS OF TEMPERED STEEL,
HER PHANTOM POWER, SUCCOR TO MY SUIT
AS FITFULLY I PLY THE LEAVES OF WEBSTER'S TOME;
NOT MODERN KNIGHT NOR VENERABLE BOWDITCH
DELVED THIS HEADY PROBLEM, VERSE TO SPIN,
WHICH TIME, FLITTING AT THIS PRESENT EVE
FROM YEAR TO YEAR, LEAVES LITLE CHANCE
FOR THOUGHTFUL CARE—THE BREEZE IS IN THE SHROUDS,
ALIGHT WITH STRANDS OF MULTICOLORED GLOBES,

AND ROUND ABOUT MORE UNITS OF PACFLEET
ALIKE ARE DRAPED WITH TRAPPINGS OF THE SEASON
TO LACE PEARL HARBOR'S SKY WITH FITTING CHEER,
WHILE DARKLING YARD AND SMALL CRAFT LURK UNSEEN.
HERE, WHILE REVELERS QUAFF THEIR CUPS OF PORT,
SERRANO'S SOBER SIDE SO NAMED FOR WINE
'GAINST SHIPYARD BERTH (OF BRAVO'S LINEAGE, TENTH),
NESTLES WITH ANOTHER, FITTING MATE,
SAFEGUARD CALLED, A SALVAGE TYPE WITH MEANS
TO RESCUE STRANDED MARINERS ON REEFS
AND SHOALS UNCHARTED, WHICH WE BRAVELY PROBE,
FOR HYDROGRAPHIC SURVEY IS OUR MISSION.
DOUBLED ARE THE STANDARD MOORING LINES
AND YOKE IS SET AS IS THE RIGOR DUE.
THROUGH ALL THE DECKS BUT LITTLE STIRS THE SILENCE
SAVE HOLLOW VOICES MURMURING A WISH....
LIKE THE SHIP, WHOSE COLD MACHINERY BROODS,
WHILE WATER, POWER, AND STEAM FROM SOURCES FAR
THE PIER THROUGH VARIOUS UMBILICALS PROVIDES;
SO ARE THESE HOPEFUL HEARTFELT GREETINGS FED
ON DISTANT DREAMS, AND ECHOING MEMORIES FRAMED
IN SPLENDID VISIONS OF GOOD TIMES. NOT LONG
WILL FLEETING FANCIES OUR HORIZON CLOUD.
SOPA, CINCPACFLT, GREAT FOUR-STARRED-CHIEF,
ASTRIDE THE HILL ASHORE HIS REALM SURVEYS;
THE MAGNITUDE OF OCEAN UNEXPLORED,
SERRANO'S TASK ENORMOUS, MEETS HIS GLANCE.
NOW HASTEN, MUSE, DEPART, I NEED THEE NOT
TO FATHOM PURPOSE NEW THIS YEAR HAS BROUGHT.

R.D. Butterbrodt
LTJG, USN

USS *New Jersey* (BB 62), January 1, 1969
[Hand-printed all upper case]

INDEPENDENTLY STEAMING OFF VIET NAM
IN SEARCH OF VICTOR CHARLIE CONG
AND NOW JUST SOUTH OF THE DMZ
SHOOTING AT TARGETS TOO FAR TO SEE
WITH ORDERS FROM COMSEVENTHFLEET
TO FIRE OUR GUNS AND KEEP THINGS NEAT
AS PART OF 70.8.9
WE WILL BE FIRING ALL THE TIME
EMPLOYMENT SCHEDULE 3-69
KEEPS US BUSY ON THE LINE
THE OTC AND SOPA TOO
IS CAPTAIN SNYDER OF "62"
COURSES VARY THROUGH THE NIGHT
BUT 090 AT 5 JUST NOW SEEMS RIGHT
YOKE IS SET, WE KNOW ITS TRUE
WE STEAM AT CONDITION OF READINESS TWO
WITH BOILERS 1, 3, 5, AND 8
GENERATORS 2, 4, 6, AND 8
WE'LL HAVE NO PROBLEMS MAKING STEAM
WITH THEM ON OUR NEW JERSEY TEAM
WE SHOW NO NAVIGATION LIGHT

FOR DARKEN SHIP THIS NEW YEARS NIGHT
LT THORNTON THE OOD
SAYS THINGS LOOK GOOD, AND WE SHOULD SEE
A SUNRISE WITH THE PASS OF TIME
TO BRING US INTO "69"
THERE ARE SOME THINGS WE HOLD SO DEAR
AMONG THEM PEACE IN THIS NEW YEAR
GOOD CHEER, GOOD LUCK, A SAFE TRIP HOME
AND WITH THAT THOUGH, I'LL END THIS POEM.
A MISTAKE HAS BEEN MADE IN THIS LOG I FEAR
FOR MORE ENTRIES NEED BE ENTERED HERE
AT TIME ZERO TWO FORTY ONE
ORDER WAS RECEIVED TO FIRE OUR GUNS
COMMENCED FIRE MAIN BATTERY TURRET TWO
AND A HAPPY NEW YEAR TO VICTORY CHARLIE TO YOU
SEVEN SALVOS RESOUNDED WITH A MIGHTY CLAP
WITH SEVEN FULL CHARGES AND PROJECTILES HICAP.
THE ENEMY IN HIS HOOTCHES AND BUNKERS WE DID ZAP
ROUNDS COMPLETE, CEASE FIRE CAME THROUGH THE PHONES
AND RELUCTANTLY WE RETURNED TO THE NIGHT STEAMING ZONE

T.J. Thornton, LT, USN

References

Adams, Emil John. [No date]. CDR EMIL J. ADAMS, USN FLIGHT LOG ID: 2300. National Flight Log Entry. Naval Aviation Museum Foundation. https://navalaviationfoundation.org/ways-to-give/national-flight-log/national-flight-log-entry/?id=2300.

Allen, Tom. (2012, October 23). "Mister President, the Navy Will Not Let You Down." Updated: February 5, 2013. https://news.usni.org/2012/10/23/mister-president-navy-will-not-let-you-down.

Allman, W.B. (2016, November 7) "USS *Murphy*: Long Service in Wartime," p. 1. *Warfare History Network.* https://warfarehistorynetwork.com/2016/11/07/uss-murphy-long-service-in-wartime/.

The Baltimore Sun. (1955, November 30) p. 18.

Bauman, Richard J. (2018, February). "The Strange Disappearance of Admiral Wilcox." *Naval History Magazine,* 32.1. Proceedings of the US Naval Institute. https://www.usni.org/magazines/naval-history-magazine/2018/february/strange-disappearance-admiral-wilcox.

Bergstrom, L.W. (1994). "The USS *Patterson* DD 392: Shipmates and Memories." Self-published cruise book.

Budanovic, Nikola. (2017, July 5). "Praise the Lord and Pass the Ammunition—The Legendary Army Chaplain of Pearl Harbor." War history online. https://www.warhistoryonline.com/world-war-ii/praise-the-lord-and-pass-the-ammunition-bc.html.

Butler, J., Blackford, M., and Dunn, J. (2016). *Onboard the USS* Mason*: The WWII Diary of James A. Dunn.* Columbus, OH: Trillium.

Carlson, Peter. "Encounter: FDR Dines with King Ibn Saud." *HistoryNet.com.* https://www.historynet.com/encounter-fdr-dines-king-ibn-saud.htm. Originally published in the December 2010 issue of *American History.*

Childs, Earl B. (2010, November 10). US Naval Academy Alumni Associate & Foundation biography. https://web.archive.org/web/20101130203450/https://www.usna.com/NC/History/ClassOf1940/C.htm

Childs, Earl Wayne Freed. (no date). [Navy Cross Award]. The Hall of Valor Project. https://valor.militarytimes.com/hero/9248.

Christensen, Arthur G. Affidavit of Lt COL (Inf) Arthur G. Christensen, II Corps, G2; RG 389, Box 2123. http://www.mansell.com/pow_resources/camplists/tokyo/tok-08b-motoyama/taikoku_maru_voyage.htm.

Clark, Alexis. (2020, August 5). "Black Americans Who Served in WWII Faced Segregation Abroad and at Home." History.com. https://www.history.com/news/black-soldiers-world-war-ii-discrimination.

Corkery, Paul. (1987). *Carson: The Unauthorized Biography.* Ketchum, ID: Randt & Co.

The Courier News, Bridgewater, NJ. (1918, April 8). "Posthumous Son Born to Naval Lieutenant's Wife," p. 9.

The Daily Item, Port Chester, NY. (1958, January 17). "Boy 5, Dies After Slipping Into Pond: Playing Child Falls Off Dam," p. 1.

The Daily Oklahoman. (1955, February 8). "Reserve Center Gets New Chief," p. 26.

The Daily Times, Davenport. (1942, May18). "Paul Kortkamp To Be Field Manager for ODT Office," p. 21.

Davison, T.W. (1942, April 10). Report of the sinking of USS *Finch*, Enclosure A. Fold3. https://www.fold3.com/image/267937180.

Davison, T.W. (1942, April 28). Letter to Navy Relief Society President, Enclosure F. Fold3. https://www.fold3.com/image/267937233.

Delich, Helen. (1955, November 30). *The Baltimore Sun.* "Ship with Polar Pet," p. 18.

De Long, E. (ed). (1884). *The Voyage of the* Jeannette*: The Ship and Ice Journals of George W. De Long.* Boston: Houghton, Mifflin, and Company.

Destroyer History Foundation. "Destroyer Squadron Twelve." https://destroyerhistory.org/benson-gleaves class/desron12/.

Dix Noonan Web. (2017, July 19–20). Orders, Decorations, Medals and Militaria (19 & 20 July 2017). Lot 760. [Catalogue]. https://www.noonans.co.uk/auctions/archive/past-catalogues/455/catalogue/295212/?keywords=fahnestock&x=0&y=0

Dorr, Robert F. (2014, November 6). "Slugging It Out in Tarawa Lagoon." Defense Media Network. HTTPS://www.DefenseMediaNetwork.com/Stories/Slugging-it-out-in-Tarawa-Lagoon/. Accessed November 9, 2021.

Edel, C. (2020, August 15). "Lessons from 'Tales of the South Pacific' for Today: The war in the Pacific holds the keys to addressing our problems today." *The Washington Post*. https://www.washingtonpost.com/outlook/2020/08/15/lessons-tales-south-pacific-today/

Edwardsville Intelligencer (Illinois). (1970, April 11). p. 3.

Emil J. Adams. Obituary. Dignity Memorial. https://www.dignitymemorial.com/obituaries/east-hartford-ct/emil-adams-7336828.

Evans, Mark L. (2015, November 12). *South Dakota* II (BB 57). Chapter 1. DANFS, Naval History Heritage Command. https://www.history.navy.mil/content/history/nhhc/research/histories/ship-histories/danfs/s/south-dakota-ii-bb57-1941-42.html

Evans, Mark L. (2017, April 26). *Enterprise* VII (CV-6): 1938–1956. DANSF. National History and Heritage Command. https://www.history.navy.mil/research/histories/ship-histories/danfs/e/enterprise-cv-6-vii.html.

The Evening Star, Washington, D.C. (1942, January 3). "Miss Elizabeth Acker Wed to Ensign W.H. Bargeloh, Jr.," p. A9.

Fahnestock, G. (1947, July 16). "Testimony from the Hearing Before a Subcommittee of the Committee on the Judiciary United States Senate Eightieth Congress First Session on S.1261. Relief for American Citizens Captured and Interned by Japanese," p. 46.

Ferro, John. (2015, June 16). "70 Years Ago a Fiery Plane Crash on Mt. Beacon." *Poughkeepsie Journal*. https://www.poughkeepsiejournal.com/story/news/local/southern-dutchess/2015/06/16/recalling-1945-plane-crash-mount-beacon/71267300.

Forester Athletic Hall of Fame. Floyd A "Duke" Gates, '42. http://campus.lakeforest.edu/foresters/fgates.htm.

Fort Worth Star-Telegram. (1953, January 25). "Corsair, Bowing Out to Jets, Holds Astounding Number of War Records," p. 16.

Fort Worth Star-Telegram. (1962, October 25). "Blockade Chief Model Officer," p. 1.

Fort Worth Star-Telegram. (1966, April 3). "Swabbings," p. 7.

Gertrude Emerson. Obituary. Find a Grave. https://www.findagrave.com/memorial/178588976/gertrude-emerson.

Great Falls Tribune, Great Falls, Montana. (1946, November 10). "Froid Girl Is Married in Maryland," p. 34.

Hartford Courant. (1942, April 23). "War Department Procurement Division," p. 19.

Hayes, Raymond Eric. (1941, June 5 and 13). [Letters]. Copies in possession of Dave Johnson.

Hill, John Clayton II. https://mightymux.com/CommanderHill.pdf.

Hodnett, William Philip, Jr. Manila American Cemetery and Memorial (Tablets of the Missing). https://www.abmc.gov/decedent-search/hodnett%3Dwilliam-0.

Holzmeister, K., and Raimy, E. (1970, April 17). "The Day the Ship Came In." *The Argus,* Fremont, CA, p 5.

Hull, Dave. (2007, December). "One Helping the Other—The Internet and the Library." *Relative Bearings,* Friends of the San Francisco Maritime Museum Library Newsletter, p. 8.

Hussey, Brian F. (1991, May 5). "The U.S. Navy, the Neutrality Patrol, and Atlantic Fleet Escort Operations, 1939–1941." Defense Technical Information Center. https://apps.dtic.mil/sti/citations/ADA245396.

Indiana Gazette, Indiana, Pennsylvania. (2000, February 13). Obituary of Lilburn C. Feldman, p. 13.

Intelligencer. (1970, April 11). "Lady Customs Inspectors to Break Tradition," p. 3.

James C. Eschen. Obituary. Legacy.com. https://www.legacy.com/us/obituaries/marinij/name/james-eschen-obituary?id=25993530.

James Delaney Boatman, Jr. *Find A Grave*. https://www.findagrave.com/memorial/10059034/james-dulaney-boatman.

James Francis Roohan. Obituary. Legacy.com. https://www.legacy.com/us/obituaries/sandiegounion tribune/name/james-roohan-obituary?pid=2538125.

"Japan Invades the Aleutian Islands." (no date). [Article] *American Experience*. PBS. https://www.pbs.org/wgbh/americanexperience/features/alaska-japan/.

Johnson, Lynnda. (1988, December 29). "The Honorable A. John Ruggeri moves on." *The Sun-Advocate,* Price, Utah.

The Kansas City Star, Kansas City, Missouri. (1990, November 12). Obituary, p. 18.

Keeshan, Alfred G. *Find A Grave*. https://www.findagrave.com/memorial/124660848/alfred-g-keeshan.

Kelly, Mary Pat. (2015). *Proudly We Served: The Men of the USS Mason*. Annapolis, MD: Naval Institute Press.

King, Gilbert. (2012, December 19). "The boy who became a World War II veteran at 13 years old." *Smithsonian Magazine*. https://www.smithsonianmag.com/history/the-boy-who-became-a-world-war-ii-veteran-at-13-years-old-168104583/.

Kitts, William W. (2009). Transcript of an oral history conducted 2009. Oral History Program Recordings Collection, University of North Texas Special Collections.

Knoxville News-Sentinel. (1950, August 10) p. 20.
Linn, James. (2017, August 9). "USS *New Orleans* Coconut Log Artifact." National WWII Museum. https://www.nationalww2museum.org/war/articles/uss-new-orleans-coconut-log-artifact.
Lionel Burton Garrison. *Find A Grave.* https://www.findagrave.com/memorial/113812043/lionel-garrison.
Logbooks of U.S. Navy Ships, ca. 1801–1940. https://catalog.archives.gov/id/581208.
Lucky Bag. US Naval Academy yearbook. *USNA Digital Collections.* https://usna.primo.exlibrisgroup.com/discovery/collectionDiscovery?vid=01USNA_INST:01USNA&inst=01USNA_INST&collectionId=81101730500006751.
Lundstrom, John B. (2005). *The First Team: Pacific Naval Air Combat from Pearl Harbor to Midway. (New ed.).* Annapolis, MD: Naval Institute Press.
Marbas, A.R. (1945, November 2). Testimony before military commission. Public trial, *United States vs. Tomoyuki Yamashita.* pp. 707–712.
Martin, Kali. (2020, October 26). "Pluck, Pogy, and Portland: Naming Navy Ships in World War II." The National WWII Museum. https://www.nationalww2museum.org/war/articles/naming-navy-ships-in-world-war-ii.
McNitt, Robert W., Captain. (1959, January). "The First Watch." *Proceedings of the US Naval Institute,* Vol. 85 no. 1, 671.
Metro Ports, A Nautilus Company. [no date]. Our history. https://www.metroports.com/history.html.
Michno, G.F. (2016). *Death on the Hellships: Prisoners at Sea in the Pacific War.* Annapolis, MD: Naval Institute Press.
Miller, David B. (1993). "Life aboard 'Battleship X': The USS *South Dakota* in World War II." South Dakota State Historical Society. https://www.sdhspress.com/journal/south-dakota-history-23-2/life-aboard-battleship-x-the-uss-south-dakota-in-world-war-ii/vol-23-no-2-life-aboard-battleship-x.pdf
Nanaimo Daily News, Nanaimo, British Columbia, Canada. (1935, September 19). "Launch Nohea Safe," p. 1.
National City Star-News, National City, CA. (1943, July 30). "Lt. 'Bob' Harbison Home On Furlough After 10 Battles," p. 1.
National City Star-News, National City, CA. (1947, October 3). "Cmdr. Harbison Attends School on Rocket Warfare," p. 1.
National WWII History Museum. (2020, June 25). "Engage Until Neutralized: USS *Texas* Battles Battery Hamburg." https://www.nationalww2museum.org/war/articles/uss-texas-battery-hamburg-1944.
Naval History and Heritage Command. (1940, July 17). DANFS. *Enterprise VII* (CV 6) 1938–1956. https://www.history.navy.mil/research/histories/ship-histories/danfs/e/enterprise-cv-6-vii.html.
Naval History and Heritage Command. (2015, February 12). "Modern Biographies. Dixie Kiefer, 4 April 1896–11 November 1945." https://www.history.navy.mil/research/library/research-guides/modern-biographical-files-ndl/modern-bios-k/kiefer-dixie.html.
Naval History and Heritage Command. (2018, February 20). "USS *Detroit:* Report of Pearl Harbor Attack." https://www.history.navy.mil/research/archives/digital-exhibits-highlights/action-reports/wwii-pearl-harbor-attack/ships-d-l/uss-detroit-cl-8-action-report.html.
Naval History and Heritage Command. (2019, April 23). "Ship Naming in the United States Navy." https://www.history.navy.mil/browse-by-topic/heritage/customs-and-traditions0/ship-naming.html.
Naval History and Heritage Command. (no date). *Norman Scott.* DANFS. https://www.history.navy.mil/content/history/archive/research-archive/histories/ship-histories/danfs/danfs-archvies/norman-scott.html.
Naval Operations. (1967). Chapter 4. Circular Formations and Screens. Bureau of Naval Personnel. Google Books.
Naworzki, J. (1981, December 6). "Pearl Harbor 40 years ago: They were there." *News American,* Baltimore, MD.
Negri, Gloria. (2004, June 24). "Richard P. Axten, at 89; was an executive at Raytheon." *The Boston Globe,* p. 33.
New York Times. (1921, Nov 27). Will Marry on Warship, p. 22.
New York Times. (1949, May 15). "Barbara Bigelow to Wed: Larchmont Girl to Become Bride of Alfred G. Keeshan Jr.," p. 87.
New York Times. (1981, May 5). "Thaddeus R. Beal, 64; Army Under Secretary Was a Boston Lawyer." Thaddeus Reynolds Beal, Jr. Obituary, Section C, p. 20.
Newport Mercury, Newport, RI. (1973, December 28). "Commissions Daughter," p. 3.
Oakland Tribune. (1938, August 17). "Socialite Heir Weds U.C. Girl: Herbert Fahnestock To Continue Studies; Shuns Wedding Trip," p. 1.
"100 Per Center: Applicant Astounds Navy Recruiters." *The Detroit News.* (1941, December 3). Clipping from Raymond Hayes papers in possession of Dave Johnson.
Pape, R. (1960). *Poles Apart.* London: Odhams Press Limited.
Paris News. (1938, June 2). "Detroit Boy Highest of PJC Grads," p.1.
Pearl Harbor Survivor Accounts. Navy History & Heritage Command. https://www.history.navy.mil/

research/library/online-reading-room/title-list-alphabetically/p/pearl-harbor-survivor-reports/uss-california.html.

Poyer, David, Captain USNR (Ret). (2019, June). "Indestructible: Dixie Kiefer." United States Naval Academy Alumni Association and Foundation. https://www.usna.com/shipmate/indestructible-dixie-kiefer.

"Prose with a Purpose: The Navy's Tradition of the New Year's Day Deck Log." *January Landmark,* January 15, 2018. Naval History and Heritage Command, Retrieved October 8, 2021. https://issuu.com/ussemorys.land/docs/january_issuu.

Purdon, E.S. (1972). *Black Company: The Story of Subchaser PC 1264.* Annapolis, MD: Naval Institute Press.

Ray, Michael, ed. (Revised 2021, October 16). "Battle of Leyte Gulf." Britannica. https://www.britannica.com/event/Battle-of-Leyte-Gulf.

Regulations for the government of the Navy of the United States, 1913. https://www.loc.gov/resource/dcmsiabooks.regulationsforgo00unit_2/?sp=967.

Richard Curtis Inghram. Obituary. Legacy.com. https://www.legacy.com/us/obituaries/pilotonline/name/richard-inghram-obituary?pid=150036363.

Rickover, Hyman G. *American Submariner,* Second Quarter, 2019, p. 27.

Ritchie, George. (1942, May 13). "Ship Which Wouldn't Sink Is Home Healing War Wounds." *The Arizona Daily Star,* p. 3.

Rock Island Argus. (1947, February 4). "Moline Man Named District Director," p. 15.

Rock Island Argus. (1951, December 24). p. 17.

St. Louis Star and Times. (1945, October 27).

San Francisco Examiner (1901, March 20). "Under the Lash a Thief Escapes: Captain James Eschen Vainly Uses Up His Horsewhip," p. 8.

San Francisco Examiner. (1913, January 14). "Prominent Homes Stricken in Sorrow by the Tragedy," p. 2.

Santa Cruz Sentinel. (1982, July 23). "Big Battle Brewed Over Beer," p. 37. Newspapers.com. Accessed February 9, 2022.

Schneider, Raymond J., Jr. (2009, September 23). Raymond John Schneider Dad. Spitzenpopper. http://spitzenpopper.blogspot.com/2009/09/raymond-john-schneider-dad.html.

Schoettler, Carl. (2002, January 2). "Military Sails Into New Year on Verse-Writing Tradition." *The Orlando Sentinel.* Retrieved October 8, 2021. https://www.orlandosentinel.com/news/os-xpm-2002–01–02–0201010060-story.html

Sheller, F.E. (2019). "My Recollections of the Collision of USS *Murphy* (DD603)." USS *Murphy* Website. http://www.ussmurphydd603.com/msgt-usaf-ret-formerly-y2c-uss-murphy-dd603/.

Soundings, Encinal Yacht Club. (2019, September/October). Friends of the San Francisco Maritime Museum Library Newsletter. The Story of the Encinal Flag Pole as Written in the July 1961 *Soundings,* p. 11.

The Spokesman-Review, Spokane, WA. (1941, December 13). "Two Seattle Ensigns Killed in Sea Action," p. 19.

Stewart, George, Captain USN (Ret). (2013, October 3). Fletcher Class Destroyer Operations—Part II. Naval Historical Foundation. https://www.navyhistory.org/2013/10/fletcher-class-destroyer-operations-part-ii/.

Stilwell, Blake. (no date). Famous Veterans: Johnny Carson. Military.com. Retrieved January 28, 2022. https://www.military.com/veteran-jobs/career-advice/military-transition/famous-veteran-johnny-carson.html.

Suciu, Peter. (2021, October 8). "USS *Texas*: The Super Battleship That Changed Everything." *1945.* https://www.19fortyfive.com/2021/10/uss-texas-the-super-battleship-that-changed-everything/.

The Sun-Advocate. (1934, May 24). Price, Utah. "Notre Dame School Holds Graduation Ceremonies Sunday."

Thorp, Jerry. (1950, August 10). "'Hit Anything That Moves,' Carrier Pilots Told in Briefing for First Korean Mission." *Knoxville News-Sentinel,* p. 20.

Times Colonist, Victoria, British Columbia, Canada. (1941, December 20). "Reported Killed, Bruce Elmore Safe," p. 1.

Toll, Ian W. (2012). *Pacific Crucible: War at Sea in the Pacific, 1941–1942.* New York: W.W. Norton and Company.

Topp, Walter. (2019, July 17). "Twenty Thousand Miles to Home—The Miraculous Voyage of the USS *Marblehead.*" MHN Military History Now. Accessed December 7, 2021. https://militaryhistorynow.com/2019/07/17/twenty-thousand-miles-to-home-the-miraculous-voyage-of-the-uss-marblehead/.

US Naval Academy. (1921). Van Bergen, Nicholas. *Lucky Bag* [Yearbook].

US Naval Academy. (1940). Hodnett, William Philip, Jr. *Lucky Bag* [Yearbook].

US Naval Academy. (1940). Perras, Louis Adelard, Jr. *Lucky Bag* [Yearbook].

USS *Alabama.* (1944, February 21). War Diary. Fold3. https://www.fold3.com/image/272060387.

USS Aylwin. (1945, August 4). Official report. https://www.fold3.com/image/300333357.

USS *Aylwin.* (1944, December 18). Official report. https://www.fold3.com/image/293471030.

USS *Boston* Cruise Book. (1958). p. 18.

USS *Buchanan.* (1944, December 18–19). War Diary. Fold3. https://www.fold3.com/image/293490352.

USS *Buchanan.* (1945, September 1–3). War Diary. World war II diaries. Fold3. https://www.fold3.com/image/300383473?terms=september,1945,buchanan,uss.

USS *Bush*. (1945, April 6). Report of Ops in the Invasion of Okinawa. https://www.fold3.com/image/295875402.
USS *Bush*. [No date]. USS Bush, A World War II Fletcher Class Destroyer. [Website]. http://www.ussbush.com/.
USS *Champlin*. (1944, April 7). Action Report—Sinking of German Submarine, 4/7/44, Atlantic. Fold3. https://www.fold3.com/image/274214216.
USS *Colorado*. (1944, July 24). Report of Operations. Fold3. https://www.fold3.com/image/279779617.
USS *Colorado*. (1944, July 24). War Diary. Fold3. https://www.fold3.com/image/279804516.
USS *Colorado*. (1944, November 27). War Diary. Fold3. https://www.fold3.com/image/293493796.
USS *Colorado*. (1945, January 9). Action Report. Fold3. https://www.fold3.com/image/295246011.
USS *Cooper*. (1944, December 3). After Action Report/Report on Loss of USS *Cooper*. https://www.fold3.com/image/292544272.
USS *Dent*. (1943, December 22). War diary. World War II Diaries. Fold3. https://www.fold3.com/image/280042740.
USS *Dent*. (1943, December 27). War diary. World War II Diaries. Fold3. https://www.fold3.com/image/280042742.
USS *Dewey*. (1942, May 7). Action Report. Fold3. https://www.fold3.com/image/267945055.
USS *Enterprise*. (1940, July 17). Deck Log. DANFS.
USS *Enterprise*. (1942, August 24). War Damage Report. Fold3. https://www.fold3.com/image/268018167.
USS *Gilmer*. (1941, December 17–18). War diary. Fold3. https://www.fold3.com/image/268362891.
USS *Glennon*. (1943, October 21). Deck log. Fold3. https://www.fold3.com/image/270524770.
USS *Idaho* (BB 42). (1945, April 12). War Diary. Fold3. https://www.fold3.com/image/296066721.
USS *Lansdowne*. (1942, September 15). War diary. Fold3. https://www.fold3.com/image/268829026.
USS *Liddle*. (1944, December 7). Report of Ops in the Landing at Ormoc, Leyte Is, Philippines on 12/7/44, Including AA Acts. https://www.fold3.com/image/293497205.
USS *Mason*. (1944, March 24). Deck Log. https://catalog.archives.gov/id/28918537.
USS *Monrovia*. (1956) Cruise Book, p. 8. https://www.fold3.com/image/307376339.
USS *Murphy*. (2016) Warfare History Network. https://warfarehistorynetwork.com/2016/11/07/uss-murphy-long-service-in-wartime/.
USS *North Carolina*. (1942, September 15). War Report. Fold3. https://www.fold3.com/image/268390238.
USS *North Carolina* BB 55, 1941–1961. Naval History and Heritage Command. https://www.history.navy.mil/our-collections/photography/us-navy-ships/battleships/north-carolina-bb-55.html.
USS *PC 1264*. (1945, August 7). Deck log. https://catalog.archives.gov/id/26078848?objectPage=41.
USS *Patterson* (DD 392). (1944, June 16). Deck Log. National Archives.
USS *Pennsylvania*. (1945, September 8–30). War Report. Fold3. https://www.fold3.com/image/300889761.
USS *Pennsylvania* (BB 38). (1942). Ship's Record. Fold3. https://www.fold3.com/image/302742550.
USS *Ringgold*. (1943, Nov 19). Action Report. Fold3. https://www.fold3.com/image/270932876.
USS *Ringgold*. (1945, March 4). War Diary. Fold3. https://www.fold3.com/image/295884659.
USS *Russell*. (1945, January 10). War Diary. Fold3. https://www.fold3.com/image/295249983.
USS *South Dakota*. (1942, October 26). Ship's action report, pp. 14, 18. Fold3. https://www.fold3.com/image/267851774.
USS *South Dakota*. (1945, May 6). War Diary. https://www.fold3.com/image/296541916.
USS *Spearfish* (SS 190). (1942, May 4). Third War Report. Scribd. https://www.scribd.com/doc/176299805/SS-190-Spearfish.
USS *Ticonderoga*. (1945, January 27). After action report. Fold3. https://www.fold3.com/image/295267259.
USS *Washington*. (1942, May 27). Official report. https://www.fold3.com/image/268228337.
USS *Yarnall*. (1945, March 4–5). War Diary. Fold3. https://www.fold3.com/image/295388673.
VAntage Point. https://blogs.va.gov/VAntage/85652/veteranoftheday-navy-veteran-gordon-chung-hoon/.
Washington Post. (2011, November 18). Daniel Elmor obituary. (https://www.legacy.com/us/obituaries/washingtonpost/name/daniel-elmore-obituary?id=5980284).
Wessells, Frances. https://en.wikipedia.org/wiki/Frances_Wessells.
Williams, B. (1998). "GM's '36 Parade of Progress." http://futurliner.org/account.htm. Accessed August 4, 2021.
Williams, John R. (2000, December 9). Testimonial to Gordan Paeia Chung-Hoon: Captain USS *Sigsbee* 14 May 1944 to 19 June 1945. USS *Sigsbee* website. Accessed November 17, 2021. https://web.archive.org/web/20030205072819/http://sjkids.scottsburg.com/Testimony%2520to%20Chung-Hoon.htm.
Wright, T.F. (1973). *Short history of the Lucky "L": USS Lansdowne DD 486, 1942–1945,* p. 5. Croton on Hudson, NY: Self-published.
Young, S. (2013). *Trapped at Pearl Harbor: Escape from Battleship Oklahoma*. Annapolis, MD: Naval Institute Press. [Published originally by Blue Jacket Press, 1991].
Zimmerman, D. (2013, November 27)." '31-Knot' Burke Gets His Nickname: The Battle of Cape St. George." *Defense Media Network*. https://www.defensemedianetwork.com/stories/31-knot-burke-gets-his-nickname-the-battle-of-cape-st-george/.

Index